MW01505435

Father John J. Hugo

YOU ARE GODS!

by

FATHER JOHN J. HUGO

See www.castleofgrace.com for more details on Father Hugo, and to order books.

ISBN-10: 1-952889-01-4
ISBN-13: 978-1-952889-01-1

FOREWORD

You Are Gods! (from Psalm 81:6) contains the first sixteen conferences of a seven-day, silent Ignatian retreat first given in the 1930s by Fr. Onesimus Lacouture, S.J. The author of this book, Fr. John J. Hugo, of Pittsburgh, made the retreat under Fr. Lacouture in 1938 and then went on to teach the retreat regularly, mostly to the laity. The most famous promoter of the retreats was Dorothy Day, co-founder with Peter Maurin of the Catholic Worker. She made the retreat many times.

Fr. Hugo said that "if the retreat must have a name," he liked to think of it as "the Folly of the Cross Retreat." His later retreat brochures entitled it "Encounter with Silence," a phrase he borrowed from a book by "new theologian" Karl Rahner (though Fr. Hugo himself was not a "new theologian"). He told retreatants that he used the phrase because of the extreme importance of complete silence in the retreat. But it turned out that retreatants would most often refer to it as simply The Retreat, and I will refer to it as such.

For those who do not know the significance of The Retreat, a brief history might be helpful. Fr. Lacouture, a French-Canadian Jesuit, first presented it in 1931 and continued to teach it for eight years. Based on the first week of St. Ignatius' 30-day retreat, Fr. Lacouture's retreat was credited by several trustworthy and eminent persons as being a phenomenal cause of renewal in the spiritual lives of thousands of priests. In spite of that, in 1939, one year after Fr. Hugo had made The Retreat, Fr. Lacouture's Jesuit superior not only forbade Fr. Lacouture to give The Retreat, but also further punished him. Fr. Hugo's book *The Sign of Contradiction* tells the history of the unjust treatment of Fr. Lacouture and of the other priests who gave it. It also tells of The Retreat's power to inspire and motivate Catholics and the reason for the opposition to that power. (*A Sign of Contradiction* is also published by Castle of Grace LLC.)

Fr. Hugo, a priest of the Pittsburgh diocese, also suffered for giving The Retreat to the laity (and often to priests as well).

Though never silenced or formally censured, he endured painful consequences. Among other things, his bishop suddenly removed him from his position as a college teacher and sent him to small rural parishes as a curate. For many years he was forbidden to give The Retreat without the express permission of his bishop. He and the other "retreat priests" were also unjustly charged, misrepresented, and even defamed, by theologians, some clerics, and the proverbial "council of whispers." Three of his books are brilliant defenses against these charges.

Why so much opposition? After all, The Retreat has consistently inspired its retreatants to follow the Gospels more closely and with a greater love for God. In addition, Fr. Hugo's book *Applied Christianity,* which contains a summary of all the retreat conferences, received an *imprimatur* in 1944 from Archbishop Francis J. Spellman. Fr. Hugo's own succinct explanation was that both his and Fr. Lacouture's "undoing was the condemnation of worldliness, especially the worldliness of the clergy." But perhaps the best response is: read this book and draw your own conclusions.

During his 48 years as a secular priest, as well as giving The Retreat whenever he could, Fr. Hugo served as college teacher, chaplain, assistant pastor and pastor, chaired diocesan commissions on the liturgy and theology, and published books, pamphlets and homily keys. He also collaborated in the preparation of a post-Vatican II catechism for adults, *The Teaching of Christ*, published by Our Sunday Visitor in 1976.

For about a decade in the sixties and seventies, The Retreat was probably not given at all. But that changed in 1976 when Sister Peter Claver, an old friend of Dorothy Day and Fr. Hugo, wrote Fr. Hugo and asked him for spiritual direction. Sister Peter Claver, a member of the Missionary Servants of the Most Blessed Trinity, had made the retreat in the past. In fact, in *The Long Loneliness,* Miss Day recalls that around 1941 Sister Peter Claver was the person who had first given her the notes from one of Fr. Lacouture's retreats, which Sister Peter Claver had received from her confessor. Sister Peter Claver's connection to the "retreat priests" eventually led to Miss Day's traveling to Pittsburgh in the early 1940s to make her first retreat under the direction of Fr. Hugo and Fr. Louis Farina.

In 1976 Fr. Hugo was a chaplain to the Sisters of the Holy
Family at Mt. Nazareth Convent in Bellevue, a borough north of
Pittsburgh. Sister Peter Claver, who lived near Philadelphia,
traveled to the convent to meet with Fr. Hugo. She was 76 and
Fr. Hugo 65 years old. Because I became friends with Sister
Peter Claver after Fr. Hugo's death, she told me about this visit
years later. During the sessions of spiritual direction, as Fr.
Hugo and she talked, he would also read aloud from the Bible
and pull down from his shelves some spiritual classic to read
aloud a passage that he had marked in years past. Sister Peter
Claver told me that she was wonderfully renewed by his words
and expressed amazement at Fr. Hugo's mastery of scripture and
the spiritual teaching of the Church. That significant visit, she
told me, was "the startup of The Retreat" once again.

Dorothy Day followed in her friend's footsteps and traveled
to Pittsburgh in August of that year to make her last retreat with
Fr. Hugo. (She died four years later.) From that re-inaugural
year until he died in 1985, Fr. Hugo conducted retreats at Mt.
Nazareth.

Printed about 1946, *You Are Gods!* contains the same
doctrine and largely the same presentation that Sister Peter
Claver and Miss Day heard in 1976. Although many years and
the cataclysmic changes of Vatican II intervened between 1946
and 1976, the essential content of The Retreat remained the same
and continued to remain the same until Fr. Hugo died.

Written evidence of this consistency is the fact that Fr. Hugo
presented the same Retreat in his 1984 book *Your Ways Are Not
My Ways, Volume II.*

I can also attest to this because I made The Retreat under the
direction of Fr. Hugo in 1981 and 1983. (I made the Retreat in
subsequent years three more times under the direction of
Monsignor Joseph Meenan and Fr. Francis Ott, both from the
Pittsburgh area, who had given the retreats with Fr. Hugo in the
1940s.) The teachings of the conferences that I heard from Fr.
Hugo—and from the other priests—were the same as in this
book.

I, too, experienced both the power and joyfulness of the
conferences, the prayerful silences and the Catholic
interpretation of the four Gospels. At The Retreat I read the

Gospels for the first time, and since then I have discovered that many Catholics have never read them.

When I arrived at The Retreat, I was the typical Baby Boomer lapsed Catholic whose pleasure-seeking youth during the Cultural Revolution had taken me from God and the Church. When I left, I was a Christian. I came back to Christ and the Church because of The Retreat. That was over 35 years ago, and I have experienced much in the Church since my return to it. I have been a Catholic journalist and teacher. I have helped my husband in his own Catholic publishing endeavors (he produced material for children), and I have reared a child in the Church. I have traversed the ideological lanes that crisscross the Church. I started out as a rather liberal Novus Ordo Catholic who years later ended up attending the Traditional Latin Mass. And now, living far from a Traditional Latin Mass, my family and I are back in a Novus Ordo parish. And I have been exposed to a fair number of the numerous groups of different "types of Catholics" in between.

The Retreat—which is nothing more than the perennial teaching of the Catholic Church—not only guided me out of apostasy and the modern mindset, but has helped to steer me through these chaotic times in the Church in many important ways. I have written about these things in my own articles. (These articles are accessible at www.ideasrealized.com.) But in this Foreword I will only note—for what it's worth—two things that struck me in this book, and I do so based on my broad and deep experience as a Catholic.

Fr. Hugo writes in Conference Thirteen about the relationship among the sacraments, meritorious actions and grace. In Conference Six he writes again on the subject of the sacraments around a similar theme, best summed up as: "a supernatural life is not a natural life with liturgical adornments." In these chapters, it seemed to me that Fr. Hugo addresses in theological and spiritual terms an attitude that I have seen prevail in both the Novus Ordo parishes and the traditional chapels and churches. It is a frame of mind—ever a temptation it seems for Catholics—that thinks that as long as Catholics get to Mass, they can live worldly lives that are largely based on wholly natural and secular principles and values.

Fr. Hugo teaches strongly against this mentality.

My second comment is that Fr. Hugo believed that Vatican II, in which he had placed his hopes of a great spiritual renewal of the Church, was a failure in the one way that he had cared mostly deeply about: evangelization, that is, teaching those living in the modern world about the new life in Jesus Christ. I remember during one of his retreats when he actually rose from his seat under the power of his emotions and told us that the "greatest failure of Vatican II" was its failure to deliver on the promise of evangelizing both Catholics and the world.

In one of his books he notes that "Paul VI in 1975 would inaugurate a world-wide program" of evangelization. "That program, however, has failed sadly," continues Fr. Hugo, "and, although it should be an unceasing effort in the Church, is already all but forgotten, without doubt the major spiritual casualty of the post-Vatican II period. Yet the failure was inevitable for want of the needed model. Evangelization, abandoned to others, had indeed become strange, shadowed by heresy, and therefore suspicious to Catholics...Catholic evangelization starts rather from the intense and joyous realization that, 'from the foundation of the world' (Matthew 15:34), God's human creatures have been destined to be 'like Him,' to share in his nature by grace, to grow in holiness, to become His children in Christ, and to extend the Incarnation and multiply its fruits."

The Retreat, writes Fr. Hugo, had "unveiled a Catholic model for evangelization." His last retreat brochure described The Retreat as "a program of self-evangelization," as well as "a scriptural retreat," and "a desert experience in the hills of Pennsylvania." He was deeply disappointed that the Church, for the most part, continued to ignore The Retreat, and he was determined, in spite of his isolated position, to continue presenting it.

As for the character of Fr. Hugo, in her book Miss Day called him "a brilliant teacher" who took "great joy in his work." She referred to "the famous retreat" as "the bread of the strong" and "a foretaste of heaven." Sister Peter Claver confided to me that "I feel a great vacancy in my life after his death. I never had a friendship like ours," and wrote in an article that "a golden stream of love flowed from his fine, clear intellect into his heart which embraced in love the cosmic world." Msgr. Meenan said that Fr. Hugo "had a great mind. He took the conferences of Fr. Lacouture and systematized and synthesized them." Pittsburgh retreatant Frank Huber remarked that "Fr. Hugo was one of the most powerful personalities that I have ever encountered in my life. John Hugo was an integral part of whatever The Retreat meant for me." Another retreatant, a friend of Sister Peter Claver who made The Retreat twice, confided in her that "in the presence of Fr. Hugo, I felt that God had hollowed him out and filled him with Himself."

On October 1, 1985, Fr. Hugo visited his old friend and former fellow retreat director, Fr. Ott, in Greensburg, Pennsylvania. Later, they drove through heavy rain to Seton Hill College to visit with a Sister of Charity who was proofreading one of Fr. Hugo's books. With Fr. Ott driving, the car hydroplaned on the slick pavement and skated off the road. Fr. Hugo was killed instantly. Fr. Ott was slightly injured. They had been talking about scripture, and the conversation is "to be continued in eternity," Fr. Ott told my brother Michael Hugo.

Fr. Hugo died two days after teaching a September retreat. His sister Cecilia found on his desk the last chapter of the manuscript *Your Ways Are Not My Ways, Volume I,* which was his second, updated account of the history of The Retreat— finished, it seemed, on the morning he had died. On his bedside table was a handwritten note. "It is a great happiness," it said, "to be spared to present this parting gift to the Church that I love and have served faithfully throughout my life...[I dedicate] this work to the Church as bride of Christ, praying that [I would] help to remove those spots and wrinkles marring her beauty."

In a telephone conversation the previous summer, he had told a friend and former retreatant that he had two things remaining to do—finish his book and his September retreat. "I remember thinking that was odd," this woman wrote to Cecilia Hugo, "because he had November retreats planned, and throughout all of 1986." When this woman heard that Fr. Hugo had died immediately after finishing both his retreat and his book, she wrote that "I feel as if the dramatic coda to a Beethoven symphony had been the finish to his life."

In publishing this book, Castle of Grace LLC hopes to continue Fr. Hugo's power to evangelize.

Rosemary Hugo Fielding (niece of Fr. Hugo)
Feast of St. Cecilia, Nov. 22, 2019

NOTE

Fr. Hugo wrote and typed *You Are Gods!* during the time he served as a curate at St. Mary in Kittanning, a small rural parish north of Pittsburgh. It was printed, with the help of his sister Cecilia Marie Hugo, on a small printing press in their parents' basement. With the exception of this foreword, the "About the Author," "Prayer for Retreatants," and "Fr. Hugo's Symbol," this book is published exactly as Fr. Hugo had printed it in about 1946.

TABLE OF CONTENTS

	Foreword	i
	Introductory	1
Introductory Conference	The Hour of the Christian Conscience Has Struck	2
Conference I	The Two Planes of Action	10
Conference II	Creation and Re-creation	24
Conference III	Some Principles for Applying Christianity	37
Conference IV	The Two Kinds of Happiness	52
Conference V	Harmony Between Nature and the Supernatural (1) Where the Harmony Lies	68
Conference VI	The Harmony Between the Two Orders (2) How the Harmony May Be Preserved	80
Conference VII	The Conflict Between Nature and Supernatural (1) The Centre of Conflict	96
Conference VIII	The Conflict Between Nature and the Supernatural (2) The Reasons for the Conflict	112
Conference IX	The Conflict Between Nature and the Supernatural (3) Why Natural Motives Must Be Mortified	126

CONTENTS

Conference X   The Two Mentalities   139

Conference XI   Jesus Described the Supernatural Life   152

Conference XII   The Pagan Mentality   169

Conference XIII   Maxims of the Pagan Mentality   181

Conference XIV   The Fruit of the Pagan Mentality   195

Conference XV   The Christian Mentality   204

Conference XVI   Imitators of God   220

                    About the Author   238

                    Father Hugo's Symbol   242

                    A Prayer for Retreatants   243

"You are gods,
And all are sons of the Most High."

(Psalm 81, 6)

INTRODUCTORY

The following conferences correspond to the chapters of *Applied Christianity,* Part One, "The Natural and the Supernatural." They are indeed the conferences of which these chapters of *Applied Christianity* are brief summaries. Thus the present book deals with only a single principle of Christian living; but this principle is absolutely fundamental.

Brevity is not always a virtue. There are matters of such importance – and such complexity – that they deserve detailed study. For this reason it is hoped that the present conferences will supplement the terse presentation of these same truths given in *Applied Christianity.*

INTRODUCTORY CONFERENCE

"THE HOUR OF THE CHRISTIAN CONSCIENCE HAS STRUCK!"

My dear Friends in Christ —

St. John Chrysostom is quoted as saying that when we look at the Gospels, then at the lives of Christians, the latter seem more like enemies of Christ than like friends and followers. Times have not changed. The lives of many, perhaps most, Catholics today are scarcely distinguishable from those of the pagans among whom they dwell, except for their observance of certain external religious practices, and this observance itself is but too often a matter of dead routine, not always faithfully carried out. Pope Pius XI, looking out from the watch-tower of the world, observed sadly that "the habit of life which can really be called Christian has in great measure disappeared." *(Ubi Arcano Dei)*

Catholic writers frequently point out that the opponent of the Church today is no longer any religious body or bodies, but rather a reappearance of that ancient pagan spirit which persecuted the Church in its beginnings. This spirit, in its modern manifestation, is called the new paganism, to distinguish it from the old; and it has been observed that while the old paganism was a growth, even when it went beyond maturity to the rottenness of over-ripeness, the new paganism is in its very nature a reversion, a retrogression, a disintegration, and is marked by the odor of decay.

A more polite and pedantic name for paganism is naturalism; but call it what you will, that which is signified by these names is without doubt the great error of the day: a denial, at least implicit, of God and of His Son Jesus Christ; and with the denial of Jesus, or of His divinity – which comes to the same thing — a denial of His mission in the world, the mission to elevate men to

2

a higher than human plane of life and so gain for them a higher than human destiny and happiness. With these denials comes a devotion to the material things of the earth, to the pleasures of sense, to the transitory goods of time rather than to the life of eternity. Worldliness is the soul of practical paganism.

These principles of paganism, but slowly taking definite shape amid the decay of a Christian civilization, and for a long time lying loosely and unformed about the world, suddenly became hardened and organized in the monstrous systems of Nazism and Communism. Now, with Nazism gone, the Church Militant recognizes in Communism, this fierce concentration of all the forces of paganism, her great contemporary enemy, and she is girded for a battle to the finish. Pope Pius XII, speaking to the Romans, and through the Romans to the world, at the critical moment when Communism, threatening Italy, threatened by that fact also to spill over and flood Western Europe, cried out, "The great hour of Christian conscience has struck!" On this occasion the Pontiff also said, "Rome now finds itself before, or better say, in the midst of, changing times which demand of the head and the members of Christianity a maximum of vigilance and of tireless readiness for unconditioned action." The Pope thus challenges and exhorts Christians: "May this conscience of Christianity be awakened to full and virile appreciation of its mission of help and salvation for a human race wavering in its spiritual framework."

In a former time of the Church's great distress, St. Dominic outlined the program needed, and the program which he intended to follow, in the startling demand, "We must out-labor, out-fast, out-discipline these false teachers!"

This is the kind of moral and spiritual effort needed also against the false teachers of today.

But while it is necessary thus to view the religious conditions of our times in bulk, as it were, in order to do what we can towards the solving of this world-problem, we must not allow ourselves to wander too far from home. If an omelet is bad, this is because it was made with bad eggs; and if our so-called Christian civilization is without spiritual vitality and corrupt, this can only be because the units that make it up – nations, communities, families, and individuals – are themselves also spiritually lifeless and corrupt. Nor need we travel far to find the marks of this corruption.

After twenty centuries of Christianity, it would be hard to find – or rather, may we not say impossible to find – even one Catholic parish in which all or even a majority of the members live in accordance with the lofty ideals set before us by Jesus in the Sermon on the Mount. Further, would it be easy to find even a religious community, all or most of whose members, although specially consecrated to the service of Christ, conform their daily lives in any adequate measure with His spiritual teaching?

Not that Jesus has no true friends; as there was a little band near the cross, so there is today and in every age a "little flock," as He Himself called it, but scattered up and down the world, one here, one there. "The number of the elect is so small," said St. Louis Grignion de Montfort, "so small, that were we to know how small it is, we should faint away with grief. It is so small that were God to assemble them together, He would cry to them as He did of old by the mouth of His prophet, '*Gather yourselves together, one by one....One from this province, one from that kingdom . . .*'"

Truly, therefore, we need not go to Moscow or Berlin to find paganism. It is close at home: can we be sure that it does not mar our own lives, that it does not find a home in our own hearts? For if it gains magnitude and momentum only when taken in the large, and is visible as a definite force, the force which the Scriptures call "the world," only then, yet its ultimate home is in the hearts of men and its ultimate form, or infinitesimal unit, is the attachment of the heart to the creatures of the world.

The basic error, then, of the world today, the general error of which all others are particular manifestations, is naturalism, paganism, or what Pope Pius XII called "black paganism." The words of the Holy Father are worth noting, not only as applicable to our era, but also as specially pertinent to our country, since they were addressed to the Eucharistic Congress held at Minneapolis and St. Paul in 1941. He said:

> "Early explorers record in their relations their utter amazement at the mighty current that sweeps down the Mississippi River. There is a stronger current of black paganism sweeping over peoples today, carrying along in its

onward rush newspapers, magazines, moving pictures, breaking down the barriers of self-respect and decency, undermining the foundations of Christian culture and education."

What is most helpful in this statement is that the evil described is pointed out in its specific and near manifestations. There is little use declaiming against the new paganism, against Communism or secularism or any of the other numerous isms that infect the modern world, if we cannot localize them and so proceed against them. A body is healthy only if its tiny cells are healthy; a disease is curable only if it can be removed from these cells. And the words quoted from the Holy Father bring home the fact, noted above, that we need not go far off to find paganism today: it is near at hand, it is imposing itself on us from every side, any of us can touch it, all of us should be able to recognize it and be immunized against it, and we can begin at once, without moving a step, to cure it: its infinitesimal unit, we have just observed, is in our own hearts, and its carriers, the Sovereign Pontiff here indicates, are the newspapers, magazines, moving pictures and other similar agencies that are breaking down the barriers of self-respect and decency and are undermining the foundations of Christian culture and education.

Nor can we leave this passage from the Holy Father's address without citing the practical conclusion he draws from it: "Only a young man and woman of self-sacrifice – We were almost going to add, heroic self-sacrifice – will escape the flood [of black paganism]."

Here is the call, repeated for our own day, to out-fast, out-pray, out-discipline the false teachers.

What is therefore needed to stem this tide of paganism is a strong affirmation, both in principle and in practice, of the supernatural character of our religion. What we Catholics can do, therefore, both to revive our own spiritual life and to make Christianity really effective for the salvation of men in a time of great need, is to fortify our minds with the principles of our religion, which is essentially supernatural, and nerve our wills for the endeavor, an endeavor that might well take the form of a Crusade, to carry out the design of the Creator and respond to His grace by living supernatural lives.

Yet engaging in such effort is more than a matter of making a mechanical resolve. Once when I had made to a group of sisters the observation repeated above, that it would be hard to find one religious community that lives according to the Sermon on the Mount, the superior, struck by this thought, afterwards came and proposed modestly that she was willing, even anxious, that her community should be the first. A commendable resolve, surely; but while praising the good intention it seemed also necessary to explain that it would not be quite as easy as putting a sign on the community bulletin board instructing all the sisters that next morning they should forthwith carry out all the directions of the Sermon on the Mount. A long course of spiritual discipline would be necessary. More, it would require a sustained pursuit of Christian perfection, and not only the pursuit of it but the attainment of it as well, for them or for anyone else to carry out fully in practice the sublime teachings of the Gospel.

We Catholics must give a more deliberate emphasis to Christian practice. Christianity can become effective only when it is lived. There is today a widespread recognition that the world's ills can be cured only through the teaching of the Gospel; and, as a consequence, many statements are made of Christian principles. What is lacking is the effort to translate these principles into action in the personal lives of Christians. Indeed, the teaching Church itself sees to the affirmation and definition of Christ's doctrine; but it remains for her children to dedicate themselves to the labor of carrying these principles into action.

What is the profit of our repeating over and over the formulas of Christian teaching if there is no corresponding effort to make them the determining influence in our lives? Will faith save us without charity? What is the use of drawing up elaborate blueprints of a Christian society, as this should be organized according to Catholic teaching, if there are so few real Christians in the world and so few are attempting to intensify their spiritual lives or will even recognize the need for such an endeavor? If, by a miracle, a fully Christian society, conforming to all the blueprints, were suddenly to come into existence, how would the vast throngs of semi-pagan, secularized, worldly Christians feel in this society? At the very least it is to be feared that they would be very ill at ease! And the institutions of such a society, assuredly, would soon deteriorate in their hands; it would not long remain Christian. Nor are we being unduly pessimistic; this is actually what has happened: the world was once Christian. As for the present – "the habit of life which can really be called Christian has in great measure disappeared" from the world.

It will require a race of Christians to create a Christian society. And therefore our first and most important task, if we are to assist in extending the Church and our needy brethren throughout the world, as well as to save our own souls, is to make the sublime truths of Christianity and the goals it opens, the living, active, superintendent force of our lives. We must become de-paganized, cease living for the goods of this world, cease allowing ourselves to be ruled by the principles of mere natural reason. We must learn to live as children of God, according to the revelations of faith, seeing to it that divine grace and charity supply the impulsion of all that we do. Then, as we become Christians-- that is, living and active Christians--we will soon create for ourselves a habitable society and show greater efficiency than we have so far done in bringing salvation to our brethren.

Now the conferences which we are here beginning are dedicated to the purpose of assisting in the task of establishing in our minds those doctrinal convictions which are necessary if we are to undertake seriously and perseveringly the effort to live truly Christian and supernatural lives.

Throughout this series of talks our purpose will be practical. And yet we will have to be ready to think, and think profoundly, since if we are to go beyond mere sentiment, we must examine the doctrinal basis of practice. And right at the beginning, it will be well to give the doctrinal context of our study. While necessarily limiting the field of our inquiry, we shall need to know the bearing of our principle on the whole body of Christian truth.

Now the great central fact of Christianity is the Incarnation-- God becoming man in order that man might return to God and share in the divine happiness. Underlying this great fact and truth, without which it would be simply incomprehensible, is the mystery of the Blessed Trinity, Three Divine Persons in one God.

The Incarnation tells us that One of these Three Persons took on our human flesh and became a man, and that therefore this Person, Jesus Christ, was truly God as well as man. His purpose in doing this was to carry out the Father's wish of giving to men the opportunity of sharing in the divine life and happiness.

Jesus, the Scripture tells us, was the firstborn of many brethren. God predestined Jesus from all eternity; He foresaw the Incarnation from the beginning; yet He did not see Jesus alone, but, with Him, all mankind. Hence, the eternal plan and decree of God was to create a race of creatures who might be elevated to share in the Divine life and in the Divine happiness. Through Jesus Christ, the Incarnate God, this plan was effected. It is clear then, that the basic fact of our Christian religion is our elevation to this new state through Jesus Christ to share in the life of God. We have been given a human life, already a precious gift; but God also planned to bestow on us a gift far greater than human life. From eternity He decreed that His human life would be the vessel of a still more sublime principle, a principle that would introduce us to a higher than human world, namely the world and universe of God Himself.

The plan of God is realized in man's elevation to the supernatural order. Man, born in the human or natural order by God's creative act, is then by a more loving paternal gesture, elevated to a still loftier plane of being. This elevation, as you know, comes through sanctifying grace. And here, then, is what sanctifying grace does—it raises us up to a level that is more than human, which is really Divine and which we therefore call supernatural. The Catechism defines sanctifying grace as a supernatural gift given by God to the soul. It will help greatly to keep in our thoughts also the definition which is given to us by the Scriptures. St. Peter in his second letter tells us that we are raised to a participation in the Divine nature; and theology adds that this participation in the Divine nature is accomplished by means of sanctifying grace. Accordingly, we may define sanctifying grace as a sharing or a participation in the Divine nature and in the Divine life. This fact, like the distances to the stars, is a thing so staggering that we can never fully comprehend it. It is worth a lifetime of meditation. Nothing, no other set of words, could give us a clearer idea of what is meant by grace, nor convey better than these to our minds, weak as they are, a more adequate notion of the immense height and dignity to which we are raised by the grace of God. Yes, we are really given a share in the Divine life.

The fact of our elevation to the supernatural order is the basis of the Christian spiritual life, and so will be the fundamental principle in our presentation of that life. And the definition of grace as a sharing in the Divine life will be the keystone in our edifice of spiritual doctrine.

And now, at the very beginning of our study and meditation, let us take as our motto and guide these memorable words of St. Paul: *"For the rest, brethren, whatever things are true, whatever honorable, whatever just, whatever holy, whatever lovable, whatever of good repute, if there be any virtue, if anything worthy of praise, think upon these things."* (Phil. 4, 8-9) Let us also think upon the things set forth in this conference. And may God bless you.

> *"O God, Who has created the nature of man in wondrous dignity, and has still more wonderfully re-created it, grant that through the Mystery of the Incarnation we may become partakers of His divinity, Who has condescended to become a partaker of our humanity, Jesus Christ, Thy Son, Our Lord, Who liveth and reigneth with Thee in the unity of the Holy Spirit, God, world without end. Amen."*

THE TWO PLANES OF ACTION

My dear Friends in Christ —

Perhaps you have read one of those stories — there are a number of them—that describe an imaginary trip to the Moon, or to another planet, Mars or Venus. That is what happens to us when sanctifying grace is conferred upon us; we are carried, all in an instant, on a more than magic carpet, to another planet, to another world, the world and universe of God Himself. When we are raised to the supernatural order, therefore, we are taken from man's world to God's: our destiny is henceforth to be worked out in the universe of the Trinity. And the fact that a trip even to Mars or to the Moon remains still a flight of fancy, which science cannot actually effect despite all the control it has gained over the forces of nature, will assist us in grasping in some measure the marvel of the feat accomplished by the mercy and the omnipotence of God when He lifts us to the supernatural order.

But this comparison with a trip to Mars, while useful in some respects, is inadequate in others. God does not raise us to the supernatural world as a man is lifted in an elevator or as he might be carried off into space by a rocket. He is elevated by a new inward principle of vitality, by his sharing in a new and higher kind of being. Suppose that some friend of yours were to need a blood transfusion and you generously supply the blood. In his weakness and lack of vitality he is revived by the energy which he receives from you: he gets new life from you. Now something like this happens when we receive grace. We receive a transfusion—new life, new energy—from God.

But of course this comparison is inadequate too. The life that you give your friend does not inwardly change him; it is the same kind as your own human life. But God gives us a transfusion of divine life, infinitely higher than our own, and that is why we call it supernatural. Moreover, the vitality that you give your friend in the blood transfusion, will not make him like you, not give him your talents, your mannerisms, your gait, your voice. On the contrary, your blood will be assimilated to his own and become part of himself. But when we share in the divine life, the opposite happens. We become as gods. We receive powers to act like divine beings. And if we allow ourselves to be molded by grace, we will come in time really to resemble divine beings; that is to say, since grace comes through Jesus Christ, we will come to conform to Christ, will become Christoform. That is what happens to saints; that is what makes them saints. And that is why St. Paul says to all of us, *"Put on the Lord Jesus Christ...."* (Rom. 13, 14)

When Adam and Eve were first placed in Paradise, in addition to their humanly happy life there, and infinitely above all their human gifts, was the gift of grace which gave them a share in the divine nature and a destiny in the supernatural order. By their rebellion they lost the gift of grace, and the destiny it involved, both for themselves and for their children. But the gift and the destiny were restored to us by Jesus Christ. This indeed, was the purpose of Jesus in coming among us: God became man in order that men might become as gods.

Accordingly, the first act in the personal history of each of us as Christians was our reception of Baptism, which communicated divine grace to our souls, and effected our elevation to the Divine life, thus giving us the opportunity of returning again through Jesus to dwell, already here in this world in some fashion, but perfectly in the next world, in the bosom of the Trinity. And since this elevation to the supernatural order is the first and fundamental fact in our personal religious history, it is the fundamental fact also in determining our religious duties and our responsibilities as Christians. Therefore, in seeking to know how we may live truly as Christians, how we may apply the truths of Christianity to our daily lives, it is to this elevation of ours to the supernatural order that we must go; from this fact in the first place we should derive the standards of spiritual conduct proper to us. The more deeply we meditate upon this, indeed, the more fully we will realize in our hearts and souls the dignity of being Christians and the responsibilities our high calling involves.

In beginning a course of the Christian life then we take frankly and explicitly man's elevation to the supernatural order as our starting-point. It will be the key to everything that follows. Therefore, the understanding of everything else depends upon our initial understanding of this idea of the supernatural. The first few conferences, attempting to explain so lofty a subject, will be of a solidly doctrinal character, and therefore perhaps a little difficult for some to understand; but it is necessary to submit to the difficulty in order to have this key to the rest of Christian teaching. Let us then arouse our minds and put them to work in the attempt to grasp as best they may the meaning of this great fact. In the present conference we will first define and then distinguish the natural and supernatural orders in reference to Christian practice.

The Two Planes of Life and Action

Life manifests itself in activity; and such kind of life has its own distinctive activity. Plants feed themselves, grow, and reproduce their own kind. Animals can move about and they also have sense knowledge. You know that a dog is alive, and that he is a dog, by his barking. You recognize a bird by its flying, a fish by its power to swim. Similarly, our human life and human nature gives us special powers; we can think, act freely and deliberately, make tools and work with them. And when we are raised to a share in the divine life, we are given further and still higher powers of action, such namely as befit divinized beings.

Suppose that you were omnipotent, and because of this, you were to give to the plants in your garden the power of moving from place to place, such as animals possess. Now, if they do not find enough to eat in your yard, they can move off and feast on the fertilizer in nearby gardens, as dogs beg for food at all the houses in a neighborhood. Or suppose that you attach wings to some pet goldfish; so that now, besides being able to swim, they are also able to fly. Or suppose you should give a pet dog the power to think and speak; now your faithful companion would no longer be dumb, but would be able truly to sympathize with your human needs and offer consolation and counsel in your difficulties.

In each case a being having one kind of life is given a share in a higher kind. But of course the examples themselves are ridiculous because we are not omnipotent. God, however, is omnipotent; He can do such things and has done so in at least one case. To us having human life, He has given a share in the divine life and with it powers of divine activity. And a dog with the faculty of speech would scarcely be a stranger sight in the universe than are we human beings with our share in the divine life and activities.

Thus in every man, as a consequence of our creation and elevation, there is a twofold principle of life and activity. The first is simply his human nature, which enables him to act as a man, on the natural plane, as a human being. The other principle is sanctifying grace, the share in the Divine nature, which elevates him to the plane of God, makes him a son of God, makes him capable of living according to a higher law, and in fact imposes on him the duty of living supernaturally, as a son of God. Nature, in a sense, belongs to us: once God made up His mind to create us, all that belongs to human nature belongs to us properly. But the supernatural principle does not properly belong to us at all; it belongs to us less than the power of flying belongs to a fish, or speech to a dog. We might have been created as true human beings without receiving the gift of sanctifying grace; that we have received it is owing to the overflowing generosity and goodness of God. Grace is God's free gift, the greatest of all His gifts, greater than health and life, and we ought ever to thank God for it before all other things.

Since both grace and nature are principles of activity, men are capable of two kinds of actions: namely, natural actions and supernatural actions. Corresponding with these two ways of activity are two ways of life: the one human and natural, the other supernatural and divine.

As to the natural life: one lives a natural life when he lives in accordance with the impulses of his nature or in accordance with the truths and laws discovered and known by the reason. When we live, therefore, exclusively by our natural powers—the senses, the bodily faculties, the will, the imagination, and reason—we live a natural life.

On the other hand, one lives a supernatural life when he lives under the impulse of grace, in accordance with his status, his supernatural status, as a child of God, when he follows, not the truths and laws given by reason, but those indicated to him by faith, by his faith, that is to say, in Divine revelation.

A natural life, therefore, is proportioned to man's natural abilities; a supernatural life exceeds all human abilities and would be completely impossible without the special help of God. God gives us the knowledge of this higher way, He elevates us to it, and He bestows upon us constantly the help that we need to live in accordance with it.

The Three Fold Distinction

So much may be said in general. Now let us try to define these two modes of living, the natural and the supernatural, more carefully and explicitly. We may do this by distinguishing them in three ways: by their make-up, or composition; by their respective guides; and finally by their destinations.

First, as to the make-up of these two orders. A man's natural life is composed of all his natural actions, that is to say, of all the actions that proceed from his senses, his body, his understanding and will. Eating, drinking, walking, talking, thinking, working— all these things are natural to man; and if one did these things, and did nothing else, he would be said to live on the natural plane.

What about the supernatural? What is the make-up of this order? That is, what is its essential constituent? That which raises us to the supernatural order and gives us a share in the divine life, we have observed, is sanctifying grace. With this grace there are infused into the soul supernatural virtues and the seven Gifts of the Holy Spirit. All of these together constitute a new supernatural organism. Grace itself is the new principle of a higher life, while the virtues, supplemented by the Gifts are active powers that enable elevated souls actually to live as divine beings. These virtues are called into action and implemented by the actual graces that God bestows on the soul incessantly according to the demands of duty and the opportunities provided by circumstances. It may be said, therefore, that grace, working through the virtues, is the make-up or essential element in a supernatural life; and we live practical supernatural lives when we exercise these supernatural virtues or when our daily conduct is governed by them. In the practical order, therefore, what constitutes supernatural action is the dominance in our actions of those dynamic; supernatural principles, the infused virtues.

Moreover, of all the virtues infused into the soul the greatest is charity. *"God is love,"* the Sacred Scriptures tell us (I John 4, 16). Not, God has love or exercises love but that He *is* love. And when we are raised to the supernatural order, we are raised to God, that is, to a world in which God is both the center and the circumference. We have compared our elevation from the natural to the supernatural order to a journey from this earth to another planet. If we were to make such a trip, we would doubtless find things in our new planet quite different from what we are accustomed to here—new forms of vegetation, new kinds of life, an altogether different atmosphere. Now when we are raised to the supernatural order we are in truth brought to another world where likewise everything is new and different: *"Behold"*—the Scriptures say—*"Behold all things are made new!"* And in this new world of God's—new for us, that is—the very air that we take in with each breath will be love. Out of love God endows us with divine grace; and He endows us with grace that we may return that love; the other virtues are given to us, and all the other duties of the Christian life are enjoined upon us, in order that we may grow and perfect ourselves in love. When we enter the supernatural world we learn that the great end for which we shall henceforth labor is union with God through love; indeed, the first word that greets our ears in this new world is that the great law which shall from this moment rule our lives is: *"Love the Lord thy God with thy whole heart, and thy neighbor as thyself."* The supernatural world, therefore, is a world in which love, divine love, reigns supreme. St. John, after stating that God is love, adds, *"And he who abides in love abides in God, and God in him."* That is, he who loves, lives in the world of God. Jesus Himself, speaking of His teaching says: *"A new commandment I give you, that you love one another."* And He makes this love the criterion of His religion: *"By this will all men know that you are my disciples, if you have love for one another."* (John 13, 35)

Charity of course does not live in solitary splendor in the supernatural kingdom. There are many other virtues: first, the other theological virtues, faith and hope; and then also the moral virtues, like humility, penitence, meekness. Yet charity sits among these as a queen among courtiers; and as a queen may attend to some matters herself, while entrusting others to the care of courtiers, so also charity acts directly by acts and works of love, but also indirectly, as occasion and duty demand, by inciting to activity humility, self-denial, holy fear, patience, penitence and all other glorious virtues that come to us with sanctifying grace.

Thus, if our lives and actions are to be supernatural, their principle must be supernatural. Without grace, and without the activity that grace and the virtues make possible, human life remains but natural. If a man lacking grace, a pagan, performs some good action, let us say gives an alms, his action is but natural because its principle is but natural. But when a Christian, in obedience to the Gospel law, gives an alms, he acts in virtue of the principle of grace and his activity is supernatural. He is exercising the supernatural virtue of faith because he sees Christ in his neighbor; he is exercising supernatural hope because he willingly gives up earthly goods in order to receive an eternal reward; and finally he is exercising charity by showing in this concrete way his love for God as imaged in his neighbor.

Of course a Christian also, although having grace, may through neglect fail to make his activity supernatural and allow it to remain on the merely natural plane by not making grace the active principle of his life and actions. Suppose that a Christian gives an alms in order to be seen by men? Will his action be supernatural? Hardly; at least Jesus speaks slightingly of such almsgiving, observing that even the pagans do this. The reason is that the influence of grace is intercepted, as it were, by an unworthy motive; so that nature rather than grace is the principle of the action. It is thus the practical task of the spiritual life to make grace, working through the virtues, and especially through charity, the active influential principle of our lives.

The second way in which we can distinguish the two orders of nature and the supernatural is by their respective guides. God gives us a faculty to guide us on each level. In the bodily order God too gives us our eyes to guide us; without sight we could not move about nor safely live in this world, would not be able to get downstairs safely in the morning. Now on the higher, properly human level, God also gives us a guide, namely, reason or intelligence. Every man has reason, and this reason is intended by God to enlighten him and guide him through life—in a word, to do for him at the human level what eyesight does for him at the bodily level. If a man lives according to reason, then we may say that he lives a human or natural life. Of course all men do not live according to reason; perhaps most men live on the level of sense. One who would live at the level of reason—we will see that truly insurmountable difficulties are encountered in the effort to do so—might be said to live a truly human life; and he would be described as a good pagan. Still, although living a good life, he would not yet live a supernatural or Christian life.

Therefore, upon raising us to the supernatural plane God gives to us an altogether new and more exalted guide.

This is faith, or the assent given by the mind to the truths revealed by God through Jesus Christ and taught by His Church. These truths are known to us and held by us through the virtue of faith. This faith is the guide which will lead us in living a supernatural life, as reason alone would have led us had we been left to live merely natural lives. If we live by reason we live as human beings; to live as Christians we must live by faith, that is, we must take the truths of faith as the principles of our actions. This may be seen in the example already given. When you give an alms to a man because he is a relative or a friend, or because you wish to secure his goodwill, you are acting reasonably, but not supernaturally. But when you give an alms to a man because you see in him the image of Jesus Christ and, out of love for Jesus, you offer this neighbor of yours the assistance he needs— that is assuredly a supernatural act. Now what is it that enables you to see Jesus in your neighbor? It is faith that gives you this power of second sight. Jesus said that *"whatsoever you do for the least of My brethren you do it also to Me."* Knowing this we are confident that in helping our brethren we are serving Jesus personally.

Or take another example—suppose that you are struck or injured by another. What is your natural tendency? Simply to strike back, that is, to have justice from your assailant. Even reason will permit this, will tell you that your anger is justified and that you have a right to have an eye for an eye and a tooth for a tooth. But if you live by faith, another rule will impose itself upon you. You will recall, you will have it ever on your mind, that Jesus said, *"Love your enemies, do good to those who hate you, and pray for those who persecute and calumniate you."* This is the rule of faith and the man who lives by faith will adopt this higher rule and, again in the words of Jesus, when he is struck will turn the other cheek. You see then that there is a vast difference between acting according to the principles of reason and acting according to the dictates of faith. To live according to reason will seem perfectly natural to us; a reasonable life is a good life; and this consideration, that it is a good life, may make us fully satisfied with it and obscure from us the other and more important fact that there is a higher kind of life and a higher kind of conduct which we Christians ought to observe, namely, living by faith.

It may be well to notice here, too, that in practice reason often falls sadly away from that devotion to truth and virtue which it ought to observe. That is to say, actual men and women are often led by passion and prejudice rather than by reason, although even then they will call upon reason to justify their conduct and do call it "reasonable." When one sees Jesus in his neighbor, we have just observed, he is acting by faith. But reason ought at any rate to realize that all men are essentially equal and good. Actually, we see how men almost universally fall into racial and national suspicions, jealousies, and even hatreds; and yet they are fully persuaded that their conduct in the matter is reasonable. If faith is immeasurably higher than even the purest reason, it rises even further beyond such false reason and is diametrically opposed to it.

So far we have considered two modes of distinguishing the two ways of life and action; namely by their make-ups and by their guides; on the higher way, faith is the headlight and charity the motor force. We may also distinguish them by their respective destinations. Every highway brings you to its own destination, and you choose this one or that according to whether or not it will take you to the destination that you desire. If you wish to go to New York, you will take one road; if to Cleveland, then another. And so we can also define the two ways of life with which we are concerned by the destinations to which they lead us. If we live according to the supernatural way of life, it will bring us to God, to God's home, to heaven. Heaven, which is happiness with God, is, we may say, the destination of the supernatural way of living.

What about the natural life? What is its destination? It would lead us to the attainment of a natural good, that is, to a natural end; and the natural end of a natural life is natural happiness. Natural happiness is such happiness as men can obtain here on earth; and in eternity the place where souls enjoy natural happiness is Limbo. It is to Limbo, as you will recall, that the souls of unbaptized infants go when they die. They go there because they have not been reborn by grace and elevated to the supernatural plane; hence they cannot enjoy supernatural happiness. And since, on the other hand, they have committed no grave personal sins, they do not deserve the terrible punishment of hell. Therefore God permits them to enter a state proper to their nature, a state something like that which all men *might* have entered had not God decreed that they should labor for supernatural happiness.

Limbo, then, or natural happiness, is the term or destination of the natural way of life; and when we live, or attempt to live, a natural life, we are tending towards Limbo. Mark—and this is important—we might think that because we are living a natural life, which is a good life, we are tending towards heaven. But this is not so; a natural life, and natural actions, are powerless to merit heaven for us of themselves. On the other hand, we do not say that a person who lives a natural life will go to Limbo but simply that he *tends* towards Limbo. No one except unbaptized infants, and perhaps some primitive and ignorant peoples who are like infants, will go to Limbo. Limbo is closed to the baptized. Nevertheless, it will help us to keep our ideas clear, and to define the natural order, if we know that the natural order of itself tends towards the natural happiness which is described by philosophers and which at least some souls enjoy in Limbo. We may say, therefore, that the destiny, or the destination, of the natural order is Limbo and the destination of the supernatural order is heaven.

To summarize what has been said so far: we can distinguish

the two orders of natural and supernatural according to their respective makeups, their guides, and their destinations. The make-up in the natural order is all natural activity; that of the supernatural is grace, which flowers in love. The guide of the natural order is reason, while the guide of the supernatural is faith. The end or destination of the natural order is natural happiness or Limbo, and the end of the supernatural order is supernatural happiness or heaven.

Faith and charity then are the two distinctive powers of the supernatural life. As swimming is proper to the fish, flying to the bird, and thinking to man, so is living by faith and charity proper to the children of God. To these we must also add hope which lifts our mind above earthly goods and causes us to seek our happiness in God, thereby preparing the way for the union with God that comes through love.

The Third Level

Alas, we must now complicate our diagram, thus far so simple and clear, by adding to it a third level, that of sin, which is below the level of nature.

Until now, in speaking of the natural life as this is guided by reason in conformity with natural virtue and the natural law, tending finally to the highest natural happiness, we have been speaking of an ideally pure and perfect natural life. In practice and in actual life, nature, when it neglects to correspond with grace, does not always act with such perfection but is often led away even from the path of reason and natural rectitude by the desire of its faculties to gratify themselves with the good things of the world. In a similar way we speak of an ideal wife or an ideal husband, including in our mental picture of this ideal all the virtues that could be desired in wife or husband. Yet in real life wives and husbands—as any husband or wife will testify—do not always measure up to the ideal. They have the failings common to all men and women, to all at least who are not saints; and therefore, despite the sincerity of their love, they are frequently deflected from the ideal of conduct proper to them.

So likewise men in general (to speak of them apart from the influence of grace) may be impelled to action by their sense desires rather than by reason; this occurs in virtue of their freedom and because they have an animal nature as well as a spiritual soul. Indeed, reason, too, may act in a manner unbecoming to its better self, violating the very laws which its own order imposes; and the will, also a spiritual faculty, may join the rebellion against true reason by loving the goods of the world immoderately and thus using them wrongfully. Of course when the senses throw off the rule of reason they at the same time rise against faith and the control of grace; and reason and will, in refusing in their turn the demands of natural rectitude, by that very fact also repudiate the higher sway of *the new man* formed by grace.

In a word, men in actual life are very prone to fall first into worldliness and then, if they continue in the desire to satisfy their senses and passions, into sin. They fall into worldliness when they allow themselves to be led by natural desires; and when their love of earthly goods has so far grown that they abuse these in defiance of God's law, then they sin.

In this manner the third or lowest level comes into existence; or, to put the matter differently, it is in this way that men descend to the third and lowest level. And, following the mode of definition used so far, it may be said that the make-up of sin, that which makes an action evil, is the fact that it is a rebellion at once against reason and against God. The appetites or desires—and neither faith nor reason—are the guide, blind guide indeed, on this lower level. Finally the end or destination of sinful activity is spiritual death, hell.

Of course in describing this tendency of natural activity to go downhill as it were, we are far from saying that all natural actions are bad or that a pagan, for example, or even a Christian, is incapable with his human powers alone of performing good natural actions. By no means: even with natural powers only, it is possible to perform some good natural actions, as for example rendering assistance to a neighbor. On the other hand, it is a Catholic teaching that without the aid of grace one cannot fulfill the whole of the natural law or remain faithful to all its precepts indefinitely. Hence, while a man by his human strength alone can perform good natural actions, this is true only of actions taken singly or in small numbers or over relatively short periods of time. Taking life as a whole and viewing actions over a long period of time, we are not able without the assistance of grace to meet all the requirements even of natural virtue and right reason. This is why one who neglects grace will go down a slow declivity, drawn by the love of earthly goods, until he eventually commits sin; and unless the whole process is reversed by an interior conversion and a sustained effort to correspond with grace by living on the supernatural plane, sin will lead to further sin, to a habit of sin, and to final ruin.

To review: our completed diagram has three levels as follows:

I	II	III	IV
LEVELS	**MAKE-UP**	**GUIDE**	**DESTINATION**
Supernatural	**Charity**	**Faith**	**Heaven**
Natural	**Natural Activity**	**Reason**	**(Limbo)**
Sinful	**Rebellion**	**Appetite**	**Hell**

(NOTE—The parentheses above indicate that limbo is a merely theoretical possibility.)

In speaking of Limbo, we always bear in mind that it is only a theoretical possibility. In fact, the whole natural plane, taken in the large, is, we can now see, but a theoretical possibility: that is to say, while one may perform some good natural actions, whether singly or for a period of time, it is not possible to remain on the natural plane indefinitely or permanently. If a man tries to stay on this plane of life—that is, if he rejects the grace which God offers to all and which would raise him to the supernatural order—then he will find himself going down a gradual declivity that will bring him at length into sin. Thus sin is not an independent level of activity; it branches off from natural activity because of the downward inclination of nature left to itself, of nature under the influence of carnal desires, while nature and natural activity in their ideal purity, because they are abstractions, have no actual destination, like a road that ends in a pasture.

Hence, while for purposes of definition it is useful to represent three possible levels of life and action, it is well to remember that, generally speaking, there are only two actual levels, the one, the ideal natural life, being in its completeness but a theoretical possibility. For this reason the Scriptures speak of only two levels; St. Paul for example, contrasts carnal and spiritual living; and he tells us (Rom. 8, 13) that those who live according to the spirit shall have life and peace while those who live according to the flesh shall die. The Apostle does not speak, as the philosophers do, of living according to reason by the natural virtues and observance of the natural law. He is concerned, not with the ideal or theoretical truths of philosophy, not with nature in the abstract but with the actual conduct of living men. And, knowing that concupiscence leads men awry when they try to live on the natural plane, he speaks derogatorily of this mode of life as carnal, according to the flesh. His judgment is that it will lead them to ruin.

Yet, despite this usage of the Scriptures, and despite the fact that apart from grace men cannot live a perfect natural life, it is by no means useless, but rather useful and also necessary, to describe the ideal natural order. Just as an airplane, while traveling above the earth, takes its rise in the first place from the earth and its altitude is measured in reference to the earth, so the Christian life, while it is supernatural, must be defined in reference to the order of nature, and its loftiness is best understood by our minds likewise in relation to that order. Thus, to understand supernatural living and conduct, we must understand the powers and possibilities of nature. To make our lives divine, we must know the meaning of the merely human and how to rise above it. Our nature and its powers are the starting-place, the point of departure, for our elevation to the supernatural plane and for our efforts to live on that plane.

Let us think upon these things. And may God bless you.

> *"We pray Thee, O Almighty God, that Thou wilt not allow us to be overcome by human dangers since Thou has gladdened us with a share in the divine life. Through Our Lord Jesus Christ Thy Son Who livest and reignest with Thee in union with the Holy Spirit, God world without end. Amen."*

(Postcommunion, 23rd Sunday after Pentecost)

CREATION AND RE-CREATION

My dear Friends in Christ —

Before going any further with our subject, let us pause to examine the truths we have been considering as they are given in the Sacred Scriptures. So numerous are the texts that deal, whether directly or indirectly, with our elevation to the divine life that it would be impossible to enumerate them all. Indeed it may be said without exaggeration that the whole of the Scriptures is concerned with this truth, and that the inspired writings are simply incomprehensible without the knowledge of it. That is why we have called it a key: it opens doors—one after the other. Without doubt one of the reasons why we find many passages of the Bible so mysterious—apart from technical difficulties—is that we have such an imperfect grasp of this fundamental doctrine of our Faith.

What we propose to do in the present conference is to take up four groups of texts which deal in different ways with our subject. Afterwards, in your own reading of Sacred Writ, you will find many other passages to place with each of these groups.

Our Adopted Sonship

The first group deals with our supernatural elevation under the figure or analogy of sonship. Who does not know those tremendous words of St. John which at the very beginning of his Gospel trumpet the staggering fact of God's Incarnation and the consequent raising of man to the exalted state of sons of God? *"And the Word was made flesh, and dwelt among us....To as many as received Him, He gave the power of becoming sons of God; to those who believe in His name: who were born not of blood, nor of the will of the flesh, nor of the will of man, but of God."* (John 1, 12)

The Apostle here clearly speaks of two kinds of generation, the natural generation of man, and a higher generation, not fleshly, but spiritual, by which men become sons of God.

Now while we have called the idea of sonship, as describing our elevation, a figure of speech, the Scriptures are by no means indulging in a mere empty metaphor when they here speak of us as sons of God; this figure is not the same as when we call a brave man a lion or a cunning man a serpent. No; we are here dealing with an analogy of a vastly higher order: it is truth: as on the natural plane we are related to our human fathers, so on the supernatural plane we are related to God. To put it differently: we are not only *called* sons of God—this is not a mere empty title of honor—but we *are* sons of God. It is St. John, again, who insists on this: *"Behold what manner of love the Father has bestowed on us, that we should be called children of God; and such we are."* (I John 3,1)

Our understanding of grace enables us to grasp this teaching. By grace we share in the divine nature; and because we share in the divine nature we are truly children of God. Sonship—the relation of offspring to parent—always and necessarily involves a similarity of nature. Dogs give birth to puppy dogs, never to kittens; cats never give birth to puppies, always to kittens; and human parents always have human children. This is the very nature and definition of sonship: the rise of a nature similar to the nature of the parent. In human children there is often, not merely a similarity of nature, but also a resemblance of their physical features to those of their mother and father. In the same way, therefore, the Scriptures call us children of God because we have a share in the divine life; and only those who thus share the divine life are truly children of God.

Jesus Himself explicitly spoke of this higher life when He told Nicodemus (John 3, 3) emphatically that *"unless a man be born again, he cannot see the kingdom of God."* Perhaps you recall how these words puzzled Nicodemus. For to be born means to receive life; and once we have received life, how can we be born again? *"How can a man be born when he is old?"* asked Nicodemus in his perplexity. *"Can he enter a second time into his mother's womb and be born again?"* Jesus explained that this second birth is to be understood spiritually; to be born *again*, we must receive, in addition to our common human life, a higher principle of living. This is accomplished, Jesus said, by water and the Holy Spirit; that is why we call baptism, in which this promise is fulfilled, the sacrament of rebirth, or regeneration: through it we receive life from the Spirit. In the same passage, Our Lord distinguishes the two kinds of life and cryptically reveals the reason for the absolute necessity of the divine life: *"That which is born of the flesh is flesh; and that which is born of the Spirit is spirit."* To enter into heaven, which is the home of God, we must be children of God, and to become children of God we must be reborn spiritually to possess divine life. The flesh and all its works cannot gain the kingdom of heaven. There is no other text in Sacred Scripture which shows us the absolute need of grace—that is, of participation in the divine nature—as this one does.

In insisting that we are truly children of God, it is to be kept in mind of course that we are not the natural or consubstantial children of God, as is Jesus Christ, the Son of God. To distinguish our sonship from His, Catholic teaching calls ours an adopted sonship. At the same time, we must note that our adoption by God is no mere legal fiction or formality, as it is when a human couple adopt a child who, despite the legal title, is not really their own. Our relation to Our Father Who is in heaven is, on the one hand, not to be confused with the infinitely more perfect relationship to Him of His only-begotten Son. At the same time, because we are given a share in the divine nature, our adoption is a reality, not a mere legal arrangement or empty title.

It should be clear from all this that the Scriptures call us sons and children of God in an altogether special sense. Sometimes these words are used loosely, and all men are described as sons of God. It is true that God gives human life to all and by His fatherly providence sustains that life. Yet the creative act by which He gives us human life is altogether different from, and lower than, the paternal act by which He gives us a share in the divine life. Making a thing is quite different from giving birth to, or begetting, a child. A carpenter makes a table, but there is not the same relationship between him and his table that there is between him and his son; and if he is pleased with his table, he will nevertheless not give it the tender affection that he gives his son. All men are creatures of God, but all men are not His sons in the sense that they are sharers in His nature. Taking these terms in their broad sense may at times be useful; but unless we are careful, it may lead to a blurring of the proper concept of divine sonship and so cause us to miss or to forget or fail to appreciate the glorious dignity and privilege he has conferred upon those who are his sons in truth. If a sculptor were to make a statue of a boy looking very much like himself, it would still not be his child; but were he able to infuse his own life into the statue, then it would become his child. If all men are creatures of God and made to His image, it is only when they receive grace that they come to life in the Scriptural and Christian sense and become His children.

Before leaving this group of texts, I would only point out further the condition fixed by St. John for possessing this status: those have the power to become sons of God, the Evangelist says, are those who believe in His name. Faith, then, is the open-sesame to the supernatural world; and the faith meant is a faith formed and made fruitful by charity. You will recall that when defining the supernatural way of life in our last conference, we put down faith and charity as its characteristics. St. Paul teaches the same thing when he says in his letter to the Galatians that *"neither circumcision nor uncircumcision availeth anything"*— that is, neither the law of the Jews nor that of the Gentiles can bring salvation—*"but faith which works through charity."* (Gal. 5, 6) St. John also makes charity as well as faith, the criterion of the supernatural life, as when he says, *"He who loves his brother abides in the light...he who hates his brother is in darkness...."* (1 John 2, 10)

Creation and Re-creation

The second set of texts speak of our elevation as a renewal. Thus, *"you are to put off the old man, which is being corrupted through its deceptive lusts. But be renewed in the spirit of your mind, and put on the new man, which has been created according to God in justice and holiness of truth."* (Eph. 4, 22-24) Manifestly, the renewal here spoken of is not one that is merely accidental or external, as when one is "renewed" by a bath and a good meal or by a day in the country. What is meant is a complete interior renovation and transformation; and this is effected in the first instance by the reception of sanctifying grace and carried to completion by the soul's correspondence with grace.

Perhaps the meaning of this renewal is best brought out by St. Paul when he says, *"If then any man is in Christ, he is a new creature: the former things have passed away; behold they are made new!"* (II Cor. 5, 17) The renewal here spoken of, then, is no mere freshening up of the mind, not simply a new outlook— although it is this also. Through Christ we are recreated, created on a higher plane; we are, in a word, new creatures, the products of a new and higher creation. And the freshness and newness of our thought and conduct should come from that fact. In the same spirit, St. Paul says that *"neither circumcision nor uncircumcision but a new creation is of any account."* (Gal. 6, 15)

To be created means to be made out of nothing. That is what happened when the world and man were created. And now it happens again on a higher level. Creation was a gigantic work, the exercise of God's omnipotence. It is a work, too, that we can in a manner imagine. Hence, to call the work of grace a new creation gives us some idea of the magnitude of the work accomplished by grace.

But how can this renewal be called a creation when man at least has existence at the time of his receiving grace, whereas creation is effected from nothing? St. Thomas explains by observing that although it is true that a man has existence at the moment of his justification, yet he has no merits of his own that are of any value in the supernatural order. In this sense, he is raised to the latter order from nothing: hence the act by which he is raised is a real creation, a second creation or re-creation.

Indeed, this second creation is an even greater work than the first. Not only was man raised to the divine plane without merit of his own, but he was raised also against the resistance encountered by divine grace in man's sinful state. But even more important, as St. Thomas also points out, this second creation is greater than the first because the first act of God raises us only to the human level while the second raises us to the divine. By the first act we became men, as the Psalmist says, *"a little lower than the angels."* The same inspired writer now cries out to us,

"You are gods...."

With all this in mind we are in a position to understand better that admirable prayer in which the liturgy of the Mass summarizes the redemptive plan of God and sets forth the basic doctrine of the Christian religion: "O God, Who has created the nature of man in wondrous dignity, and has still more admirably re-formed it, grant that through the mystery of this water and wine, we may become partakers of His divinity, Who has condescended to become a partaker of our humanity, Jesus Christ, Thy Son, Our Lord, Who liveth and reigneth with Thee in the unity of the Holy Spirit, God, world without end. Amen."

Darkness and Death; Light and Life

Another class of texts speak of those who live on the divine plane as being in the "light" or having "life," while all others are in "darkness" or "death." For example, Jesus once said, *"Amen, amen, I say to you, he who hears My word, and believes Him Who sent Me, has life everlasting, and does not come to judgment, but has passed from death to life."* (John 5, 24) Again, a little further on in the same Gospel, He is reported as saying, *"I have come a light into the world, that whoever believes in Me may not remain in the darkness."* (John 12, 46)

What is of significance in these texts, in addition to the clear distinction of the two planes of life and activity, is the criterion whereby Our Lord distinguishes those who possess supernatural life. Many persons, reading these texts hastily, and interpreting them in accord with the general tendency to regard practical Christianity as a mere avoidance of grievous sin, rather than as also a rising above nature, would understand by those who are in darkness or in death as persons who sin mortally. But that is not what Jesus says. He does not state that those who avoid grave sin have life and those who commit such sin are dead; rather He says that those who have faith, as we have already declared, have passed from death to life, from darkness to light. In other words, not only men who commit mortal sin are in darkness and death but those also who, in defiance of God's plan for our supernatural happiness, remain on the natural level, following reason and rejecting the higher guidance of faith.

This interpretation will seem surprising, if not scandalous, to some who, invoking the truths of philosophy—which we of course do not deny, but which must take account of actual circumstances in being transposed to the practical order—will remind us that nature and reason are God's creatures and therefore good. Nevertheless, if you scrutinize the texts under consideration, you will see that in the teaching of Jesus, it is only those who live by faith who are on the road to salvation.

In truth, if man had been created in a state of pure nature and left there, with the duty of laboring for the fulfillment of a merely natural destiny, then without doubt he would have been expected and required to regulate his life by reason. But man was not created and left in the natural order; he was re-created and given a supernatural destiny; so that if, proudly complacent in his natural powers, he prefers to rely on his own resources and to be guided by his own reason, rejecting the truths of faith, which he does not understand, he is guilty of rebellion, is liable to punishment, and so is truly in darkness and in death. In other words, considering man in his actual supernatural state, any determination to live by reason alone is an act of rebellion.

As an example, consider a little boy who each day stops and looks in various store windows, eyeing the things that interest boys—marbles and tops, baseballs and bats and gloves. He looks at them greedily, but alas he has no money. Suppose that one fine day, his father gives him money, a large sum. The boy's imagination leaps with delight and he begins to think of all the things he can get. But just as he starts out to satisfy his desires, we will suppose, his father calls him back and gives him a small savings bank; the money, the father tells him, is to be put in this bank and saved for his future schooling, that he may some day enjoy a career as a doctor. If the boy, in spite of this instruction, defiantly spends the money on toys anyway, he will at once commit an act of disobedience and deprive himself of a higher good.

Now our heavenly Father deals with us in some such fashion as this. He endows us with natural powers, surrounds us with natural goods, gives us a natural appetite for these goods. It is then quite natural indeed for men to set out in pursuit of them. But now God intervenes. He tells us that He plans a career for us on the supernatural level, and that our natural faculties, activities, and appetites are to be consecrated to that higher purpose. If we obstinately insist, in defiance of God's plan, upon seeking natural goods, then we, like the boy, besides depriving ourselves of the Supreme Good, are guilty of grave disobedience. This is why if, in view of our present elevated state, we remain on the plane of reason, we are in darkness and in death. And this is also why St. John of the Cross, following the same line of thought, tells us that, not only those who commit mortal sin are in darkness, but also those who retain any natural affection or attachment for creatures, although this affection in itself is not sinful. Men who retain an affection for creatures are defying, more or less, the plan whereby God would have us renounce the desire for natural goods and dedicate our talents wholeheartedly to the pursuit of our supernatural end and good.

Thus, while to avoid any depreciation of even God's natural gifts, we must recognize the goodness of nature and reason considered in themselves, we must at the same time, in ascertaining or describing the conduct proper to Christians, take into account a tendency of nature and reason to veer from the norm of rightness in their actual behavior. Although reason in itself is good, in actual practice it tends to live by its own principles on the natural plane; and if it follows this tendency, rejecting the guidance of faith, it is without doubt in "darkness."

Those who, above all, prefer to follow their reason to acceptance through faith of the truths of the supernatural order, are rationalists in the narrow sense, and are guilty of the sin of infidelity. We may also call this sin rationalism—or naturalism. In the first place, this was the sin of the fallen angels and of our first parents; and it led to all other sins, as we have seen that the attempt to live on the natural plane still leads invariably to sin.

In a broader sense there is also among Catholics—not indeed infidelity, by which they would cease to be Catholics—but a spirit of infidelity by which, while giving a vague speculative assent to the truths of the faith, perhaps reciting the Apostles' Creed regularly, they fail to make the truths of faith active in their daily lives. On the contrary, they take their practical principles of conduct from the world, which communicates its maxims to them in the most attractive way, through newspapers, magazines, popular novels, moving pictures, the radio, and, first and foremost, through the pressure of constant companionship with worldly people. Thus we find Catholics quite at home among worldlings, often outdoing the latter. They are pleasure-seekers, follow the styles of the world without restraint or discrimination, are devoted to wealth and the wealthy, are habitually guilty of human respect and snobbishness in their dealings with others. In a word, they live as though there had never been an Incarnation, as though they had never received the gifts of grace and faith; and they can only justify themselves by appealing to the broad prohibitions of the natural law. Even their observance of the natural law often would stand no very close scrutiny. These persons are spiritually blind as a result of their self-indulgence, and so they think that they have satisfied the natural law if they have not been guilty of any gross infractions against its more rudimentary precepts.

Such practical infidelity or practical naturalism—both names are correct—would reduce Christianity to a mere body of speculative truths and a system of natural morality. In the individuals whom it infects, it causes, as we see everywhere, spiritual blindness, tepidity, mediocrity. Its effort to reconcile Christ with the world is a scandal even to the world. It weakens and corrupts the Mystical Body of Christ by weakening and corrupting Christ's members; and it thus makes the action of the Church ineffective in the world at times of great crisis like the present. Lastly, it does not stop at lukewarmness but frequently ends in open infidelity, as we see in the case of those who, as a result of weakened faith devote themselves to the pursuit of natural goods, and end by rejecting the faith altogether in order to gain or hold such goods, for example, desirable marriages, business advantages, pleasures and comforts. We see the same thing on a wider scale in the so-called Christian world's infidelity to the teachings of Christ.

The remedy for this evil is a spirit of faith, gained by loving meditation on the truths of the Gospel and a persevering effort to apply these truths to the smallest practical problems of everyday life.

Texts Dealing with Practice

A final group of texts that we will now consider are those that deal most immediately with practice. Certainly all the passages that we have studied have their practical implications, and in some cases these implications are more or less clearly indicated. There are others which deal explicitly and directly with the practical consequences or our elevation to the supernatural order. It is necessary for our purpose to give deliberate attention to these latter texts.

In this connection we should first observe that the phrase "supernatural life" may be used in a twofold sense. It may refer to the endowment of grace received by the soul from God; or it may refer to the exercise of that grace: to the principle of supernatural life, or to the use made of this principle in everyday practice. Or, to put the matter differently, it may mean the original capital received from God, or the investment of that capital for spiritual profit and a further increase of wealth.

Now very often, Catholics, while acknowledging the necessity of the supernatural life, limit their notion of that life to the first meaning; that is they limit it to the principle of supernatural life, and ignore the need of an effort on the soul's part to activate that principle in a truly divine manner of living. As a consequence, they view grace and the sacraments in a rather speculative or theoretical manner. They eloquently describe the efficacy of the sacraments and the excellence of grace, but do not show much industry in making that excellence and efficacy really effective. They point out that sanctification is the work of grace and that grace comes from God; and that therefore sanctification is the work of God. This is of course true, but it is not a truth that relieves us of spiritual effort.

Grace comes from God but it becomes effective only through our cooperation; just as, on a lower plane, food also comes from God, and obtains its power of nourishment from Him, yet this power is utilized on our behalf only when we eat and digest the food.

The result of such an attitude is that, in seeking for the foundation of the duties of the spiritual life, these Catholics invoke right reason and the laws of natural morality. Often, too, as we have seen, as a result of worldliness, they have an attenuated notion even of natural law. In any case, they tend to reduce Christianity at best to a mere moral system, to a code of natural ethics. They thus compromise and lose the specifically supernatural character of Christian teaching and the mode of living that depends on that teaching. By meditating on such texts as we here mark, we will correct that too natural tendency. We will learn to derive our religious duties from our supernatural elevation; and we will come to realize how immeasurably higher are our duties as Christians than the ethical conduct proper to good pagans.

We are concerned here, then, directly with texts that point out the duty of really practicing and living a supernatural life. Of course the Scriptures are filled with moral exhortations; and it may be affirmed further that the basis, at least implicit, of all these exhortations is primarily man's elevation to share the divine life, and not right reason or the natural law. But our interest here is with passages that make our elevation or re-creation the explicit basis of moral teaching.

Perhaps the passage in the Gospels which comes most quickly to mind in this connection is the one which suggested the example, just given, of a man investing capital. You recall the parable of the talents: how two men were rewarded because they put out their talents at interest, while one who buried his talent to preserve it was punished. Too often this parable is understood materially, as though it referred only to human or natural gifts and endowments. But manifestly, in the mind of Jesus, it refers primarily to our spiritual gifts and especially to sanctifying grace. And the punishment of the man who buried his talent is a terrible warning to those who think that they may leave their sanctification entirely to God and do nothing themselves to use the grace and spiritual gifts which He so liberally bestows on them.

We may mention here also those passages in which Sacred Scripture enjoins on us a standard of behavior that is really divine and Godlike, as for example, when Jesus says that *we should be perfect as the heavenly Father is perfect*" or when St. Paul lays upon us the equally amazing injunction to be *"imitators of God."* (Eph. 5, 1) Such words would be incomprehensible, not to say impossible in their demands, had

34

we not been elevated to the divine life. Indeed admonitions like these, addressed to mere men, could produce but spiritual exhaustion and despair; they are fittingly addressed to us now, because as the Psalmist says to us, *"You are gods, and all of you the sons of the Most High."* (Psalm 81, 6)

Obviously, too, the basis of our duty to imitate Christ is the fact of our elevation to divine life. Otherwise the effort to imitate Him would be sheer madness. For Jesus, although truly human, was also divine; even His human life was divine in its ultimate principle—the divine personality—as in the wisdom that guided His steps, the motivation of His actions, and the Spirit that dominated His entire career. We can imitate such a life only because we also have been given through Him, a divine principle of life and action.

There are other places in which the inspired word appeals explicitly, not to reason or to natural law, but to our special state as Christians as the foundation for our spiritual lives. I will mention two. St. Paul writes, *"I therefore, the Prisoner in the Lord, exhort you to walk in a manner worthy of the calling with which you were called."* (Eph. 4, 1) The Apostle goes on here to urge us to the practice of such specifically Christian virtues as humility and love. A little further on he appeals to a conception with which we are now familiar, namely the idea of light. He says, *"You were once darkness, but now you are light in the Lord. Walk, then, as children of light (for the fruit of the light is in all goodness and justice and truth), testing what is well pleasing to God; and have no fellowship with the unfruitful works of darkness, but rather expose them."* (Eph. 5, 8-12) To walk worthy of the light—that is, to become holy: this is our duty as Christians.

The other similar passage not only indicates that the spiritual duties of Christians derive from their association with the Incarnation of Jesus but also states bluntly the nature of these duties. *"Therefore, if you have risen with Christ, seek the things that are above, where Christ is seated at the right hand of God. Mind the things that are above, not the things that are on earth. For you have died and your life is hidden with Christ in God."* (Col. 3, 1-3)

You see here the duty that follows immediately from our

incorporation into Christ: detachment— not only from sin; but from all the goods of the natural world: *"Mind not the things that are on earth."* Indeed, the Saint tells us our response to the goods of earth, should be like that of a dead man, which is not to respond at all. Alas, that so many Catholics are dead to Christ and live habitually for the world! Yet there can be no doubt that, as we are risen with Christ, we should reverse this attitude and set our hearts wholly on the things that are above.

We will conclude these citations by noting the examples with which the inspired word illustrates the fundamental law of the supernatural world, the law of love. The first we have already observed; since we are children, our relationship to Him and our duties towards Him are akin to those that issue from the strong and tender love of children for their father. Then our Lord also calls us friends, here likewise in a different manner appealing to love, this time a love of equality as the explanation of the bond that He would establish between Himself and us, *"I will not now call you servants: for the servant knoweth not what his lord doth. But I have called you friends...."* (John 15, 15) It is because we now share in the divine life that we can now enjoy such equality with the Son of God as to be in truth His friends.

The final example is that of married love. Following the tradition of the Old Testament, Jesus represents Himself as a bridegroom, while the Church, and of course the souls within the Church, are the bride. In this comparison with the most tender and most intimate of human loves, God gives us, as we shall have many occasion to see, the most perfect way of knowing our duties towards Himself.

Let us think upon these things; and may God bless you.

> *"Grant us, we beseech Thee, O Almighty God, that we who have obtained from Thee the grace of a new life may ever glory in Thy gift. Through Our Lord Jesus Christ Thy Son Who livest and reignest with Thee in union with the Holy Spirit, God world without end. Amen."*
> (Postcommunion, Second Sunday after Easter)

SOME PRINCIPLES FOR APPLYING CHRISTIANITY

My dear Friends in Christ—

Let us suppose that you have accomplished, at least in imagination, the project suggested in an earlier conference. Let us suppose that in virtue of extraordinary powers you have equipped your cabbage and tomato plants with feet and legs; your gold fish can now fly; and Rover is able to converse with you in cultivated accents. What would you expect of these creatures, thus raised by your goodness to a higher order? Certainly gratitude at least, as well as promptitude and eagerness in using their new abilities. But if your plants refuse to move about and care for themselves, requiring that you still serve them, if the fish obstinately refuse to fly, preferring the water; if Rover maintains a sullen silence, or, worse yet, reverts to barking, how would you feel? Disappointed at least; perhaps angry enough to dissolve the dream.

Now God raises us to the supernatural order and gives us supernatural powers expecting us to use them. There are duties and responsibilities, as well as privileges, following from our elevation to share the divine life. It will be our task to discover and describe these responsibilities and duties in detail. But even now, from the truths we have already studied, certain broad practical principles emerge. We will consider them in this conference, setting them down as axioms or easy reference rules of conduct. Six such axioms may be distinguished.

The First Axiom

The first is this: the supernatural life urges us to adopt standards of conduct higher than such as are involved in the avoidance of sin. Or better, practical Christianity does not consist merely in the avoidance of sin. If we seek only to avoid sin, particularly mortal sin, and aim at nothing higher, neglecting the supernatural teachings of the Gospel and ignoring the requirements of charity and divine grace, then we are content to live as pagans rather than as Christians—good pagans perhaps, such as described by the ancient philosophers, but pagans nevertheless, following a natural and rational standard of conduct. Note too that we can practice all the natural virtues—prudence, justice, fortitude, and temperance—such as those described by Aristotle, and still act as pagans. These virtues in themselves, although good and desirable, belong to the natural plane. It is the supernatural virtues, above all faith, hope and charity which make it possible for us to act supernaturally as Christians; it is in the exercise of virtues that we live really as Christians.

Of course we have already noted the difficulty, not to say the impossibility, of remaining on the natural plane indefinitely without grace; what we wish to say now is that even though it could be done, it would not satisfy the requirements of supernatural conduct.

It is therefore insufficient for us to take as a guide for our conduct the rule to avoid mortal sin. If we make this our maximum of conduct, we will not get beyond the merely natural standard of behavior proper to the good pagans. We have already seen from our diagram of the three levels, that we might avoid sin and still be on the good natural plane. Moreover, if we take this rule, to avoid mortal sin, as the norm of our conduct, we will be apt to slip into the belief that, provided we avoid mortal sin, it will be perfectly all right for us to abandon ourselves to worldly pleasures and the love of creatures. That is why so many Catholics, although claiming that they are observing the standards of Christian conduct, live worldly lives. The truth is that they are observing the standards of only a natural life. If they were living supernaturally they would be much more mortified and detached from the goods of this world. For a Christian, then, the avoidance of mortal sin is an absolute minimum of conduct not a maximum. It is the least that we can do; and of itself, that is, apart from faith and hope and charity, it is not sufficient at all; our vocation is much higher, namely the vocation to conform to Christ and to conduct ourselves as sons of God. Suppose a wife considers that she is being neglected by her husband and reproaches him. And suppose that in reply he protests his love for her. When she asks him the extent of this love let us imagine him as saying, "Well, my dear, you see I do not divorce you." Would the wife be satisfied with such a declaration of love? It does contain some love, but a minimum; and it is certainly not what is to be expected of a true lover. When we take as our rule the avoidance of mortal sin, while neglecting the higher demands of love which should rule our lives as Christians, we are just like such a man; we are saying to God that of course we love Him since we are so careful not to divorce ourselves from Him. But our reluctance to do anything more than avoid divorce is no strong argument for the sincerity and ardor of our love.

It should be clear then that a mere obedience to the commandments of the natural law does not of itself make us act as Christians. The natural law, you know, comprises all the commandments which men know by reason, that is to say by studying the inclinations of their own nature. For example, "Thou shalt not kill," and "Thou shalt not steal" are laws of nature. Men would know these laws without Christ or Revelation, although Revelation has made them more easily accessible and clear to all men. But in themselves they are laws known to reason, and it is a great mistake to confuse them with the much higher standards taught by the Gospel. By the mere observance of the commandments of the natural law we cannot be saved, that is, we cannot enter into supernatural happiness. These commandments, if kept, would help us to realize to the full the possibilities of our nature; but they can never raise us to the level of a supernatural life, and by their observance we would merit at best a merely natural happiness. The Christian life consists in following the movements, not of nature, but of grace. No doubt, as we shall see, in living a supernatural life we will also keep our human nature and our natural activity intact; but we must learn to rule them in accordance with the requirements of grace and love.

The terrible mistake of the Scribes and Pharisees was that they reduced the law of God to a mere observance of natural law, forgetting the great commandments of love, which were given already in the Old Testament. Their great sin, therefore, from which their other sins followed, was a sin against the supernatural. And the insufficiency of their teaching, for salvation, is evident from the words of Jesus to the rich young man who was able to boast that he had kept all the commandments of the natural law. *"One thing is still lacking to thee,"* was Our Lord's reply; and He went on to state, as a further requirement, the commandment of love. We repeat the error and the sin of the Pharisees when in our practice we reduce the whole law of God to the law of nature and gauge our conduct as though we were now living in a mere state of nature.

To be sure, one who is in the state of grace, which is accompanied always by infused charity, and has faithfully observed the natural law by avoiding grave sin will be saved. But it is the grace and charity that save him—not the natural law. The point to be observed here is precisely that only a supernatural principle and supernatural activity, that is to say, actions which proceed from a supernatural principle, can merit salvation.

Christianity, therefore, is not to be put down as a mere system of morality; it is not to be confused with natural ethics. Yet this mistake is frequently made. Christianity takes natural morality as a starting-point and then goes far beyond; it is essentially a supernatural religion.

It was not Our Lord's special mission to teach us the natural law. The great pagan teachers did this in large measure. We Christians are under a heavy debt to the enlightened pagans, like Plato and Aristotle. And of course we ought to be thankful to God that in His Revelation He made even the natural law clearer for the greater number of men. Nevertheless we must never confuse our supernatural religion with even the highest natural law and natural religion.

The Second Axiom

Since obedience to the natural law is not the distinctive mark of Christian conduct, the question then arises, "What, then, is the supernatural law?" The answer of course is that the great commandment of Christianity is the commandment of love or of charity. When the lawyer asked how he might enter into eternal life, Jesus answered, *"Love the Lord thy God with thy whole heart, with thy whole mind, with thy whole soul, and with all thy strength. This is the first and greatest commandment. And the second is like to this: Thou shalt love thy neighbor as thyself."*

Moreover, not only is love the first and characteristic law of the supernatural world, but its fulfillment is also necessary for salvation. St. Paul leaves us in no doubt of this: *"If I should speak with the tongues of men and of angels, but do not have charity, I have become as sounding brass or a tinkling cymbal. And if I have prophecy and know all mysteries and all knowledge, and if I have all faith so as to remove mountains, yet do not have charity, I am nothing. And if I distribute all my goods to feed the poor, and if I deliver my body to be burned, yet do not have charity, it profits me nothing."* (I Cor. 13, 1-3) It should be noted that even what is called baptism of desire is really an act of charity and not simply a desire for baptism: it is desire for God, and desire is the first movement of love; it is a preference for God above all things because of His goodness, together with the resolve to do all that God asks. Thus, no one can be saved without charity: it is an absolutely indispensable means of salvation.

St. Gregory the Great sees in the wedding garment spoken of in the Gospel parable a symbol of charity. You recall how the man without the wedding garment was expelled from the feast and punished. Now St. Gregory says that this wedding garment could not refer to baptism or to faith; for these are required even to obtain entrance into the feast, that is, into the place where the feast is prepared, into the Church. And since the man in the parable had already been admitted to the feast, he must stand for those who have faith and have been baptized but lack some other quality necessary for salvation. What they lack, says St. Gregory, is charity, without which no one can enjoy the feast of eternal love in heaven.

It is true that the charity required is in its substance an infused virtue; that is to say, not a virtue that we acquire, but one poured into our souls by God. Just as the light from an electric lamp comes from a distant source and, after giving us illumination, returns to that source, so the power of affection which we return to God in the first place comes from God.

Nevertheless, charity, although infused, is given to us to be exercised: that is what every virtue or habit is for. A man cultivates the habit of typing in order to use it, or the habit of swimming in order to swim. The same is true of these supernatural habits or virtues which God gives to us. The only difference is that we do not labor to acquire these; still, of their very nature they tend towards action. God rewards us precisely for utilizing our supernatural powers; it is through exercising them that we earn or merit supernatural happiness. Should an infant die immediately after baptism, in which he has received an infusion of charity, he will be saved in view of that infused charity. But an adult is expected to make his charity active. St. Francis de Sales says that "charity being an active quality cannot be long without acting or dying." He remarks also that the Fathers compared it to Rachel, who also represented it. Now Rachel said, *"Give me children, otherwise I shall die."* So also charity "urges the heart which she has espoused to make her fertile of good works; otherwise she will perish."*(Love of God,* IV, 2)

The Third Axiom

The third axiom follows immediately from the second and is inseparably connected with it, being indeed but another aspect of the same principle. It is this: Hatred of the world belongs to the essence of Christianity. Or we may put the same truth this way: hatred of the world is the reverse of the love of God; and the love of God involves and requires a hatred of the world. Only by raising ourselves above the natural order do we become Christians. To do this, we are to love God with our whole heart, our whole soul, our whole mind and our whole strength. This means that we are to detach ourselves, not only from love of sin, but also from the love of all the goods of the natural world. To give our whole love to God means to withdraw this love from the things of the world. We have only one heart, and God requires all of it. It doesn't take a knowledge of higher mathematics to see that if we give all the love of this one heart to God, we have nothing left for the world.

Because our faculties and their desires naturally seek their own natural and sensible objects, we are prone to become absorbed in the creatures of this world and to become attached to them. This tendency is to be mortified by deliberate effort. The natural inclination towards attachment must be corrected and canceled by an opposite supernatural movement towards detachment. Accordingly detachment or contempt for the things of the world is the very keynote of Christianity and its practice an unmistakable mark of Christian behavior. Avoidance of mortal sin, we said, is conformity to the natural law and is therefore already demanded by natural religion. But the characteristic of supernatural religion is the ability to rise in our affections above all the goods of creation. In other words, the Christian life is not only super-sinful but literally super-natural; it requires, therefore, not merely an abandonment of evil, but also a renunciation, to be accomplished at least by interior detachment, of all the goods of the natural order.

If a man says that he loves his wife more than he loves some offensive creature, like a toad or a lizard or a reptile, or if he tells her that he loves her more than he loves filth, she is not likely to be overcome by this flattery or to be carried away by such a declaration of love! What he must say, what she expects of him, is that he loves her more than every other person, more than all other women. He may not even say that he loves her more than all other women except a few especially attractive ones. There must be no exceptions—the very fact that others are attractive is the reason why his wife demands, as a proof of love, his preference for her. Love, you see, is a preference. The husband and wife show their mutual love for each other by preferring each other's companionship above that of all other persons.

Sin is spiritual filth. While we must of course avoid sin, we do not flatter God very much, not nearly as much as His goodness urges, when we can but say that we love Him more than we love the filth of sin. Like the lover or husband, we must rather show God that we love Him more than all other creatures, including attractive creatures, and we might say especially attractive creatures. It is the very fact that creatures are attractive that makes our act of preference for God a true expression of love. St. John of the Cross lays it down as a principle that the higher is the excellence of any created good, the greater is the love we show for God by renouncing it for His sake. When a

Catholic says that his only object is to avoid sin he is choosing God merely in preference to filth.

Some persons are scandalized by the phrase "contempt of the world" or the similar phrase "to despise the creatures of the world." They assure us that creatures were made by God and are therefore good. We recognize that truth and do not challenge it. Rather we insist upon it. And we are going to choose God above these good creatures, above any creature, however good. And by this fact, and by insisting on the goodness of these creatures, we make our preference for God a true act of love. Obviously then, the phrase contempt for creatures does not imply that creatures are evil. That many persons think it necessarily carries such an implication illustrates how far a merely natural or pagan mentality has taken possession of our thinking. Supernatural thinking is so strange that we do not understand it and even Catholics misinterpret it when it is heard. Should any of our hearers be disturbed by the phrase, we suggest that they look into their Missals. Here they will find it occurring time after time, particularly in the Collects and Postcommunion prayers. Let us cite just one example, the Collect from the Mass of the Sacred Heart, the very feast of divine love: "May Thy holy mysteries, O Lord Jesus, impart to us a divine fervor, whereby having known the sweetness of Thy most tender Heart, we may learn to despise earthly things and love those that are heavenly." Those who use the Missal daily will find over and over this petition—*despicere terrena et amara caelestia*—to despise things earthly and to love things heavenly: this is the refrain of many of the prayers which our Holy Mother Church puts on our lips at Mass. And yet Catholics who presumably repeat these prayers at Mass are distressed when they hear this phrase out of Mass. They should be more attentive to the meaning of the prayers they are reciting! By these prayers the Church is teaching us what we ought to seek at the hands of God.

It is clear then that the maxim "enjoy the world as long as you do not commit mortal sin" is incompatible with practical Christianity. Such a maxim is rather pagan than Christian. To be sure, the avoidance of mortal sin is already a great good; but the search for enjoyment in the things of the world is not Christian or supernatural. Paul, we have seen, tells us that we are *not* to mind the things that are upon the earth but should rather seek the things that are above. This is Christianity.

The contempt for creatures, then, is the reverse of the love of God; just as the lifting of darkness is but the opposite aspect of the coming of light, and you cannot have light without the dispersal of darkness, so detachment from creatures is but the underside of the love of God and you cannot practice the love of God without withdrawing the heart from creatures. If a man moves towards New York, then in the very fact of approaching that city he makes a greater distance between himself, let us say, and San Francisco. Similarly in moving towards God, we move further away from creatures; and we cannot move closer to God without detaching ourselves from creatures. Those who wish to love God more, and still retain all their love for the world and for the pleasures of the world, are attempting an impossible thing. They are trying to go forward without moving, trying to get to a distant place without stirring from the spot on which they stand.

Some say that if it were true that we should despise creatures, then we would be expected to hate our parents, brothers and sisters, husbands and wives. Now manifestly, when we speak of hating creatures, we refer to what the Scriptures call the vanity, the riches, and the pleasures of the world. The commandment of love does not release us from our natural duties to our families. At the same time, in acknowledging this, let us not forget that Jesus did once say that we should hate father, mother, sister, brother, wife and husband. In time we will see what this means. For the present it is enough if we realize that God expects us to prefer Him to all the good things of the world without exception and that the practice of charity therefore involves detachment from all these goods.

It must be added that not only does God ask us to love Him above creatures, but He asks of us an exclusive love for Himself, complete detachment from creatures. In other words, He is jealous of our love. Love is that way—exclusive in its demands, jealous, A husband is not willing to share the affection of his wife with other men; he demands all of it. Similarly God tells us that we should love Him with our whole hearts. Some are disturbed by the statement that God is jealous as they are by the phrase "contempt for creatures." But it is God Himself Who

says, *"I am a jealous God";* and the commandment of charity, as
God gives it to us, requiring our whole heart and mind and
strength, is the most forceful possible statement of an exclusive
and jealous love.

The Fourth Axiom

An action and its reward are proportionate to each other. Or,
an action and its reward are on the same plane of activity. If I
desire to enjoy the pleasure that is to be obtained from eating an
apple, I must eat the apple; and I do not expect to get that
particular kind of pleasure, let us say, from drinking a cup of
coffee. There is, in other words, a proportion between actions
and the pleasure or reward coming from them. On the basis of
this fact, we may say that only a natural reward will come from
natural actions, If we desire a supernatural reward, then must we
perform supernatural actions, A man who is employed by Jones
will not expect to be paid by Brown. If he goes to Brown, asking
for his wages, the latter will send him back to Jones. Similarly, if
one works for the world, he must be satisfied with the pay which
the world gives; he cannot reasonably expect to be paid by God.
If we wish to be paid by God, by receiving supernatural
happiness, we must work for God. This is the significance of Our
Lord's words spoken in the Sermon on the Mount concerning
those who work for worldly motives: *"Amen I say to you they
have received their reward."*

St. Paul gives us the same rule in a slightly different form:
He says, *"For what a man sows, that he will also reap. For he
who sows in the flesh, from the flesh also he will reap
corruption."* (Gal. 6:8) If a man sows wheat, he will expect to
reap wheat, not rye or corn. If he desires corn, then he will sow
corn. The rule is as simple as that. We would not question it in
the natural world, but we forget it when dealing with spiritual
matters, foolishly expecting supernatural fruit from natural
sowing. But if we sow in the flesh we will reap in the flesh a
merely natural pleasure—St. Paul says indeed that we shall reap
corruption, which indicates his opinion of these natural
pleasures; and we know why he says this—since living
according to the flesh, that is, according to our natural desires,

leads us away from virtue into sin, we in truth reap corruption. And if we, as Christians, desire the supernatural happiness for which we are destined, then we must sow in the spirit, that is, give ourselves over to supernatural activity.

The Fifth Axiom

The fifth axiom states: Heaven is not primarily a place, but rather a state, a condition of soul. This rule is necessary to avoid a childish way of thinking of heaven. It is true that we necessarily speak of spiritual things in human terms, and form our ideas of them according to the categories usually employed by the mind. But we must also constantly endeavor to correct our inadequate human words and concepts, just as scientists must correct their instruments to compensate for changes in temperature. To think of supernatural happiness as if it were a place above, and of hell as a place below, is to fall into the danger of misleading ourselves. Eternal happiness consists in the knowledge and love of God, namely, union with God. Therefore our happiness consists essentially in love, and it depends in its degree on the degree of union which we enjoy with God.

Hell, on the other hand, is likewise primarily a condition of soul, a condition in which the soul is deprived of God—although there is also a punishment of sense, according to Catholic teaching. It is then best to think of heaven and hell, first of all, as a condition of soul: heaven a condition in which man enjoys God in an eternal embrace of friendship and love; hell a condition in which man, craving for infinite and eternal love, suffers from an everlasting insatiable thirst.

Souls in Limbo are also deprived of the Beatific Vision; but their appetites have never been sharpened by grace to expect this vision or to miss it, so they are content with the merely natural happiness that they possess.

Suppose that a group of people scattered all over a hillside are watching a sunset. Those on the summit of the hill get the best view; those down a little farther can see also, but their vision is poorer the farther they are from the top. Those towards the bottom cannot see the sun at all, although they still have light; those deep in the valley below are in total darkness.

God is the Sun of Justice. The saints are those who stand on the top of the hill and enjoy the fullest measure of the Beatific Vision. The souls of the just who are lesser saints are those who, a little farther down, also possess, though not so resplendently, the vision of God. The souls in Limbo are those who have happiness of a kind but are excluded from the glorious vision of God that comes as a reward for supernatural living. Those in darkness are the souls in hell. Clearly, then, the souls in Limbo are "lost," in the sense that although enjoying some measure of happiness, they are forever deprived of the supernatural end and good which God intended for all men. There is thus an infinite difference between those in Limbo and the least of the saved. At the same time, even among the latter there are great differences according to the degree of charity to which they attained during their earthly probation.

After the resurrection, our souls will be rejoined by our bodies, and we will again occupy a place in space. In this way, then, heaven may also be said to be a place, where the glorified bodies will dwell, but primarily and essentially it is the soul's state of eternal bliss. It is love, it is friendship with God: a love that has an infinity of degrees. Our own degree through all eternity will be determined by how we have on earth corresponded with God's grace by loving Him.

The Sixth Axiom

The sixth and last axiom is this. Death changes nothing; death simply immortalizes what is in us. If we wish to enter into the kingdom of heaven, we must live a supernatural life on earth. As we have seen, heaven is a condition of soul, a condition of love and union with God; and we will remain for all eternity in that condition of soul in which we are caught at death, like sculptured figures of men dancing or working, embracing or fighting, and fixed forever in the position in which they have been carved. And the moment of death fixes our condition of soul forever; there will be no changing after that. To put it differently: we will carry into eternity the degree of love that we have when we leave the earth. If one has five degrees of charity, then he will have five degrees of charity throughout all eternity;

if he dies with three degrees of charity or love, throughout all eternity he will remain with these three degrees; if he dies without love then he will never possess any love in eternity. God will give to us the "light of glory" in eternity, which enables us to enjoy the vision of God there face to face, according to our measure of love; but He will not then increase our love. Of course death itself is a most important part, indeed the very climax, of our trial on earth and so gives us a last-instant opportunity to increase our love wonderfully. Still, our happiness in heaven will be what we merit here: and our love in heaven will be but the blossoming and fructifying of the love that, through His grace, we have possessed on earth.

The reason for this is that earth is our place of probation, and our period of meriting increases of grace and love ends at death. After death we can merit no longer. During this life we can and should increase in the love of God every day. After we have yielded up our souls to God we can never again perform meritorious actions; in eternity we will but gain the fruit of what we have planted here on earth. He that sows in the Spirit will reap of the Spirit—will reap life and peace.

Suppose that a man walks across the room holding five dollars in his hand, and, while he is walking, someone turns out the light. He will still have five dollars in his hand when he gets to the other side. Turning out the light has no effect on the sum of money.

If a Frenchman gets on a ship in Europe, he will still be a Frenchman when he gets off in this country. If he is German or Italian when he embarks, he will be German or Italian when he arrives. Crossing the water will make no difference in his nationality. Now there are only saints in heaven; every naturalized—or rather supernaturalized—citizen in the kingdom of heaven is a saint. To obtain such citizenship, we must likewise be saints; that is why St. Paul says we are all *"called to be saints."* Now if we wish to arrive in eternity as saints, we must leave the earth as saints—the mere passage into eternity will not transform us. Sanctity must be achieved in our lifetime on earth. We are in fact placed on earth for no other purpose than to grow in holiness as a preparation for eternity.

Many persons seem to have a false notion of what takes

place after death, and with it, a false notion of purgatory. They seem to think that they can live rather careless, worldly lives on this earth, candidly acknowledging and even boasting that they are not saints and expecting some magical transformation, it appears, after death. There will be no such transformation. Death changes nothing. We must make the transformation in ourselves, with the help of God's grace, now. As regards purgatory, purgatory will not change the essential condition of our soul; nor will there be any meriting in purgatory. If our eternal happiness depended on the performance of one small supernaturally meritorious act, to tip the balance in our favor, we would not be able to perform that act after death.

Purgatory, therefore, will not increase our charity—for charity is increased only with meritorious actions. Hence if a man does not love God when he dies, but rather loves the world, no miraculous change will come over him after death. *"If the tree falls to the south,"* the Scripture says, *"or to the north, in what place soever it shall fall, there it shall be."* St. John, quoting Jesus, puts the same doctrine in different words, *"Night is coming when no one can work."* A farmer with much work to do in the fields tries to do it before daylight wanes, knowing that after dark he will be unable to see and therefore unable to work. Jesus here compares our lifetime to the daylight in which we are to work; and after dark, that is after death, we can work no longer.

Accordingly, if we anticipate the supernatural pleasures of heaven, we should cultivate a taste for them here. If Christians who take great delight in the things of the world are serious in their wish for eternal happiness with God, why do they not fill themselves with things of God now? What makes them think that their tastes will suddenly change after death? Death changes nothing; death simply immortalizes what is in us.

Let us now think upon these things: and may God bless you.

"May Thy holy mysteries, O Lord Jesus, impart to us a divine fervor, whereby having known the sweetness of Thy most tender heart, we may learn to despise earthly things and love those that are heavenly. Who livest and reignest

with God the Father in union with the Holy Spirit, God world without end." Amen.

(Postcommunion, Feast of the Sacred Heart)

THE TWO KINDS OF HAPPINESS

My dear Friends in Christ—

Suppose that in making a trip to a distant city, you come upon a crossroad at which turning one way would put you on a wide super-highway while the other road looks little better than a wagon track. Naturally you choose the superhighway, thinking the other is but a side road. You then speed along for many miles, delighted with the scenery and with the smooth driving. But suddenly, without any warning, a sign looms up ahead. You apply the brakes, and read: "Road closed: dead end." The super-highway comes to an end in a field.

This is a good illustration of what would happen to those who might attempt to lead a natural life. Such a life is both good and pleasant. Nevertheless, because of the actual design of God to elevate us to a higher destiny, the natural way of life is a road which leads nowhere. Even if we were to succeed in staying on it—we really cannot for long—we would eventually come to a sign which says, "Road closed: dead end." The reason is that the term, or destination, of the natural way of life is natural happiness; in the next world, Limbo. And Limbo is closed to the baptized.

On your trip you would have been saved time and disappointment had you known that the beautiful highway would not take you to your destination! It will likewise save us a great deal of wasted effort and a truly fatal disappointment if we know from the beginning that the natural road of life is a road which leads nowhere. We ought therefore to know something about this fair-seeming highway and be apprised of the fact that its connatural destination has been taken away. To do so, it will be of help to know more about natural happiness and about Limbo.

We are still concerned very largely with doctrinal matters; and if it seems a little dry and heavy, I hope that the importance of the subject and your desire to please Our Lord will keep you attentive.

It was God's design from the beginning, we have seen, to elevate man to the supernatural plane. For this reason He gave us a nature capable of receiving grace and of being elevated through grace to share in the Divine life. Now let us suppose that things had happened differently. Let us suppose that God had created man and left him on the natural plane, without raising him to a participation in the Divine life. In that case man would have lived, and would now live, in what philosophers call the State of Pure Nature. Of course, it did not happen that way; but we can learn some useful lessons from imagining what our life on earth would have been like if it had. God certainly could have done this had He wished; He is free and under no constraint to give us the privileges of grace.

In the State of Pure Nature man would have been guided by reason alone, without being expected to submit to the higher rule of faith. His life would have consisted in the exercise of his natural activities and there would not have been any need to raise these to a higher plane. These activities, when ruled by reason, would have led him to a perfectly natural happiness. We know from our knowledge of human nature and human life what that happiness would have been. It would have been something like the natural happiness that worldly men seek now. Sensual men, it is true, are prone to have a rather gross and faulty notion of this natural happiness; but philosophers, judging by reason and looking at human nature at its best, teach us that true happiness consists in the exercise of our minds and wills, that is to say, in the knowledge of truth and the love of good. After death, this natural happiness proper to the State of Pure Nature would have continued, since the human soul is immortal, and would have then reached its final fruition in the knowledge of the highest truth and of the supreme good, which is God. But such cold intellectual knowledge of God, and the imperfect, distant love proceeding from it, would be vastly different from the intimate personal love of friendship promised in the Beatific Vision as the reward for a supernatural life.

This place of natural happiness, in the other world, is the place that we have been calling Limbo. We can never go there. But unbaptized infants go to a place of natural happiness, or at any rate into a state which is very much like that of natural happiness. We need not enter into the discussion of theologians concerning the precise nature of Limbo; sufficient for us to know that the condition of unbaptized infants after death is at least very much like the natural happiness spoken of by philosophers. In defining the supernatural order in the first conference, we have brought in the idea of Limbo; and we wish now to speak of it further.

At first it might seem useless to do so—and that is the reason why so many of us have simply dropped Limbo from our thinking. Since man in fact has been given a higher than human destiny and therefore does not actually tend towards mere natural happiness in eternity, it may seem at first sight unnecessary and useless to consider the matter at all. But the reverse is true. Even though the possibility of a merely natural life and happiness is only theoretical, at any rate for the baptized, it still aids our thinking concerning our actual destiny and our efforts to define the supernatural order to keep this possibility in mind, while of course we should also keep always in mind the fact that for us it is but theoretical or hypothetical.

When a person enters a religious community—to take a somewhat similar case—he gives up marriage and family life, and takes on himself a wholly new set of obligations. Marriage, as an end in life, is closed to him; and yet it is certainly not useless for him to know something about marriage; without such knowledge, at the very least, he would have a very inadequate idea of human nature—indeed he would be unable even to understand difficulties in his own way of life and the nature of the sacrifice that he himself is making. Likewise, although we cannot go to Limbo, we will have an inadequate idea of the natural order if we do not have a clear notion of what is meant by Limbo. The possibility of our entering Limbo, it is true, has been removed. But our natural activity has not been taken away, nor has our reason and the possibility of living by reason. In other words there is a natural road of life still open to us, at least within certain limits; although of itself it can lead nowhere since the proper term of this life— Limbo—has been taken away by the divine decree which raised us to the supernatural order. It is a dead-end road.

In saying that, despite our supernatural elevation, we can still live on the natural plane—within limits—you will recall what is meant. We mean that man is still capable of becoming absorbed in human things and of relying on reason chiefly or solely for guidance. We do not mean that man, by his natural powers alone, is capable of observing all the natural law or practicing fully all the natural virtues. In our present state, the help of grace is needed to conform fully even to the standards of natural goodness. At the same time, while we cannot observe all the natural law or practice all the natural virtues without supernatural assistance, we can perform some good natural actions. That is to say, in some actions and over at least short periods of time, we can, even without grace and by our natural powers alone, perform morally good natural actions. While, if we take life as a whole, the living of a naturally good life is only a theoretical possibility, it is an actual possibility in limited areas of life and over short periods of time. The fact that we can perform some good natural actions, together with the circumstance that we retain our powers of natural activity and reason, fosters in us the delusion that we can live good natural lives. The effort in the long run is doomed to failure but the delusion remains; even repeated and bitter experience often cannot seem to shake it. This delusion is further strengthened by pushing the notion of Limbo from our consciousness. Because the kind of life that we are living, or trying to live, is not outrightly evil, we forget that we are traveling a dead-end road. If we were to keep clearly in mind the idea of Limbo as the proper destination of natural life, we would be prevented at the start from taking this foolish course.

We will now set down five reasons for taking Limbo into our consideration, five reasons why doing so will enable us to come to greater clarity of thought concerning the supernatural way of life and our supernatural destiny.

First: It Aids Clear Definition

First of all, the idea of Limbo helps us to define the natural order. We might even say that it is the best practical way to define the natural order. The simplest and most practical way to define anything is to tell its purpose or end. If you were asked to give a definition of the eye, you might flounder in a lot of technicalities trying to explain its construction from muscles and tissue and so forth. But if you would say simply that the eye is an organ given to man for the purpose of vision, you give an immediately understandable definition. In the same way if you were traveling, the first thing that you would want to know about any highway would be its destination—where it would take you. The destination—New York, or Chicago, or Philadelphia— would define the highway in your mind; and you would take this or that road according as it would lead you to the place desired. Scenic beauty and the kind of paving would be secondary considerations if there is a definite place you wish to reach. Having fixed upon a destination—New York, we will suppose— you select the road that will lead you there; and you will take a second or third rate road which will bring you to where you wish to go rather than a first rate road which will take you in a different direction. Now similarly, if we wish to know the difference between the natural and the supernatural ways of life, the best procedure is to have a clear notion of where these two roads lead. The natural way of life leads towards natural happiness—in the next world, Limbo; the supernatural way of life leads to supernatural happiness, Heaven. If you wish to go to New York, you must get on the road that leads to New York; and if you wish to reach the supernatural destination which God has designated for you, you must get on the supernatural way of life. The natural way of life will not take you there.

Across the whole United States there are two great parallel highways, Route Thirty and Route Twenty-two. Traveling from west to east, you might take either road, because both are good. But if you wish to get to New York, you will take Route Twenty-two because it is the one that leads to New York. If you get on Route Thirty and stay on it, you will have a pleasant trip and see many fine cities; but you will not get to New York. If you wish to enter into the kingdom of heaven, you must likewise get on the supernatural way of life. You are free to attempt to live a natural life—it is a pleasant way and even a good way, but it does not lead to heaven. The idea of Limbo, defining the natural way of life, will help you bear this in mind.

Second: It Shows that Christianity Is Not Just Avoidance of Mortal Sin

Secondly, the idea of Limbo shows us very clearly that the Christian and supernatural way of life does not consist merely in the avoidance of sin. A Christian, we have already seen, must not only rise above sin; he must also rise above nature, that is, above natural standards of conduct and above the desire for the natural goods of the world. If he rises only above sin, he may still be on the natural plane of living, and in this case is tending, not towards supernatural happiness, as he may fancy, but towards natural happiness—that is, towards Limbo. Since there are three kinds of life—plant, animal, and human—it would be incorrect to infer that because a living being is not a plant it is therefore a man; it could be an animal. Since for man there are three possibilities of action—supernatural, natural, and sinful—it is equally incorrect to infer that because an act is sinless it is necessarily or automatically supernatural; it may still be natural. And if it is only natural, it is impotent to help us attain supernatural happiness.

When you take a trip, before you step on the train, you first ask the attendant where it is going. You wish to know its destination before you get on the train. It would be too late to ask the conductor where it is going eight hours later. For the same reason, buses and trolley cars carry the name of their destination on the front, so that you can see it as they come along the street. You want to know your destination before you start. So also, we ought to know the destination of the road that we are taking as we begin to plan our course in life. We ought to be clear in our minds that the avoidance of sin against the natural law, of itself, does but place us on the natural way of life; and this way, which of itself tends towards Limbo, is not the way that we want. We ought to realize that the natural way of life does not of itself lead to heaven, although at its best it avoids mortal sin. Then we will make sure from the very beginning we are on the supernatural way of life.

This consideration is important. If you reflect, you will have to acknowledge that there is a very common error among

Catholics in thinking that by merely rising above sin they are doing all that is expected of them and that they are on the supernatural plane of life. For this reason they easily drift into a natural life, are much attached to the world, and show little concern about supernaturalizing their actions. They take it for granted that their actions, because not sinful, are carrying them forward towards heaven. Yet these actions, if natural, do not of themselves merit heaven but only a natural happiness. We ought to rid ourselves of this confusion and recognize clearly and explicitly the nature of the effort that is required of us if we aspire to supernatural happiness. And Limbo, kept in mind as the term of natural action, will keep us reminded that our efforts should be supernatural.

Third: It Clarifies the Notion of Happiness

Thirdly, the idea of Limbo helps to give us an accurate notion of supernatural happiness. It is to be feared that many have a very inadequate and confused notion of this happiness. The word happiness, you know, is an ambiguous one, and we are prone to think of it simply in a very broad sense, as though there were only one kind of happiness, or as though all happiness were of the kind that we know in this world, that is, merely natural happiness. Thus we come to confuse natural happiness with supernatural happiness, as if the latter were like the former, which we know at first hand. If we forget about Limbo and think about only two possible terms for our activity on earth, namely, about heaven and hell, we are likely to form or retain such a false impression. When we think of only these two terms, forgetting Limbo, we may come to imagine vaguely that heaven is just one step above hell; and thereby we confuse heaven with merely natural happiness. But if we keep Limbo in mind as the normal term of natural activity, then we will recognize that there is a third possibility between heaven and hell; we will be unable to forget that heaven is immeasurably above hell since it is also immeasurably above all natural happiness. Thus to forget about Limbo is to risk confusing natural happiness with heaven. Keeping Limbo in mind enables us to remember the immense height of heaven. Supernatural happiness is infinitely higher than natural happiness: it is a clear vision of the divine beauty, the possession of God in a love of friendship.

It was remarked a moment ago that there are two possible ways of thinking about natural happiness. There is, first of all, the way in which philosophy defines it, as the contemplation of truth and goodness. Then there is the grosser way in which the more popular paganism of sensual men thinks of it. You recall how the Indians imagined the next world as a kind of a happy hunting ground—a place where they would enjoy the endless delights of hunting and fishing. Other pagan religions conceive of the happiness of the next world in the same gross way. And I fear that many more sophisticated people think vaguely in a similar manner. That is to say, they think of the happiness promised to us in the next world as something very much like the happiness which men seek for and enjoy in this world: they project human ideas of happiness into eternity. This is why they fail to discern that the search for worldly pleasures is not a good preparation for eternal happiness with God; that is why they think it unnecessary to renounce the mere enjoyment of creatures, and seem to expect that the joy in the next world will be a kind of continuation and extension of the joys of this world.

There is a sermon of Cardinal Newman's in which he brings out in a very graphic way the difference between worldly joy and heavenly joy, and the incompatibility of the former with the latter. He points out, in the first place, that the happiness of heaven consists in friendship with God, and, that, so far as we know, in heaven men will be eternally occupied in praising and loving God. He gives a concrete picture of such happiness and of the way in which a worldly person would regard it by observing that a Church, and the prayer and the worship that goes on in Church, may be taken as symbol and anticipation of the joys of heaven. Now how do worldly men regard going to Church? Do they take pleasure in it? Do they not rather identify prayer and worship with dullness and tedium? If they were seeking happiness would they go into a Church? At best, when from sense of duty they attend Church, do they not simply submit to it with resignation, impatient until the ceremony is over when they can resume their accustomed search for comforts and pleasures?

Now (suggests Newman) let us imagine such a man in heaven. Everyone there is preoccupied with God. No one will talk to this worldly man about the only things that he is interested in. He wanders from court to court, looking for boon companions, and he finds none. All are engaged in the one topic and in the one occupation which, throughout his life, brought him only boredom and disgust. He will be very lonely in heaven, even unhappy there! Yes, Newman says, heaven would be hell for a worldly soul. It is a strong statement, but undoubtedly true. Heaven *would* be hell for a worldly soul.

Therefore we must be purified of worldliness and of the desire for worldly pleasure if we are to be truly happy in heaven. We must correct our ideas of happiness. We must clearly recognize that the kind of happiness we are working for is supernatural. Then we must prepare ourselves by mortifying our sensual appetites and cultivating a taste for the joys of the spirit. To do this it is most useful to keep before our eyes the possibility of a merely natural happiness and the great inferiority of this happiness to that which is promised to us in heaven. Then, from the beginning, we will raise our effort to that plane of activity on which alone we can attain the divine end God has designated as ours.

Not only sensual or worldly happiness, but also the loftiest kind of natural happiness described by the greatest philosophers is infinitely below supernatural beatitude. The idea of Limbo, which is natural happiness at its best, but is still far below heaven, reminds us of this also. Otherwise we might forget it. For the terms with which we describe both natural and supernatural happiness are so much alike that we might easily fail to observe sufficiently that they really express an infinity of difference. Natural happiness is the knowledge and love of God; but this knowledge and love are natural. Supernatural happiness is also the knowledge and love of God; but here the reference is to knowledge and love of a supernatural kind. As the heavens are exalted above the earth, so is the latter exalted above the former.

To grasp something of the difference between the natural knowledge and love of God and the supernatural knowledge and love, contrast a verbal report of a fine symphony with the experience of actually hearing that symphony played by a great orchestra; or contrast the knowledge of a lovely countryside that you might obtain from a map with that which you would gain by the experience of seeing that country yourself; or again, contrast the dry knowledge of a man one might find in an atomic chart of bones and muscles with the personal knowledge and love that you have of a friend or that loving spouses have of each other. All of these examples will help in some measure to see the difference between the kind of love that follows from the abstract, remote knowledge which natural reason has of God, and that beatifying love that the soul will have in heaven when it shall see God as He is, face to face, loving Him eternally as friend and embracing Him eternally as Spouse. Yet all of these comparisons are really inadequate, for both terms of each of them belong to the same human order, whereas supernatural beatitude takes us clear out of the human order and raises us to a kind and a height of joy that we cannot now even imagine. Trying to give our minds an adequate idea of supernatural happiness is like trying to describe a symphony to an audience of cats.

Fourth: It Shows What Grace Will *Not* Do

A fourth reason for retaining Limbo as a working concept is that it shows us what sanctifying grace does not do. There are certain things which sanctifying grace does do for us, and there are other things which it does not do. And if it is important to realize what this grace does do, it is almost equally important for practice to realize what it does not do. Otherwise we shall expect of it that which God does not intend it to accomplish, and we shall fall into laziness, thinking that grace will effect everything, without any spiritual labor on our part. Now what sanctifying grace does do is this: it raises us to the supernatural level of life; it gives us the power of supernatural action, raising our faculties to the divine plane by means of the virtues of faith, hope, and charity; it thereby also opens to us the possibility of working for and meriting supernatural happiness.

This is what sanctifying grace does; now what is it that it does not? It does not automatically supernaturalize natural activity in the moral order, that is, in the direction and orientation of our activity; this depends upon our own free disposition of our actions. After baptism our wills remain free, and it is the task of the free will, operating under the inspiration of grace, to refer our natural activity to the supernatural end fixed for us by God. Grace does not do this for us; if our wills are not aroused to do their share, then grace will not bear fruit in our lives.

Here is a parallel that will help in understanding this matter. An idiot's action is human in the physical sense inasmuch as it is performed by a human being. But it is not human in the moral sense because it is not fully informed by reason, is therefore not deliberate and free. So all the actions of a baptized person are, physically, the activity of a Christian, the activity of a person who has been raised to the supernatural order; but they are nevertheless not truly Christian activity, do not attain to the supernatural order in the moral sphere, the sphere of human freedom, unless they are referred by the will to the supernatural end of life.

Even a man with the use of reason may perform actions thoughtlessly; these would then be the acts of a man but not true human acts. Similarly a man may have grace but act apart from grace under the impulse of nature. And when he thus fails to cooperate with grace, he does not perform fully supernatural actions although he is in a supernatural state.

Two elements may thus be distinguished in our natural activity. First, there is the physical activity itself, such as eating, or working or thinking or praying. Then there is the moral aspect, or core, of these activities, the spiritual use and disposition that is made of them, their reference by the free will to some chosen end. When we are elevated to the divine plane, our faculties are elevated too, so that henceforth all their activities may be supernaturalized and made meritorious of eternal life. This is accomplished when they are referred to the supernatural end of life; then they become supernatural, not only physically, but in the moral order also. But when they are engaged in for some natural end, as from the desire for earthly goods, this is but natural action though it is done by a Christian in the state of grace.

A man who is a good carpenter before he receives sanctifying grace will remain a good carpenter afterwards. If he can paint or sing or is a skilled mechanic, or has any other abilities, he will retain them also afterwards. Only now, since his soul and its faculties have been elevated, he will be able to make all this natural activity supernatural; by means of his daily actions he will be able to merit an eternal reward. Still he is free, and he is human and defectible, so that even after his reception of grace he may be still inclined to exercise his faculties from mere human ambition or the desire for earthly goods, neglecting to refer his actions to his supernatural end. In this even his actions are not supernatural. Grace does not force or circumvent his freedom; nor will it be operative in his life so long as this neglect continues.

A man may give his son an automobile, but the gift will be of no value to the boy unless he gets in and drives it. So God, in the gift of grace, gives us a powerful principle of action; but it remains up to us to decide whether we will utilize this new capacity. Only when we cooperate with grace will its power become efficacious in our lives, influencing our conduct, meriting eternal happiness for us by giving an eternal value to each daily action. But this cooperation is necessary. We cannot look for any effortless sanctification. God gives the grace, but we must work also; He does not, when bestowing grace, take back the liberty He has also given us. Housewives today put their dinners uncooked in special stoves, and when they return hours later the food is ready to be eaten. Spiritually, we sometimes try to do the same thing. We seem to think that it is necessary only to receive God's grace in the sacraments and that this will take care of everything, while we need do nothing. Certainly this is not so; and this is why we are so often kept waiting, never making any real spiritual progress. The gift of divine grace is not a dispensation from effort; it is on the contrary a summons to the most strenuous effort.

In a word, sanctifying grace and the infused virtues do not automatically supernaturalize our actions in the moral order, the sphere of our personal freedom. This remains for us to do under the influence of the actual graces that are rained upon us each day in order that we may act in accordance with the status and the powers conferred by sanctifying grace and the virtues.

And the point of particular interest at present is that the idea of Limbo, by keeping us aware that the proper result of natural activity is but a natural reward, will make us alert, now that we have been elevated, freely to direct our natural activities to our supernatural end. Thereby we make them supernatural in the fullest sense of the word; but grace does not accomplish this for us mechanically. We are still free to live in accordance with nature, thus tending towards Limbo.

Fifth: It Reminds Us of the Three Possibilities

A fifth and final reason for taking Limbo into our consideration is that, if we pass over it, we are likely also to pass over and to forget the whole natural order, and to have a very confused idea of the relationship of this order to the supernatural life. Limbo, you will recall, is the term of natural activity and helps to define the natural order with precision; to discard it is to throw away a most useful means of defining and thinking correctly of the natural order. Hence, once we lose the notion of Limbo, the next thing that happens is that all natural activity drops out of our thinking. That is, we forget about it. It is in this way that we come to conclude that simply by avoiding sin we are living on the supernatural plane. We have forgotten that the supernatural life is in fact supernatural; it has in our minds been reduced to being super-sinless. The natural order, for all practical purposes, has disappeared from our thoughts. We have now a distorted picture of the Christian life. Instead of thinking in terms of three possible levels of action—supernatural, natural, and sinful—the possibilities for us have been reduced to two, supernatural and sinful. As a consequence, we relax our energies and no longer try to nerve ourselves for truly supernatural action; we take it for granted that all that is not sinful is by that very fact supernatural. This is the origin of what may be called "the sin mentality"—that outlook which reduces the practice of Christianity to an avoidance of sin, neglecting the duty imposed by love of inwardly renouncing all the goods of the natural order.

Thus we can see how a wholly falsified picture of the Christian life is formed in our minds as a result of eliminating Limbo from our thought. So far as our practice is concerned we have lost hold of the all-important fact that Christianity is specifically supernatural.

Our minds, like all of nature, abhor a vacuum; and the place vacated in our thinking by the concept of the natural plane of life is soon filled by the supernatural order. The supernatural order drops, as it were, to the level of nature, so that our conception of this order is inadequate and our idea of supernatural conduct much diminished. If three tables were placed one upon the other, and a man were to climb to the highest table, and then, in something of the manner of a circus trick, the middle table were to be suddenly whisked away, it is clear that the man would make a quick descent; he would fall down one level, one level at least! In something of the same manner, when even the possibility of natural action is removed from our diagram of the three ways of life and action, then the man on the supernatural plane drops to a point just above sin; and it seems as though supernatural conduct is but the avoidance of sin and that any action which is not sinful is of itself sufficient to merit a supernatural reward. We have lost hold of the principle that there must be proportion between means and end: that you cannot expect a carrot to sing nor a bird to write poetry nor a natural action to produce supernatural fruit.

Suppose that you were to find a tool, new and strange, whose purpose you do not know and cannot discover; let us suppose it is a precision instrument of great value. After studying the tool for a while, you lay it aside, having no use for it, not knowing its purpose. Later, while engaged in some household task, say, fixing a door, it occurs to you that this tool that you found could be of some service; and so now you use it for your own private purpose, regardless of what the tool was originally made for, and probably ruin it. So also, if we forget about natural happiness as the purpose and end of natural activity, we are likely to lay aside, as it were, natural activity itself; or rather, since as Christians we are laboring for a supernatural end, to attempt to utilize our activity for attaining this end without seeing to it that it is fully elevated to the supernatural plane; in other words, we try to use it for an end for which it was not intended—and which it cannot achieve without being directed towards that end by our free correspondence with grace. We have forgotten about the natural order, forgotten that we can perform natural actions and can to an extent live natural lives; without troubling ourselves to supernaturalize our actions in their moral being, we take it for granted that we are moving towards the supernatural happiness of heaven. And all these erroneous twists of thought have taken place, you will remember, because in the first place we forget about the concept of natural happiness and Limbo. It reminds one of the old ditty:

> For want of a nail, the shoe was lost;
> For want of a shoe, the horse was lost;
> For want of the horse, the rider was lost;
> For want of the rider, the battle was lost;
> For want of the battle, the army was lost;
> For want of the army, the country was lost;
> And all for the want of a horseshoe nail.

At this point, we may profitably stop to summarize. Throughout these first four conferences we have been concerned with but one subject viewing it in different relationships and from various points. The subject, of course, is the fundamental distinction between nature and the supernatural. In the first conference we defined these orders and marked their distinction according to make-up, guide, and term. Then we studied how this distinction is described in the Scriptures. Thirdly, we derived from the distinction a number of principles of action. Finally, in this conference a more careful consideration was given to the difference between natural and supernatural happiness which are the ultimate determinants, respectively, of the natural and supernatural ways of life. These truths, fully mastered, should help to make our duties as Christians much clearer.

Let us therefore think upon these things. And may God bless you.

> *"Having been filled, with Thy food of spiritual nourishment, we humbly beseech Thee, O Lord, through our reception of this sacrament to teach us how to spurn earthly goods and to love those of heaven. Through Our Lord Jesus*

Christ Thy Son Who livest and reignest with Thee in union with the Holy Spirit, God world without end. Amen."
(Postcommunion, 2nd Sunday of Advent)

THE HARMONY BETWEEN NATURE AND THE SUPERNATURAL: WHERE THE HARMONY LIES

My dear Friends in Christ —

The practical relationship between nature and the supernatural may be stated in the rule that nature is to be mortified. Now to mortify means to make dead, to kill; therefore the whole duty of the Christian life is to kill or mortify nature. So, St. Paul says that, *"he who by the Spirit mortifies the deeds of the flesh shall live."*

But I have no doubt that you will wish to hear this assertion explained more fully. And indeed that is precisely our next task. Having in mind the definitions of nature and the supernatural, and the distinction between them, we pass logically to a study of the relationship existing between these two orders. Our elevation to share the divine life, we know, requires a renunciation, not only of sin, but of natural goods. And such a renunciation, in a spiritual sense, is a death; for death is precisely a passing from this world and from the things that we love in this world. This is why, in practical terms, we can express the relationship of the two orders by means of the axiom: mortify nature.

However, it is necessary to know precisely how to go about this. We wish to mortify nature in a spiritual sense, as just stated, but we do not wish actually to destroy it. An example will bring out our meaning. A surgeon, when he performs an operation, must know the human body; he must know which organs can be removed and which cannot; also the difference between a healthy organ and one diseased; finally, he must know exactly where to find the removable organs or the disease and how to cut these away. If he cuts away any vital organ or works clumsily or does not understand the human anatomy, he will destroy and not heal.

Likewise in mortifying the natural man, we must know what we are about. It is not our duty or our intent actually to destroy our human nature—if this were so, then we would have to conclude that the simplest and the quickest way to live a supernatural life and gain our supernatural end would be to commit suicide, which is absurd.

Two elements are to be found in natural life and activity: first of all, there is the good element, which is in perfect harmony with our supernatural destiny and therefore does not need to be removed or mortified. There is, however, another element which is in conflict with our supernatural calling; this it is which must be cut away. Accordingly, just as a doctor must be able to distinguish between a living organ and the parasitical disease infecting it, so must we be able to distinguish between what is good in natural activity and that which, since it is in conflict with our vocation as sons of God, should be removed. Lack of proper knowledge will lead to mistakes: it will cause us either to remove too much in our operation on nature; or to remove too little. The Jansenists made the first mistake, namely, of removing too much; the popular paganism of today makes the second mistake, and removes too little, or rather denies that anything need be removed at all.

Let us then distinguish from the outset between what in our natural activity is in harmony with our supernatural destiny, and that which, if not definitely evil, is at any rate an obstacle to the operation of grace and hence interferes with the supernatural life. Moreover, this second element, which is in conflict with our supernatural calling, although not evil, tends towards evil, as we have already indicated and will further explain in future conferences,

In our present talk we are going to be concerned with what in nature harmonizes with our supernatural calling. To do this, we may imagine that we are like surgeons who study the human anatomy in order to know and distinguish organs that are living and healthy. We are not going to mortify what in nature harmonizes with our supernatural calling, any more than a surgeon would remove healthy organs; whatever in nature is good and in harmony with the supernatural, we will rather preserve and utilize when seeking that supernatural health, holiness, which is the object of all our endeavors. But we must know where the harmony is found and what is to be preserved.

Or take a different example. When a builder plans to erect a house, he obtains heavy stone for the foundation. In doing this, he throws away any stone that is cracked or broken. He retains as the foundation of his building only the stone that is solid and strong. Now we can compare our spiritual efforts to such a building process. In our work of construction we are going to begin with our nature and our natural actions—these are the materials immediately at hand. Upon these we are going to raise the edifice of a supernatural life. And so, like the builder, we must distinguish between those materials which are strong and capable of supporting the superstructure, and those which are weak or inferior and would give way under strain. In our present discussion we are concerned with marking out the good materials; afterwards we will separate those which are inferior.

Observe that because of this twofold element in nature and natural activity, there is a double relationship between it and the supernatural. Because of what is good in the natural order, we speak of its harmony with the supernatural. Because of the other, the corrupt or imperfect element, we speak of a conflict between natural activity and the supernatural. Our present concern is with the harmony; after considering it, we will take up the subject of the conflict between the two orders.

I trust that you realize the importance of this subject. Here we define terms and state the doctrines that provide a solid basis for the practical principles to follow. Accordingly even though what we have to say may seem dry and abstract, I urge once again that you give it the closest attention, in order to eliminate, from the start, any possibility of misunderstanding what follows.

The Area of the Harmony

The present task is to mark out the area of harmony. To do this, we may indicate three ways in which there is harmony between natural and supernatural: first in regard to human nature itself; secondly in regard to natural activity; thirdly, in regard to natural reason and truth.

First, in Regard to Human Nature Itself

Human nature was created by God, and whatever is created by God is good. Therefore human nature is good and we need not destroy or injure it in order to live a supernatural life. We need not, and we may not, maim or disfigure or in any way damage our bodily or rational powers in order to become holy. That is why we do not mortify ourselves outright, finally and completely by ending our lives. That is why we know that when our Lord says, *"If thy right hand scandalize thee, cut it off and cast it from thee,"* He is speaking figuratively and His words are to be understood in a spiritual sense, as enjoining upon us the duty to avoid whatever leads us away from God however near or dear it may be to us.

On the other hand the fact that nature is essentially good does not mean that we are simply to leave it as it is. God Himself does not leave it as it is; as we have seen, He has divinized it by giving it a share in His own life. And, in conformity with the divine intention, it is our duty to see that our whole lives and all our activity are divinized, that is, transformed by grace and charity. The reason is that our human nature, although good, cannot of itself merit a more than human happiness; to accomplish this it must He informed by a higher principle that will raise its activity to a loftier plane. For God's plan requires that we labor for a supernatural end. Still, even when divinized, our human nature always remains essentially what it is—human nature, and this no matter how far the process of divinization has gone.

A blacksmith plunges steel into a fire and applies the bellows. Under the action of the flame, the metal first reddens, then comes to a white heat, and finally turns liquid. Throughout the process, even when the mass of metal becomes liquid, it remains essentially the same; it is steel now as it was before. Yet it has been changed too; it is wholly transformed, and in this new condition, it can be readily worked and shaped into all kinds of implements. So human nature and human life while they will remain substantially the same throughout the transformation effected in them, yet, as the divine action more and more accomplishes its work, nature will become malleable and therefore capable of receiving the Godlike, or Christ-like, form that grace would impose on it.

And thus, far from remaining merely human, our nature and our whole lives should be penetrated throughout by the divine principle of grace, together with the supernatural virtues and the Gifts of the Holy Ghost. Nature of itself, in view of God's plan to divinize man, is imperfect: it is to be perfected; and it is to be perfected by grace and, on man's part, by his endeavor to promote the work of grace.

Second, in Regard to Natural Activity

The second way in which we can say that there is harmony between nature and the supernatural is in regard to natural activity. Our physical activity—the activity of our senses, intellect and will—is good; it proceeds from human nature, and therefore it does not in itself conflict with our supernatural destiny. We can, therefore, engage in this activity without compromising our supernatural lives or abandoning our supernatural destiny. There is no need to mortify--in the sense of to destroy or to injure--this natural activity in the interests of a mortified Christian life. For example, in order to mortify our eyes, as is recommended by spiritual writers, we need not stare at the sun and destroy our sight. Nor need we cut off our ears or our tongues to mortify these members although they must certainly be mortified. Indeed, we must not injure ourselves by any wrong-headed "mortifications" because, as we know, the fifth commandment forbids us to damage or destroy the gifts which God has given us.

Nevertheless, we are not to leave this activity on the merely human and natural level. It must be elevated to the supernatural plane, and there it can merit eternal happiness for us. Indeed, it is precisely by this natural activity, elevated and divinized, that we can work for and earn our eternal happiness with God. Of course it is not we ourselves who elevate it to the supernatural level; it is God, by means of sanctifying grace, Who effects this elevation. But the point of practical importance to be grasped is that God, while elevating us to the supernatural plane, leaves us free; so that we can refuse to remain there, or we may fail to correspond with the divine principle of activity which is offered to us on the higher level. In order to make our activity truly supernatural, there is a need for cooperation on our part. By the exercise of our freedom, meshing with divine grace, we can make this natural activity truly supernatural.

What we are to do with our natural activity may be illustrated by the example of the farmer who grafts a branch from a fruit tree to the stock of another kind. We have, of ourselves, only natural activity; but this natural activity must bring forth supernatural fruit. How may this be accomplished? By grafting our natural activity to our supernatural life; thus our works, while remaining in themselves human and within the power of our natural faculties, become divine in their principle and possess a supernatural value. For, as St. Francis de Sales says, "the fruits of grafted trees always follow the graft, for if the graft be apple it will bear apples, and if cherry it will bear cherries; yet so that these fruits always taste of the stock." And of course they also get their vitality ultimately from the stock. In our spiritual lives, our activities are natural; but these natural activities are grafted to a supernatural principle of life. As a consequence, the works themselves will follow the graft — that is, will in their material content be simply human and natural; but the life of these works will follow the stock, hence will be supernatural and divine, giving to these fruits an interior, invisible, supernatural vitality that is meritorious of eternal life.

Third, in Regard to Truth

The third way in which there is harmony between nature and the supernatural is in regard to truth. This means that there is no discord between the truths of natural reason and the mysteries of faith. These two sets of truths belong to wholly different orders, and the latter are infinitely above the former, but they do not contradict each other; both come from God, Who is very Truth, One and Eternal. Theologians say that the truths of faith are above reason, but not contrary to it. In the same way the knowledge of our minds is superior to that of our senses, although the latter is true enough as far as it goes; accordingly, there can be no contradiction between sensible knowledge and intellectual knowledge: what our mind knows about an apple, for example, completes and perfects what our eyes tell us about the apple.

The mystery of the Blessed Trinity, which teaches that there are Three Persons in one God, is not opposed to the truth of mathematics which says that three times one is equal to three. Nor is the doctrine of the Incarnation, which reveals that there are two natures in the one Person of Jesus, contrary to the fact that in arithmetic two times one is equal to two. Nor do these mysteries contradict anything that philosophy teaches about "nature" and "person." Again, the facts of biology concerning man's bodily origin are not in conflict with the truths of religion which state that man's soul was directly created by God. For this reason Catholics were never much disturbed by the discussions over evolution and the assertion on the part of scientists that evolution destroys belief in the inspiration of the Scriptures. Catholics know that any contradiction between biology and theology is only apparent and will always disappear with further study, since the same God is Author of both nature and the supernatural world.

At the same time, to rise above reason and to assent to the truths of faith presents great difficulty to reason. We have a tendency to hold on to reason--it is, as we have seen, our guide in the order of nature. Therefore, to live by faith is a mortification to reason. Thus when God told Adam and Eve not to eat of the forbidden fruit, but gave them no reason for the command, we say that He was trying their faith. We might also say that He was exercising their faith and thus trying and mortifying their reason. Had God told them not to eat of the forbidden fruit because it was poisonous, they probably would not have done so; in that event God's command would have seemed to them reasonable. But because the divine command, although we know it did not contradict reason, strained the ability of reason, therefore it was a trial to them. In the same way Abraham, when very old, was promised a son, and promised also that he would be the father of a great nation; and then, when contrary to any reasonable hope, the son was born, the great patriarch, a veritable hero of faith, was told by God to kill that one child upon whom all his hope rested. Faith told him to make the sacrifice of Isaac; reason told him that by such a sacrifice he would lose the only chance of having any posterity at all, much less a numerous posterity. In this case also, living by faith was a trial to reason.

We may add that living by faith is always a trial to reason. The fact that reason does not contradict our faith should not close our eyes to this fact, so significant for practice. Even such a speculative truth as that there are three Persons in one God presents a trial to our reason despite the conviction that faith cannot contradict reason. Only faith in God can compel us to accept this teaching, which, at least apparently, contradicts our reason, but which in truth is simply far above it. Perhaps the immediate personal difficulty is—I will not say, greater, but more acute—in the case of practical commands, such as were given to our first parents and to Abraham. Thus it is hard for reason to accept the fact that we should renounce the good things of the natural world, or that we should love our enemies, or that we should return good for evil. And the difficulty remains even after God, apparently dealing with us less strictly than with Adam, gives us in His revelation some explanation for these commands. In any event, to live by faith we should learn from the failure of Adam, as from the faith of Abraham, to obey God without asking Him the why of His commands. Were we to understand His commands perfectly we would no longer be living by faith.

Thus, to live by faith will mean in practice a trial, a mortification of reason. St. John of the Cross teaches that it is through faith that God seeks to purify our reason. This, then, is one aspect of the mortification of natural activity. Reason is good; we must use it; we will use it even in trying to understand, as far as this may be, the truths of theology. But yet the truths of theology—the truths of faith—carry us so far beyond mere human powers that the human powers will be prone to faint and falter in this rarefied atmosphere.

All this has an immediate practical bearing. Some Catholics, in what appear to be over-zealous efforts to reach unbelievers, showing them the reasonableness of the Faith, seem almost to reduce Christianity to a mere rational system of thought. Instead of stopping at the demonstration that Faith does not conflict with reason, they seem almost to say that the truths of faith are within the range of reason and that Christians are asked to accept nothing or to do nothing that cannot be fully explained by reason. This is certainly not true. Reason cannot measure or completely explain or exhaust the truths of faith; even when it allows itself to be led by the truths of Revelation, it can move but slowly and clumsily, in the dimmest of lights, in that higher world where faith points out a way that, although certain, is not very consoling or enlightening to reason. And apart from submitting to such guidance from the truths of faith, the best that reason can do by itself is to make a few preliminary steps, preparing a rational statement for itself to show why it ought to make an act of faith. But when, thus prepared, it makes this act, it takes a daring plunge into the unknown, a great leap into what St. John of the Cross boldly calls the darkness of faith. When you look at the small white host and say that it contains the body and blood of Jesus Christ, you are making a wonderful act of faith, but you are in complete darkness so far as reason is concerned. Or when, making an act of faith in divine Providence, one gives up all his possessions, he is going against what is ordinarily called a reasonable course of conduct and making an audacious jump into a darkness and insecurity that would paralyze most men with fear.

It may be profitably recalled at this point, furthermore, that if faith is high above the purest reason and a mortification to it, then assuredly the life of faith is an even greater trial and mortification to the darkened and false reason which so often guides, or misguides, men in actual life. For reason too often descends from its lofty but arduous quest for truth to engage in the easier and more pleasant task of a pandering to sense desires and passions; it becomes a sort of low cunning put at the service of that art of nature which is lower than itself. Thus we see how men use the energies of their minds to gain earthly goods and pleasures, or to justify their desire and affection for these. To such false reason as this, faith is diametrically opposed; and the life of faith will be doubly a mortification and a purification to it.

While thus impressing on ourselves the fact that faith is infinitely beyond reason, we must understand, on the other hand, that living by faith neither asks nor permits that we should violate reason, that we should become irrational in the illusion that we are rising above reason. This means that we should not attempt to act foolishly under pretext of devotion.

There is a story of a great scholar who, touched by God's grace, left the university world where he had been an outstanding figure and, entering into a religious community, sought the most menial tasks in his desire to imitate the humility of our Lord. His brethren, on the other hand, wished to avail themselves of his outstanding talents, and once, when all the religious were assembled, he was asked his opinion concerning several scholarly books, and also to decide which was the best of those offered. He wished to be considered foolish and of no account; and so, when he had made a selection and was then pressed for a reason by those who desired to have the opinion of so sagacious a man, he gravely answered that he had chosen this particular book because it had a fine binding!

We need not doubt the sincerity of such humility nor, in view of the circumstances, that God would be pleased with this holy religious. Nevertheless, it may be affirmed as a general truth that we should not and may not indulge in follies in order to live by faith. Most of us act foolishly enough without any special effort in this direction! It will be enough if we bear the humiliation of our unpremeditated follies! In any event, to live by faith means to rise above reason, not to go below it, to become super-rational, not irrational.

Since our reason is good, we should follow it as far as it can usefully guide us; certainly we should utilize it to the full in solving all our daily problems. Even in living a supernatural life, we will use our reason, but a reason now enlightened by the higher and more penetrating light of faith. When distinguishing reason from faith, therefore, we do not for a moment imply that a Christian should in any way be unreasonable. We make this contrast because faith is so high above reason. But, at the same time, the virtue of faith dwells in our reason and illuminates its workings; so that what we mean by faith is reason illuminated by faith. Our business, then, is to take the great truths of faith, meditate on them, demand of our reason that it study and understand them as far as possible, and then apply them to our daily lives.

These considerations show that in living the life of faith we should not cultivate deliberate eccentricities, whether of thought, or speech, or dress, or manners, or behavior. Sometimes pious people get the idea that they should be carefully and deliberately different; and so they set out to make themselves conspicuous. It is easy to see how they might thus be led into self-advertising by pride rather than by humility. It is well for us to adopt the good and reasonable customs of the place where we happen to live or of the persons with whom we habitually associate, refusing to conform only when this would mean really compromising some principle of the Gospel ideal.

In practice, it is necessary to add, there is often some difficulty in determining what is or is not an eccentricity. Some Catholics are all too willing to compromise, to go along with the attachments and fashions of the world, pretending that their motive is to avoid singularity. They wish to reconcile God and mammon, heedless of the Savior's warning that it cannot be done; they therefore condemn as singular any action or practice on the part of the fervent which embarrasses or reproaches the worldly conduct of themselves or their companions. They are like Peter in that, posing as friends of Jesus, they in reality deny Him to retain the good opinion of worldly-minded associates. Thus in the matter of fashions in dress--or undress--many Catholics, especially women, but men also, follow along in adopting styles that are but dubiously modest at best and at times downright immodest. Or, if modesty is not offended, conformity to style may at any rate be dictated by vanity rather than by the desire to please God. The defense is that we must keep up with the times, that we must not be eccentrics, that to do otherwise would be to expose ourselves to ridicule and even to bring opprobrium on the Church. Such persons are likely to be bitterly critical of others who out of principle and the desire for perfection refuse to conform to the evil or dubious fashions of a pagan society.

A great supernatural prudence is thus frequently required to distinguish what may be in truth a singularity from what may be a mere compromise with the world and a submission to human respect. These two opposite vices, singularity and submission to human respect, must both be equally avoided by a soul that desires to live spiritually. The Christian must learn to keep a straight course, guided by the Spirit of God, avoiding the rocks on the one side and the shoals on the other. It is true that in a certain sense a Christian should be inconspicuous; he should not seek to draw attention to himself, since this is the ambition of pride, by violating accepted conventions or by disregarding established and legitimate customs--in a word, by being deliberately odd. In a different sense, he should be very conspicuous; by the purity of his life and a steadfast devotion to virtue regardless of consequences to himself; he should be easily distinguishable in a corrupt pagan or semi-pagan society. *"If I were still trying to please men, I should not be a servant of Christ."* (Gal. 1, 10)

To summarize these thoughts: To live as a Christian means to live by faith; and living by faith, although not contrary to reason, is still to rise far above it. Moreover, men of the world, judging by worldly and false prudence, will find a real contradiction between their corrupt reason and the life of faith.

There is, then, to conclude, full and perfect harmony between physical nature, together with its activity, and our supernatural vocation as Christians. This harmony exists in nature itself, that is, in its substance; in the activity of the natural faculties; and, finally, in the exercise and fruit of reason. This great and important truth opens up to us the possibility and the way to supernaturalize and sanctify all that is good in human life. How this is to be done will be the topic of our next conference.

Meanwhile, let us think upon these things. And may God bless you.

"Be merciful, O Lord, to our humble pleading, and receive kindly these offerings of Thy servants, both men and women, that what they have each offered for the glory of Thy name may be of profit to the salvation of all. Amen."
(Secret, Fifth Sunday after Pentecost)

THE HARMONY BETWEEN NATURE AND THE SUPERNATURAL: HOW THE HARMONY MAY BE PRESERVED

My dear Friends in Christ—

Let us suppose that a child asks his father for an orange which is on a shelf beyond the little fellow's reach. The father lifts up the child so that the latter may himself put his hand out for the fruit. If the child then takes the orange, he will benefit by its nourishment; but his arm is left free and he need not reach for the orange, and, if he does not, will not enjoy its goodness. In a similar way God raises us up to the supernatural order where we may receive His grace and utilize it in sanctifying our lives. But God leaves us free; He does not constrain our wills to accept His gifts. We may refuse divine grace or fail to use it profitably: and then we forfeit the opportunity of divinizing our lives.

A truly Christian and supernatural life requires that we accept and correspond with grace. This, indeed, is our immediate practical task, our every day labor in the spiritual life. And now we are prepared to address ourselves to the problem of how this task may be accomplished. Since we have before us the truth that nature and its activities are good, although not in themselves belonging to the supernatural order in which our destiny is cast, we are ready to study how our ordinary daily human actions, our natural activity, may be raised to the divine plane where it alone can help us towards our supernatural end.

Remember, God does not do this for us, nor does His grace accomplish it automatically. He gives us grace, but He leaves us free either to use this grace or neglect it. God, upon elevating us to the supernatural plane, does not by-pass or circumvent or suppress our freedom. St. Paul warns us, through Timothy, that we should not neglect the grace of God which is in us, thus indicating that we may neglect it. (I Tim. 4, 14) Elsewhere he tells us (II Tim. 1, 6) that we should stir up the grace of God that is in us, showing again that the fruitfulness of grace for us depends on our use of it. Although the Apostle is here primarily addressing bishops and priests, the principle he lays down is valid for all.

Nor do we sufficiently correspond with grace by attending Mass, by receiving the sacraments, or by other practices of devotion, if at the same time, our daily actions are merely natural. A supernatural life is not a natural life with liturgical adornments. We are abusing the sacraments and the liturgy if we fail to allow their spiritualizing power to exert its influence over the whole of our lives, if we rather use them to give respectability and religious sanction to a manner of living inspired by pagan principles. This is religious externalism, the sin of the Pharisees—using religious practices to camouflage unreligious hearts and lives, thus becoming guilty of hypocrisy.

Some there are who seem to think that if they attend Mass on Sundays, and perhaps practice a few other acts of devotion, they are leading supernatural lives, although their other actions are habitually inspired by merely human principles and motives. They make no effort to have their religion influence all these activities and are in fact prone to resent what they consider its intrusion upon matters outside the limited sphere of formal religious practice. They mark out an area for religion—the precincts of the Church—unconsciously imitating the conduct of those tyrants who, to destroy the influence of Christianity, tell priests that they must stay in their sacristies. On the other hand, these persons mark out a much larger area—that of their work, their business, their political action, their dealings with their neighbors, their recreation—which they frankly call secular and guard jealously against the interference of religion. To do otherwise, they say, is to carry religion to an extreme, to become fanatical. Thus, under a supernatural formalism, they are really devotees of naturalism. And while paying their dues at the Church door, they are paying a far heavier tribute to secularism, that great error of the day, so often condemned by the Church.

Let us be honest. All of us tend to be somewhat niggardly in our dealings with God. We pay Him what we consider His due, and often begrudgingly, giving no more than what we deem is necessary. We expect thus to appease Him. But alas for our worldly comfort, God is not so easily satisfied!

If a man were held up by bandits, we can imagine that he would offer his purse to his captors, hoping to get off thus lightly. But the bandits might not be content with this: they might take also his clothes and his car; perhaps they would hold his wife and children as hostages; and himself perhaps they would take into slavery or kill. God is like such bandits. He is not satisfied with the little we wish to offer Him, the little we deem His due. He wants all! He claims everything in our lives. And of course He is no bandit. He claims all by right. He is our Creator and Lord and Eternal Father.

A supernatural life, then, is one wholly changed and illuminated by grace, as a pane of glass is illumined by light. The use of sacraments and the liturgy should not be limited to occasional ritualistic observances. They are the sources of the light that is given to illumine all our lives. Their radiation should not stop at the Church door but should shine through on us as we move about in the world outside.

The practical spiritual task is thus to know how we may effect the necessary transformation in our everyday lives, that is to say, how we may raise all our actions to the supernatural plane.

The answer to this problem will be outlined in the present conference under the following three headings: (1) How to Supernaturalize Actions; (2) The Great Principle of Practical Charity; (3) How To Keep Harmony Among the Three Lives.

How to Supernaturalize Actions

Before explaining how this is to be done, we must, at the outset, observe that what we are here studying are the fully supernatural actions performed by baptized Christians. These we call fully supernatural because their principle is sanctifying grace and their motive force is charity and they are meritorious of eternal life. There are also other imperfect or incipient supernatural actions performed under an impulse of actual grace by the unbaptized or by those who are in the state of sin; such actions are a preparation for receiving sanctifying grace and charity. These latter acts are called salutary; we do not speak of them here, but rather presuppose them. Our concern is to discover how the baptized may live supernaturally; hence we wish to know how they may make their daily actions supernatural and meritorious, that is, how they may bring us to our supernatural end and secure for us the reward of eternal life.

The principle and rule which gives us the answer to our question follows from truths already considered. The supernatural world, we know, is God's world, just as the natural world is man's; and when we pass from the natural to the supernatural order we pass from man's world to God's. It is sanctifying grace that raises us to the supernatural world and establishes us there, while the virtues infused with grace are the dynamic principles that enable us to act supernaturally, to live divinely, to conduct ourselves as children of God. Thus to make our lives supernatural, we must see to it that grace, working through these virtues, becomes the active principle of our daily lives. And since charity is the greatest of the virtues, we must above all see to it that grace becomes active and operative in love.

Charity unites our wills directly to God and thereby joins us directly to our last end; and it is for this reason that it is the highest virtue. The rest of the virtues, faith and hope, as also the moral virtues, humility, penance, and the others, prepare the way for charity, serve charity, express charity in particular circumstances. *"Charity,"* says St. Paul, *"is patient, is kind.... believes all things, hopes all things, endures all things...."* (I Cor. 13,8) In the physical order our hearts supply blood to arms and legs that these may be active; and, conversely, when we engage in any strenuous activity with arms or legs, the movements of our hearts also become quickened, they beat rapidly and we breathe more quickly. So in the baptized Christian, faith and hope, humility, patience, and meekness receive their divine vitality from charity; and conversely, when special occasions demand the exercise of these other virtues, they in their own activity draw also on the energy and vitality of charity since it is through charity that they are united to God as their last end.

Accordingly, it may be said that we can make our lives supernatural and divine by bringing it about in our daily lives that our actions are ruled by grace acting through the infused virtues, especially through love.

On the other hand, the natural life is one that is ruled, in any rate in practice, by the love of creatures. The thing that marks a natural life, the special characteristic of paganism, at least of popular paganism, is the love of creatures. The leading maxim of paganism is "Eat, drink, and make good cheer." Accordingly, the characteristic note which identifies and betrays a merely natural mode of living is the love of the creatures of this world and the pursuit of enjoyment in them. When our actions are customarily ruled or motivated by the love of creatures, even when this love is not so great as to carry us to the extreme of mortal sin, we may so far be said to live natural lives.

A man's life is formally and completely ruled by the love of creatures when he takes a creature as his last end; for one's last end determines every action contributing to it, as the destination of a journey determines every action leading to that destination. At the same time, one may, without formally rejecting God as last end, neglect Him, pretty well forget about Him, stop to enjoy all the wayside flowers of the world, perhaps also its wayside taverns, and instead of going forward towards his end, dallies along the way wandering far from the main highway in numberless little excursions that promise immediate pleasure. This is what is done by a baptized Christian who, although he does not formally repudiate God by grave sin, is mainly interested in seeking enjoyment among the pleasures afforded by the world.

What is necessary, then, to make our lives supernatural is to see to it that they are dominated and ruled by the Christian virtues, especially by the love of God. And how can we make sure of this? By seeing to it that our lives and actions are motivated by love for God.

The motive for an action determines its end; or, more accurately, the good which we seek as an end determines our motive: a motive or intention is the will's grip on the good which it chooses as its end. If you desire to make a trip, then you form an intention to make the trip; if you desire to eat an apple, then you form an intention to eat the apple. If you have no motive, if you form no intention, you will neither take the trip nor eat the apple. In the same way we may say that the kind of a good we seek, from a religious point of view, will determine whether our motives are natural or supernatural. If our end—the good we seek—is natural, then our motives will be natural. If the good we seek is God, then our motives should be supernatural. By bringing all our actions then under the influences of a supernatural motive, especially the motive of charity, we make grace operative in our lives; we divinize and supernaturalize them from within; we make sure that the vitalizing power of grace reaches our daily lives. If, on the other hand, our motive is merely natural and selfish, even though we are in the state of grace, grace and charity do not impel our actions. These are then rather motivated by the love of pleasure, of comfort, of some sensible good. As a result, grace, although present, remains inoperative. In this case, although we have been elevated to the supernatural state, we are not utilizing the supernatural powers with which we have been endowed; we remain on the human or natural plane, and our actions, considered in themselves, are such as would merit only Limbo or natural happiness.

Examples show how easily supernatural motives are recognizable as the distinguishing feature of a supernatural action or a supernatural life. Suppose a Christian gives an alms, but only in order to be seen by men; suppose he prays or fasts, but only in order to be seen by men. Are his actions supernatural? Surely not; Jesus condemns such actions. But suppose he fasts or prays or gives alms out of love for God? Then doubtlessly the actions are supernatural. What makes them supernatural? The physical actions—fasting, praying, almsgiving, are the same in both cases. What makes them natural, on the one hand, is the merely natural motive of love for creatures, which reveals that they come from a natural principle. What, in the other cases, marks them as supernatural is the fact that they proceed from the virtues of faith, hope, religion, penance, and finally and especially, from love. This is clearly indicated by their motives: they are done in view of a supernatural end, for God. We may thus sanctify our actions by removing from them, as their motive force, the love of creatures, replacing this earthly motive by one that is supernatural, one which refers the actions to God. This, indeed, is the way in which we can make religion the living principle of our whole lives. This is a principle which opens to us the wonderful secret of attaining to sanctity simply by performing for God our small and commonplace duties.

Not only actions like fasting or almsgiving, which are intrinsically good, can be made supernatural. Any good natural action, any performance even of a simple duty, although it has nothing directly to do with religion, can be made supernatural by means of a supernatural motive. All the prosaic deeds of every day, all the tiresome duties we must perform, can be made divine, meritorious of eternal life, and pleasing to God, provided they are ruled by a supernatural motive, especially by divine love. What a wonderful consolation is this for us ordinary folk! Most of us are engaged in very routine duties, in tasks of no great significance to the world at large, however necessary they may be for us in our own small sphere in order to support ourselves or in order to carry on the large work of which ours forms but a trifling part. And yet, once we realize the greatness of charity, we can see that the least action of our daily routine can be tremendously important spiritually, part of a drama eagerly witnessed by the very angels, watched indeed with a fatherly and interested eye by the great God Himself.

Observe, we are not saying that supernatural motives are necessary under pain of sin; nor that natural motives are in themselves sinful and that therefore, by acting out of natural motives, men are liable to punishment. By no means. We are trying to demonstrate that you should rise above even natural actions and natural motives because you are Christians. We are trying to explain the real meaning of Christianity; and we are hoping that you who hear us, being Christians, will not rest satisfied with less than the fullness and perfection of Christian life, which is holiness.

The Great Principle of Practical Charity

What we have been saying here may have come as a surprise to some who have perhaps taken it for granted that, because a man is in the state of grace, all his actions are made supernatural and therefore sanctified, as it were, automatically. A moment's reflection should be sufficient to convince one of the difficulty of sustaining such an opinion. It is surely possible to have a talent and yet not use it; and to assume that, because God gives us grace, all our non-sinful actions are supernatural, is really to deny the fact of our freedom by failing to take any account of it. In a parallel way, every man is endowed with reason, but every man does not use his reason in every action, as when one absently kicks a pebble aside or scratches his head. These movements are the acts of a human being but they are not true human acts, in the sense of being fully rational; they do not proceed from reason as from their principle and source. So also, a Christian has grace, but this grace does not necessarily impel his every action. He may perform what we have called natural actions; and these, while they are in that case the act of a Christian, are not Christian actions.

But—it may be objected—you say that a truly supernatural and meritorious action is one that proceeds at least ultimately from charity; and every Christian receives charity from God together with sanctifying grace. This is of course true. But, once again, we may have charity and not use it; charity may lie inactive and quiescent in the soul. Charity is a habit in the will; and just as you may have other habits without exercising them— say, the habit of typing, or swimming, or driving a car—so may you fail to exercise the supernatural virtue of charity. Yet charity in its very nature is an active or operative habit. That is to say it tends towards action and its nature is frustrated if it is kept inactive. If not permitted to act, it is likely to decay and fall into ruin, St. Gregory is quoted by St. Thomas as saying that "the love of God, if present, does great things; if it does nothing, it is not present." And St. Thomas explains these words, which at first might seem surprising, by observing that one of the ways in which charity may be lost, although indirectly, is through lack of exercise; for if charity is inactive, this can mean only that other forces, the passions and appetites, in practice rule the soul and will surely undermine the sway of charity.

But still—it may be pointed out against the statement that the love of God and affection for creatures are mutually opposed—one may have sanctifying grace and supernatural infused charity while still acting from merely natural motives and retaining a love of creatures; as when one in the state of grace eats some candy from a willful and habitual desire for pleasure it affords: and this fact contradicts what you have said about the love of God and the love of creatures being opposed to each other. In other words, we can be in the state of grace, and therefore have true charity, while at the same time indulging in affections for the creatures of the world. To say otherwise would be equivalent to maintaining that every pleasure taken because of an attachment for some creature—every bite of chocolate, every puff of a cigarette, every sip of beer indulged in from a natural motive—would deprive us of charity. Yet this is absurd since we know that only mortal sin destroys charity. How then can it be asserted that affections for creatures are opposed to divine charity?

The objection is a good one; the truth that it contains—for it does of course contain some truth, but not the whole truth—not only hinders many persons from exercising charity, but lulls them into a deep and dangerous spiritual sleep. Half-truths, because they give us a false sense of security, are often more dangerous than outright errors. In any event, by answering this objection we shall discover the rest of the truth and also come upon a principle of the greatest importance for practicing charity and therefore for the whole spiritual life.

In the first place, although we said that the love of creatures is opposed to the love of God, we certainly did not say that all love of creatures is sinful. We distinctly affirmed, and now reaffirm, the opposite. The love of creatures may become sinful but it is not always or necessarily so. A man who gets intoxicated loves a creature sinfully; one who likes ice cream at every meal very likely has an attachment for that creature but he does not commit sin. What is meant then when it is said that the love of God and the love of creatures are opposed to each other is that the love of creatures, even when it is not sinful, hinders the exercise and increase of love.

Remember that we are concerned with how to apply Christianity; we are talking about how to *act* as Christians. It is true that our affections may be actively engaged in the enjoyment of creatures while charity, which is infused by God into our souls without any labor on our part, and which ought to direct all our affections towards Him, is slumbering quietly in the soul. But it is not true that we can act at one and the same time as pagans and as Christians; we cannot, in one and the same act of the will, be moved by the love of God and by the love of creatures. We may keep charity and some affection for creatures in our soul at the same time, just as we may pour oil and water into one container. But oil and water really do not mix; and neither do the love of God and the love of creatures mix in one and the same action,

A musician may use his violin to play either popular or classical music; but when he is using it to play the melodies of tin-pan alley, he cannot at the same time employ it to render the more serious works of Bach or Beethoven. In the same way our wills may exercise themselves either in the love of God or the love of creatures; but if as a matter of fact they give themselves to acting from the love of creatures, they are by that choice prevented from making the love of God active in our lives. We may say, then, that while the love of God and the love of creatures may lie side by side within the substance of the soul—although they are in truth strange bedfellows even there—they cannot mingle in the activity of the soul or in the exercise of its faculties.

No doubt an action may proceed from mixed motives, as when one performs an almsdeed primarily out of love for God, although some worldly or human motive, as the desire to be known, may creep in also. But in such a case there are really two acts of the will: one an act of love for God, one an act of love for the creature, self; their apparent unity is derived from the fact that both are directed towards one object, almsgiving, just as two cooks may collaborate to bake one pie. Therefore, to the extent that an action proceeds from the love of a creature, it does not proceed from the love of God; and conversely, to the extent that it proceeds from the love of God, then the love of creatures is excluded. In this sense, then, the love of God and the love of creatures are opposed and mutually exclusive. The love of creatures, in the comparison of St. John of the Cross, is darkness, while the love of God is light; and as St. Paul asks, *"What communion can there be between light and darkness?"*

We are thus brought to an important principle, which must guide our efforts to practice charity. Let us view it as it is set down by St. Thomas Aquinas, who is simply restating what he had seen in the writings of St. Augustine, while of course the ultimate source of the teaching of both doctors is the revealed word of God. The principle is this: Man is placed midway between the goods of earth and those of heaven; so that the more he is attached to one set of these goods, the less does he cling to the other. Therefore, if we wish to grow in the love of God, we must become progressively more detached from the goods of earth.

St. Thomas states this truth several times in slightly variant forms. For example he says in one place, "It is manifest that the more intensely the human heart gives itself to one object, the more will it withdraw itself from many others. Hence the more perfectly the human soul gives itself to the love of God, the more will it withdraw from the love of things temporal." *(De Perfectione Vitae Spiritualis, VI)* Elsewhere, speaking of how to increase charity, he gives as the first means "the separation of the soul from earthly things" and then offers the following reason for this: "The heart cannot attend perfectly to diverse objects. Hence no one can love God and the world. Therefore, the more the soul separates itself from the love of earthly things, the more is it strengthened in divine love." *(De Praecefitis Caritatis)*

St. John of the Cross takes the same teaching and makes it central in his spirituality; he teaches that "affection for God and affection for creatures are contraries, and thus there cannot be contained within one will affection for creatures and affection for God." *(Ascent* I, 6) Likewise St. Francis de Sales uses this principle in explaining how the soul may grow in love: since man has but a finite capacity for love, he teaches, then the more of this love he squanders on creatures, the less will he have for God. "Whoever desires something which he desires not for God," wrote this Saint, "that much less desires God." Many centuries before, St. Augustine had used almost identical words:

"Too little does any man love Thee, who loves some other thing together with Thee, loving it not on account of Thee." *(Confessions*, X, 19)

In affirming and taking account of the opposition between the love of creatures and that of God, we are thus following the guidance of the greatest spiritual masters of the Church. And these in turn were following the inspired word of God; as when St. James tells us that the friendship of this world is enmity with God and calls those adulterers who try to combine these two opposed loves; or as when Jesus Himself says that no one can serve two masters.

Only such complete and exclusive love of creatures as is involved in the commission of mortal sin is opposed to charity in the sense of being absolutely incompatible with it. But all merely natural love of earthly goods hinders the activity of charity and prevents its growth.

Hence the practical procedure to be followed in increasing charity is to empty the heart of earthly affections. Only in this way can we free it from obstructions to the practice of divine love and thereby also enlarge its capacity for containing new infusions of that love.

Let us add that the principle is true not only of individual actions but also of habits. Not only is the violinist unable to play classical music while he fiddles one popular song; if he is habitually or usually or always playing popular airs, then he will be habitually or usually or always hindered from learning or playing the compositions of the great masters. Moreover, his preoccupation with music of an inferior kind prevents him from getting the practice and developing the skill which he needs to render properly the more difficult and intricate works of the great composers; indeed this preoccupation is likely to foster the growth of a different set of habits altogether, which may in some measure incapacitate him for more serious effort. In the same way, not only do we preclude the possibility of acting from the love of God when we act out of love for creatures, but also, if we form a habit of acting from the love of creatures, we are *de facto* hindered from occupying ourselves habitually with God and from forming the habit of acting to please God; and, in addition, by developing our sensual tendencies and the custom of acting from natural motives, we are rendered less prompt and able to form spiritual aptitudes and habits.

A radio may be used indifferently for listening to athletic events or symphonic music. But if someone at your house keeps it tuned in all day every day on baseball games or other sporting activities, it keeps you from hearing your favorite symphonies. So also the hearts of the baptized remain free to devote themselves to earthly things or heavenly; but if as a matter of fact they are continuously occupied with things earthly, they will be kept from attending to the things of God or from receiving grace and inspiration from heaven. Of course the opposite is also true. If you keep the radio tuned in constantly on symphonic music, your brothers or uncle or father will fret because they cannot hear the baseball games. And if you form the habit of acting always to please God and of using creatures, not out of affection for themselves, but in reference to God, then, it is consoling to know, you will so far be retarded from acting from natural motives and from falling into a merely natural mode of action; on the contrary, you will form a habit of supernatural action and will gain readiness and facility in keeping all your natural activity on the supernatural plane.

How to Preserve Harmony between the Three Lives

Let us bring to a close our discussion on the harmony between the two orders by noting how we can preserve this harmony.

There is in each of us an animal life, a human life, and a divine life. Of course there is in everyone but one soul and one person. Nevertheless, because of our composite nature and our elevation to the divine, we can distinguish the three possibilities of action within ourselves. We can act as animals, living by appetite; we can act as human beings or as pagans, living by reason; and we can act as divine beings, living by faith and charity, and then we are conducting ourselves as Christians.

God has created a harmony among these three elements and He intends that it should remain. But we are free and can and very often do disturb this harmony. It is our duty to help carry out the plan of God.

If a man, instead of conforming to reason, acts as an animal, we can readily see how he destroys this harmony. Accordingly, good parents, in rearing a child, try to teach him to behave, not as an animal, but rather as a human being. Nor are they satisfied until he does so behave. Because they are human, and he is human, they demand that the child measure up to human standards. They will not be offended when they see an animal act as an animal, because an animal has no higher principle to guide him; but this is not the case with the human child. The child must eat; and this is an animal activity; and if he receives no training, he will eat greedily, like an animal. Good parents teach him the rules of etiquette, by which these animal appetites are restrained and disciplined. But let us go a step higher. Let us consider the case of Christian parents. They will not be satisfied, or should not be satisfied, although their child conforms to reason. They will perceive that, even then, he is still far below the level of action which is proper to him as a child of God. And, as pagan parents would be dissatisfied with a child that acts as an animal, so will Christian parents be dissatisfied with a child that remains on the merely human plane. They will wish him to put a third element, namely, the divine element of love, into his actions to make these supernatural. Then they will be satisfied; and then also God will be satisfied that His child rises to the standard of conduct befitting a child of His. The parents know that even eating should not escape the influence of grace and charity. They know that St. Paul has said, *"Whether you eat or drink, or do anything else, do all for the glory of God"* (I Cor. 10, 31) Hence, besides teaching their child good manners, they teach him to get in the third element—love of God; rather they teach him to eat and practice good manners out of love for God, so that the third element will be the vital principle both in regulating his health and in practicing courtesy towards his neighbor.

We can thus summarize the whole business of keeping a harmony between the three elements in our lives by saying that we should "get in the third element." We may well take this as a slogan: "Get in the third element." Any action, however good it looks exteriorly, or however reasonable it may be, is incomplete unless it contains the third element, the divine or supernatural element, which elevates it in the practical order to the supernatural plane and makes it an action worth of a child of God.

Many examples besides eating could be given. All our actions as a matter of course contain the first two elements, the animal and the human, although the human element also needs cultivation. Even such an activity as thinking, since it depends on our senses, involves our animal life. It is our task, in correspondence with divine grace, to get in the third element.

Let us take one more example. In our dealings with others we can act as animals, as human beings, or as divine beings. If we act as animals, we will be in continual strife with our neighbor, our unrestrained appetites bringing us into collision with them. If we act as men, we will learn and observe the rules recommended by the conventions of politeness. But if we get in the third element, we will treat our neighbors with divine charity, the second-sight of faith enabling us to see God in them.

What is thus true of our relations with others in general is also true of the marital relationship; this fact is particularly worth noticing. The Old Testament gives us a striking example in the story of the younger Tobias. When the elder Tobias was about to die, he wished to send his son to a distant debtor to collect some money which the boy should inherit. Unfortunately the young Tobias did not know how to get to this distant place. But God had taken this pious family under His special care; and an angel, in the guise of a beautiful young man, came to Tobias and offered to be his guide. Tobias accepted and they started out on their journey. As they went along, the angel, who was Raphael, told Tobias that in a nearby town there lived a certain woman by the name of Sara and that he should ask her father for her in marriage. Tobias replied that he had heard of this Sara and also that she had already been married to seven husbands; and that a devil had killed them all. Consequently, he was not very eager to follow his unknown companion's advice. The angel, however, assured him that these seven husbands had suffered this terrible fate at the hands of the devil was because, in marrying Sara, they had *"shut out God from themselves, and from their mind...and gave themselves to their lust, as the horse and the mule"*; and over such as these, Raphael said, the devil has power. He then told Tobias that, upon marrying Sara, they should spend the first three days of their married life in prayer, consecrating themselves and their union to God. The angel promised that, if he would do this, the devil would have no power over him. Tobias did as he was told, and God blessed his marriage with Sara.

Here we have a clear illustration of the principle which tells us that we must "get in the third element." Here is an explicit statement of the fact that an action is incomplete which lacks this third element. We are here shown a further important fact, namely, that when we leave out this third element, and live on the mere level of our desires, the devil has power over us. Doubtless, the teaching illustrated by this instance will explain the high divorce rate of the present day. Men and women are now marrying as did the seven husbands of Sara, like the horse and the mule, shutting out God, excluding the third element. And over such as these the devil has power, a power that is always manifested in hatred, envy, division. Divorce is assuredly the devil's work, just as love and peace are God's. Men and women marry to gain happiness in marriage and they frequently find only misery, and the reason is clear—they leave out God, they forget the third element, the divine element, which should be the living principle of every action.

Getting the third element, the element of divine charity, into our actions is thus the means at once of supernaturalizing all our natural activity and of preserving harmony among the three kinds of life in us and therefore also between the natural and supernatural orders.

Let us think upon these things. And may God bless you.

> *"Humbly do we pray Thee, O Almighty God, that we whom Thou dost refresh with Thy sacraments may also serve Thee by a manner of life that is pleasing to Thee. Through Our Lord Jesus Christ Thy Son Who livest and reignest with Thee in union with the Holy Spirit, God world without end. Amen."*
>
> (Postcomnunion, Second Sunday of Lent)

THE CONFLICT BETWEEN NATURAL AND SUPERNATURAL: THE CENTER OF THE CONFLICT

My dear friends in Christ--

At this point we are like the doctor who has completed his preliminary tests and knows his patient's general condition as well as the organs that are sound and do not need surgical attention. We have satisfied ourselves that nature is good and that there is harmony between nature and grace. Moreover, we know precisely where this harmony is found and how also we can preserve it in the area of our own freedom by keeping all our activity on the supernatural plane. And, as the surgeon's next task is to localize the place of infection and operate there, so ours is to discover what it is in us that hinders us from fulfilling our true vocation, what holds us back from staying in our daily lives on the divine plane, what elements of our actions, in a word, conflict with our supernatural destiny. Having discovered the exact place, it will then be our spiritual task to remove the conflict.

The purpose of this conference, therefore, is to indicate the center of the conflict and draw some practical principles of action from our discovery.

The Centre of the Conflict: in the Motive

We have noticed in the previous conference that the conflict does not appear, or at any rate disappears, and that there is full harmony between the three kinds of life in the Christian when he acts from a supernatural motive. The reason for this fact, which is the needed clue to the answer we are seeking, is not hard to discover. God indeed raises us to the supernatural order; but He leaves us free; He does not constrain us to live supernaturally; despite our elevation, we are free to live, or to attempt to live—

you recall the difficulties in the way—on the natural plane. In this matter God, we said, is like a father who lifts up his child to reach for some food on a high shelf. The father holds the child up, leaving his arms free. If the boy wants the orange, or whatever it may be, he is free to reach out and take it; if he takes it, he will get enjoyment and nourishment; but if he does not reach out, then he will not get the orange nor be refreshed by its goodness. God, in giving man grace, raises him to the divine plane, but does not force him to live a divine life. This remains for man to do; he may reach out and accept the opportunities which God gives him, the graces which are offered to him every moment of his life, or he may, in virtue of his gift of freedom, refuse them. Grace will have its effect, will supernaturalize his life and sanctify his soul, only if he uses his freedom to obtain the grace to cooperate with it.

On the other hand, we may act according to nature. That is to say, we may follow its inclinations and desires; we may allow our actions to be influenced or even ruled by concupiscence, by the desire for sensible and earthly goods. It is then natural desire or affection, not grace or divine love, that rules our actions; and our actions and our lives are then natural rather than supernatural. And moreover, when we thus live merely natural lives and habitually perform actions that are merely natural, we may be said truly to be in conflict with our supernatural destiny and with God's design that we live supernatural lives. Our actions in this case conflict with our supernatural calling. A close analysis will reveal precisely at what point the conflict occurs.

A supernatural motive prevents or removes the conflict; on the other hand, a natural motive creates the conflict. If a man in the state of grace eats out of love for God, his action is supernatural; if he eats out of love for food, or even out of a desire to obtain good health, his action is natural. The conflict is not in the act of eating, for, as we have seen, natural activity can be supernaturalized, and even saints must eat. The conflict is in the motive force, the motive behind the natural activity: the reason why he eats. The explanation of this fact is that our motives are the chief area of our freedom. God leaves our wills free, and it is in choosing and determining our motives that we above all exercise our freedom and dispose our actions. We are free, but we are not free in everything. A man is not free to refuse to eat; but he is free to determine the motive for his eating. He is not free to refuse to work—if he refuses to work he is avoiding a duty and in any case will hardly survive in this world—but he is free to determine the motive for his work. Our freedom is a great gift, but the actual area of our freedom is very small, although certainly most important. Most of our actions are imposed on us by necessity, imposed upon us, that is, by nature. Eating, sleeping, walking, talking, studying, reading, thinking, the performance of our daily duties, caring for the various requirements of bodily nature—all these are things which could not be escaped even in a Carthusian monastery. But nature, while fixing most of our actions, does not impose upon us any motive, any end or goal as the final determinant of these actions. We are free to choose our own goal, free to fix the goods to which we will consecrate our labors. It is in making this choice of a final good, and in directing all our actions towards it, that we exercise our freedom—and form our motives; for a motive is the will's grip on a good which it chooses as its end. If then we wish to direct all our actions towards God, we will act from supernatural motives. If earthly goods or creatures are the goods that we desire, then we will act out of human motives. Motives are the chief area of our freedom. Externally there may be no difference between the Christian and his pagan neighbor; both may perform the same kind of natural human actions. The difference is within, within their hearts: the kind of love dwelling in their hearts decides the motives that impel their actions.

We now have located the center of opposition between nature and grace: it is in the motive. What we must do in order to eliminate the conflict is to remove the natural motive and to replace it with a supernatural motive. Note that there are two aspects to our effort. It is not enough simply to introduce supernatural motives into them. We must, in the first place, remove the natural motives; it is only to the extent that our hearts are freed from natural motives that they can be filled with supernatural motives and the love of God. We must cease clinging by natural motives to created goods, in order that by supernatural motives we may cling wholly to God.

What God wants, then, in our actions, is our motives. Consider an example. You have a plate of food before you. Eating is an action natural, necessary, and good. But like all natural actions it should be elevated to the supernatural plane. How can this be accomplished? As we have seen, you can do it by eating from a supernatural motive; you thus make the action supernatural and meritorious of eternal life. And the food remains for you, while God is content with the motive.

Nor is the example ridiculous. Every action of our lives should be made supernatural. If we live as Christians, we will not break off our religious exertions for the week after Mass on Sunday mornings; nor will we be content merely with performing certain devotions at more frequent intervals. We will seek to transform our entire lives, raising all we do to the level of supernature; we will strive to make our actions, not super-sinful only, but truly supernatural. So St. Paul says, *"Therefore whether you eat or drink, or whatsoever else you do, do all for the glory of God."* (I Cor. 10, 31) And again he says *"Whatever you do in word or in work, do all in the name of the Lord Jesus."* (Col. 3, 17) Notice in both these texts the words "whatsoever" and "all." Nothing in our lives is too small to escape the influence of grace, or too insignificant to be raised up to the divine plane. And observe again what God wants is only the motive. The food, the act of eating, the taste He leaves for us; what we should give to Him is the motive, which is the kernel, the marrow, the center of our freedom, the dedication of our hearts, the one thing which we can give Him that He desires.

Remember, too, that it is possible for a motive to be good and still be natural. Our endeavor should be to make our motives, not only naturally good, but supernatural, remembering always that a Christian life is a life above nature. "The Imitation of Christ" points out that all men desire what is good but that many are deceived by the appearance of good. That is to say, men, in judging what is good for them, will often be mistaken; and this may happen even when, as they think, they desire some natural good only because of spiritual benefits they hope from it. Thus, what appears to us to be good, may appear so only because of our desires and passions and is not a real good. The only safe thing to do, as it is the most perfect thing to do, is to act from some supernatural motive, and finally, for the love of God. By purifying and supernaturalizing our motives we intensify our charity, we increase our merit, perfect our conduct, and constantly draw closer to God.

If we meditate seriously about the principles here described, we will find that they will gradually work a great change in our whole attitude towards the spiritual life and redirect all our efforts. They will teach us that our preoccupation should be, not simply to overcome evil, but rather to eliminate natural motives. We will take our motives as the area in which to conduct our chief spiritual endeavors. When people simply wish to avoid sin, they limit their ordinary actual effort to combating sin and evil, apparently unaware that there is a higher fight possible, as well as a deeper source of trouble. They should rather attack natural motives; by concerning themselves with these they would be perfecting their freedom and growing in love. Therefore, instead of bothering about whether actions are sinful or not, let us look inward, into our hearts, and there purify the springs of action This way we are certain to stay at a very great distance from evil, but we will also rise to the plane which is proper to children of God.

We can see too, from these principles, that the matter—the building materials, so to speak— of our spiritual lives are the ordinary naturally good and indifferent actions of everyday. It is certainly wrong and unfortunate to be so preoccupied with sinful actions that our only moral and spiritual efforts are directed towards the avoidance of sin. Such an attitude is inadequate; it relaxes our spiritual energies when it is the responsibility of a true spiritual life to intensify them; and it makes the spiritual life negative. Our minds would do better to mark out the indifferent actions, like eating or walking or studying or working, in order to supernaturalize them; or we should attend to good actions, like the performance of our duty or doing good to our neighbors or praying or fasting, in order to sanctify these actions inwardly by purity of intention.

Attention to our motives, seeing to it that they are supernatural, would free us from the depressing burden of a merely negative spirituality—preoccupation with evil, a life in darkness, like that of creatures under the earth. It would bring us into the light, would make over lives into careers of dedication, of love, of joyous and free service, offered willingly to a most lovable Creator and Father.

You see now what we mean by a conflict between natural and supernatural. Our human nature's goodness and its essential harmony with the order of grace is such an indisputable truth— one which we ourselves have just spent two conferences in affirming—that to some the notion of a conflict may at first sight seem surprising. But this will not be so, and you will grasp at once that what we are here doing is to give an exact statement to a very old truth indeed if you have pondered that famous and important chapter of the *Imitation of Christ* on the diverse movements of nature and grace, movements which are there said to be "much opposed" to each other. Only notice carefully that the *Imitation* does not state that the opposition is inherent in nature itself but that it is rather to be found in the motions or movements of nature. In other words, the conflict is not in the substance of our nature or the physical make-up of our faculties, it is rather in the practical orders. It may be seen in the mind's deliberate deflection from divine truth and its formation of a worldly wisdom or false prudence at variance with faith. But finally and above all it is to be found in the will, that is, in the sphere of personal freedom when the will neglects to refer natural activity to the supernatural good which God has fixed as the final end in life.

Or we may put the matter this way: The harmony between nature and grace is God's work; it is the effect of the excellence which God has given to nature. On the other hand, the conflict is man's work, his sorry contribution to the universe, and it is the result of neglect, carelessness, tepidity, worldliness. The conflict, therefore, arises only in the area in which the will enjoys free exercise and control; and as the will, in neglecting the grace which urges it to act and live on the supernatural plane, is responsible for the conflict, so also—and this at least is encouraging—the will, by corresponding with grace and keeping its conduct on the supernatural plane, can restore the desired harmony.

Of course the background of the conflict is to be found in that tension between flesh and spirit which is the consequence of man's dual nature and of which the Apostle speaks: *"For the flesh lusts against the spirit and the spirit against the flesh, for these are opposed to each other. . . ."* (Gal. *S*, 17) Yet this tension or opposition between the diverse tendencies of flesh and spirit breaks into open conflict only when the will, seduced by the desire for worldly happiness, fails to refer all human activity to the supernatural end which God has established for human life. This failure is manifested in the will's habit of acting from natural motives; for since motives are the area of our freedom, it is by means of motives that we dispose our actions towards their end. Conversely the will removes the conflict when by means of supernatural motives it orients its activity and its use of creatures towards the true supernatural end of life.

Thus we see that by such a simple means as acting from supernatural motives, while discarding such as are merely natural, we may prevent or end conflict between our natural activity and our supernatural destiny, preserve the pre-established harmony between the two orders, live fully supernatural lives according to the divine plan, and fulfill in every action the purpose for which we were created and elevated.

Applications of the Principle of Motivation

From this great principle of supernatural motivation which we have now established, it will now be possible to derive a great many useful and practical lessons. For example, it becomes clear that, just as we ought not to be content with avoiding grave sin, so we should not rest satisfied with ourselves because, as we believe, we are in the state of grace. In other words, we have not finished our spiritual efforts when we have brought our souls, or perhaps helped the souls of others, into the state of grace. It is a great mistake to speak of the state of grace as though its possession were the maximum of the spiritual life—as though once we enter into the state of grace, there is nothing further for us to do. On the contrary, just as in keeping the commandments of the natural law we are fulfilling a minimum, not a maximum, since we thereby exclude from our souls only what is opposed to the very lowest degree of charity, so also should we regard the state of grace as the minimum, the starting-point of all supernatural effort; for when we receive grace, we receive with it our initial infusion and lowest degree of charity. From then on grace and charity, and all the other virtues, should grow even until death. When we receive grace we have not ended our spiritual progress. Once we have the state of grace, on the contrary, we can *begin* to live a supernatural life, begin to live as sons of God, begin to labor with the purpose of increasing and accumulating grace. The gift of grace resembles earthly riches in that the more we have of it, the more desirable is our condition. Rich men never tire of making money; and Christians should never grow weary of storing up treasures in heaven. Jesus, in the Sermon on the Mount, tells us to do just that: *"Lay up for yourselves treasures in heaven."* (Matt. 6, 20)

When parents have brought a child into the world, they do not feel that their work is finished; they know that their work has just begun—that they must now raise the child to maturity. In the same way, our original endowment of supernatural life, which we receive when first placed in the state of grace, cannot be considered the perfection of this life. We may not cease caring for and developing our supernatural life once we have obtained it any more than parents may abandon their infant as soon as it is born. When we have received this new principle of a higher life in our souls, our spiritual task, like that of parents, has just begun. We must now take care of this new life; we must nourish it and increase it and bring it to maturity; and the maturity of Christian life is sanctity. Saints are grown-up Christians; the rest of us are dwarfs.

Accordingly we should not fancy that Jesus is pleased with us just because we are able to say that we are in the state of grace. He is pleased with us when we are in the state of grace if we are also living as Christians. But He is not pleased with us when, having grace, we live as pagans. Precisely because we are in the state of grace, God expects us to live, not on the natural plane, but on the supernatural. But if, having been raised to the supernatural, we continue on the lower level, then certainly He is displeased with us, since we then refuse to accept and utilize the unspeakably precious gift that He has given to us. Suppose a mother has a child who is mentally defective; the mother is sad, and we wish to console her. Could we console her by saying that, although the child acts like an animal, she should reflect that he really has reason? He has reason potentially, we might say, although he cannot use it. That would scarcely be a consolation. The mother already knows that her child has reason: that is precisely the reason for her grief. She sees a little pet dog acting as a dog, and she is not sad, but rather laughs at it; she sees a canary acting like a canary and she enjoys watching it. She does not expect the dog or the canary to behave according to the principle of a life higher than their own, a life which they do not have. But when she sees her child, endowed with intelligence, but living on the lower plane of mere animal behavior, then indeed she has reason for grief.

Similarly if, as we may imagine, God had created men and left them in the state of pure nature, then it would have been expected of such men that they should act naturally and God would not have been displeased with them for so doing. But when He sees one whom He has raised to the high state of a child of God, living or wishing to live as a mere pagan or worldling, forgetful of his higher calling, then surely He is not pleased but rather displeased.

Let us, consequently, when we live natural lives, neglecting grace, not be so confident of God's favor nor so careless about our eventual salvation, as though it were a thing assured. Nor let us be complacent about ourselves as though we have done all that is necessary and all that is expected. By habitually neglecting the gift which God has given us, we may finally end by losing it. A teacher may not be able to fail a talented student who is lazy, as long as the student studies enough at least to fulfill the minimum scholastic requirements. But if the student, in his carelessness, falls below the minimum, then he will fail despite his superior talent. So in the same way, the one who is in the state of grace, provided he retains the grace, is sure of salvation although he is not perfect; yet if he is habitually careless, certainly he cannot expect that the God of holiness takes pleasure in his carelessness and neglect, while by the very fact of such carelessness he risks the loss of grace itself and therefore of eternal life. We know, too, that when we live according to nature, we will not remain on the natural plane long but will soon begin a descent that will end in sin. Not to make progress is to retrogress. Carelessness and negligence is the beginning of a backward movement that may well bring us to ruin. The parable of the talents shows very conclusively that God expects us to make use of our talents. The grace that we have, like capital, must be put to work to produce more grace.

These considerations bring us into sight of another great advantage gained by the effort to purify and elevate our motives. By so doing we will be cooperating with grace in the most practical and effective way possible. The great practical work of our lives is this one of cooperating with grace; yet it is one which is seldom spoken about, for which careful plans are rarely made, and for which we have thought out no definite practical procedure. Our books and sermons and meditations tell us all about grace, tell us where it may be obtained, described its beauty, enumerate its fruits; but they very frequently neglect to teach us how to utilize this grace, how to correspond with it. And since God leaves us free, it is most important that we know how to make use of grace in our actions. Indeed we may say that this is the most important practical task of a Christian life, that is, how to correspond or to cooperate with grace. God gives us grace, and we need not fear that He will fail in carrying out His part in our sanctification; but we do need to fear lest we fail to carry out what is necessary on our side. Suppose that you were to give a talk exhorting a group of students to correspond with grace. And suppose that your talk were very effective and fruitful, and, in the course of it, or after it was finished, one of your hearers would come to you and anxiously ask, "How may we correspond with grace?" What would be your answer? I fear that the answer is seldom given and doubt whether the question itself is often formed. We take it for granted that in having the sources of grace, and in knowing where they are, we have enough. This is not so.

The principle of supernatural motivation gives us a practical, simple, and effective way of corresponding with grace. By charity we correspond with grace; and since through a supernatural motive, especially a motive of love, we make our charity operative, then by every action motivated by the love of God we are corresponding with grace, meriting new grace and new charity, and advancing steadily towards eternal salvation.

St. Thomas it is who teaches that the principle of merit is charity; that is to say, the cause of merit, the precious inward life which makes our actions of value in the sight of God is the fact that they spring from charity. The practical task, then, is to make active the charity which God infuses; and how can this be done better than by exercising our charity in supernatural motives, in doing all out of love for God? In this way every deed becomes an act of charity; charity is constantly active, ever alert and laboring for the increase of grace.

So, to correspond with grace, we need merely act out of love; and all day long, as we perform an endless series of indifferent or good actions, and do them to please God, we can enjoy the assurance that we are, not occasionally, but continuously doing all that we can to make the grace of God operative and effective. We ought all to be holy; the reason that we are not is no stinginess on God's part—He gives His grace to all. The reason that we are not holy is that we fail to make use of God's grace. Here is a simple way in which all of us can make every daily action count for eternal happiness.

To be sure, there are some theologians who do not accept St. Thomas's teaching that charity is the principle of merit. They think that the activity of any infused virtue, or any impulse of actual grace, produces meritorious actions in the baptized soul. But this difference of opinion does not affect the practical rule which we give here concerning motives. For although we praise charity as providing the most perfect motive, still what is urged is that you act from any motive that is supernatural, that is, from a motive derived from any of the Christian virtues—humility, patience, hope, penitence, or any other. And of course, apart from the fact that charity is active, even though secretly, in these other virtues as their source and principle, it is also clear that the rule which shows us how to make charity active applies equally to all virtues. That is to say, what better way—and, one might ask, what other way—is there to make these lesser Christian virtues operative influential forces in our lives than by deriving the motives of our actions from them? And what better way than this is there to correspond with actual grace? By supernatural motives we open our souls up to every heavenly influence, as flowers unfold their petals to receive the light and warmth of the sun.

How wonderfully consoling and encouraging is this doctrine! It means that no matter who we are, no matter how humbly situated, no matter how simple or uneducated or poor or unimportant, we have within our reach a most powerful means of exercising virtue, of growing in love and increasing in grace, of coming ever closer to God. We are all called to be saints, but too many people have a false idea of what is meant by sanctity. They fancy that to be saints they must perform miracles, or have visions, or to be called by God to the performance of extraordinary works. It is true that God does sometimes give His saints such special gifts. But the essential thing, the main thing in sanctity, is love, and a saint is one who is filled with grace and united most closely to God in love, a love which flowers also into the other virtues. This is very apparent in the lives of saints like St. Therese, the Little Flower. There was nothing extraordinary in her career, no miracles or gigantic works. Even the sisters with whom she lived wondered what could possibly be said of her in the simple obituaries that were published after each sister's death. She did nothing extraordinary and yet by a tremendous love she made every action extraordinary.

We must strive to do this also, that is, to fill every action with love and thus make every action a long stride towards holiness and heaven. It is the motive that counts—not so much what we do as why we do it. Of course some works are more important than others, and some actions are higher than others. There are, we have seen, merely indifferent actions, and they are given spiritual significance chiefly by their motive, while others, like prayer, are intrinsically good, good in their own right, and even among these good works there is a hierarchy. If we do these more important or higher works with love then will we obtain the greatest possible merit. Nevertheless, there are some men engaged in the highest work—for example priests and bishops— who perhaps gain little merit, while simple lay brothers, engaged in humble tasks, obtain great favor with God and are honored by the Church as saints. Let us therefore take this principle, this secret of sanctity, and apply it immediately and always to our lives.

Answers to Objections to the Principle of Motive

Some persons might object that this effort to supernaturalize motives would be very irksome, that as a method of spirituality it would impose great difficulty on souls. We answer such an objection simply by contradicting it. To super-naturalize one's motives means simply to think of God and to refer all one's actions to God; and this is anything but difficult for one who really loves God. It is no hardship to think of someone we love. Lovers do not think it difficult or tiresome or unpleasant to think of each other—although they sometimes find it difficult to think of anything else! If we love God, the thought of Him will be a joy and a refreshment, not a heavy task. If we find it tiresome to turn our thoughts to Him, therefore, it can mean only that our love for Him is very small. Where the heart lies, there is our treasure also. If we are worldly-minded and our hearts are filled with affections for creatures, then indeed, to think of God will we have to brace ourselves, as for an effort contrary to our nature, to oppose the usual tendency of minds occupied with creatures and to change the habits of hearts filled with creature affections. But for the man detached from this world, for the true lover of God, there is no difficulty; the problem simply disappears; for him supernatural motives come "natural."

It may be objected, further, that such vigilance over motives would tend to make souls introspective, and that therefore it would also incline them to become scrupulous and self-centered, involving them even in a danger of contracting some neurosis. These dangers are imaginary; the method we propose is in fact calculated to remove them. If the argument of those who make this objection seems plausible, this can only be because it is such an audacious perversion of the truth. The devil, with whom we are undoubtedly dealing here, is the father of lies.

Yet, in a sense, although a very different sense, it is true that this kind of spirituality would make people introspective. It would tend to turn their eyes inward; it would cause them to live an interior life. But it would not make them introspective in the sense of being morbidly interested in analyzing the interior processes of the mind. On the contrary, it would turn them away from preoccupation with self. It would turn their gaze inward in order to fix it on the divine Presence dwelling within every Soul that possesses God's grace. It would cause them to become in time wholly oblivious of self, wholly absorbed in God. Christianity, in this sense, is truly an interior life; and such an interior life is the best possible cure for a morbid introspective life.

This indicates the answer also to the charge that concern for motives would cause us to be self-centered and selfish. It would cause us to be God-centered; and by teaching us total surrender and total dedication to God, would empty us of selfishness and bring us to utter selflessness. Moreover, by instructing us how to love God in deed and in truth, by uniting our wills to His will, it would cause us to embrace in divine love, rather than in sensual and selfish love, all that He loves, all His creatures, especially all men, who in a special way bear His image. Thus the Christian interior life turns one's affections to the external world in the most generous and the most fruitful way possible. The love of neighbor, after all, is a corollary and a reflection of the love of God. Those Catholics, and there are unfortunately a number, are guilty of a monstrous absurdity, not to say a blasphemy, who find, or claim to find, an opposition between the interior life and the active apostolate, between the pursuit of personal perfection and the loving service of neighbor—in a word between charity towards God and charity towards neighbor, between the first and second commandments. The men most devoted to the interior life are the saints; and the saints have ever been the greatest benefactors of their fellows.

As to the assertion that a careful watch over motives would make one scrupulous, we answer by a flat denial. Such a statement is sheer nonsense. Scrupulosity is preoccupation with sin and an over-zealous vigilance to find sin where none exists. Now how can a rule which urges souls to turn their eyes away from preoccupation with sin, result in over-preoccupation with sin? If the method would have any faults, these should work in the opposite direction! The very point that we have been making is that Catholics, on principle, and as their habitual policy, ought *not* to occupy their attention with sin; their concern should be with good and indifferent actions, their effort should be to elevate these. Scrupulosity is a disease that comes from ignoring this wholesome positive method, which would keep the mind high above the sin level; scrupulosity is rather the extreme state of that false mentality which identifies Christian practice with the avoidance of sin. Far from causing scrupulosity, vigilance over motives will prove itself a most powerful and efficacious cure for this disease. We urge scrupulous souls and their directors to try it. No type of penitent gives directors more trouble and anxiety than the scrupulous; none are more difficult to help. Because the judgment of the scrupulous is so inaccurate, they must be put under obedience: all directors know that. But then what? What is the next step?

Most books end their counsels here; but the actual problem only begins here. What such souls need is a spiritual procedure that will give free scope to their sensitive consciences and their desire to please God, while releasing them from the paralyzing fear of sin in their every action. The answer to this need is emphasis on the purification and elevation of our motives. This gives the soul the highest spiritual ideal, while removing the sense of guilt from their failures. They learn that their customary faults are not sins at all but lapses to the natural plane, and therefore imperfections—to be overcome indeed, but not making us liable to punishment.

To the charge that this doctrine of motives would lead to neuroticism we answer again by a simple contradiction: the reverse is true. The best way to procure inward tranquility and peace of mind, to free one's self from the interior turmoil and tensions caused by conflicting desires, is to purify these desires. St. John of the Cross devotes a section to treating of the evils that result from retaining natural desires and affections for creatures. Two of these evils are relevant here. These desires weary the soul; for, says the Saint, "they are like restless and discontented children, who are ever demanding this or that from their mother, and are never satisfied." Moreover, these desires torment the soul: "in the same way wherein one that lies naked upon thorns and briars is tormented and afflicted, even so is the soul tormented and afflicted when it rests upon its desires.... and the more intense is the desire, the greater is the torment which it causes the soul." Yes, natural desires and affections weary and torment the soul. Let us reflect a little; we have not time now to study the holy Doctor's full treatment of these ideas, which themselves represent great psychological insight; but we can pause over them for a moment and each of us from our own experience can bear testimony to their profound truth. We are made discontented, and wretched by our warring, petulant, insistent desires; to purge ourselves of them is to enter upon the way of inward tranquility. In ridding ourselves of natural motives we cut these desires out by their tiniest roots and shoots, while by means of supernatural motives the peace of God grows and takes possession of our souls. The doctrine of motives here recommended would destroy at the source those emotional conflicts and tensions that always bring misery and may in truth end in neurosis.

Finally, to those who would assert that the urging such vigilance over motives would be to place too great a burden on the shoulders of the faithful, we answer that what we offer to the faithful is love, and love is joy. True there is a burden; and Jesus Himself quite candidly acknowledged that He was imposing a burden on us, comparing His teaching to a yoke. But He said: *"My yoke is sweet and My burden is light."* Love it is that makes it sweet and light.

Let us now think upon these things. And may God bless you.

> *"May the action of this heavenly gift control our bodies and souls completely, so that, not our own inclinations, but rather its graces may prevail in us. Through Our Lord Jesus Christ Thy Son Who liveth and reigneth with Thee in union with the Holy Spirit, God world without end. Amen."*
>
> (Postcommunion, Fifteenth Sunday after Pentecost)

THE CONFLICT BETWEEN NATURE AND THE SUPERNATURAL: THE REASON FOR THE CONFLICT

My dear friends in Christ--

Perhaps you know the story of Pinocchio. Pinocchio was a marionette made by Geppetto from a piece of firewood. He was, however, no ordinary marionette, but was destined to become a real boy if he would accept the conditions and endure the probation required of him. But alas, Pinocchio's career was filled with failures and infidelities. He wanted to be a boy, but he found it more fun to be a mischievous marionette. Once he said that the best trade is to eat, drink, sleep, and amuse oneself. At another time he was so bad that he even lost his status as a marionette and became a donkey. But eventually, by dint of hard work and obedience to the command to be good, Pinocchio was changed into a boy.

Now for a marionette, the promise given to Pinocchio to become a boy was a kind of supernatural destiny. His antics when he behaved as a marionette rather than as a boy may be compared to our lapses to the natural plane where we act as pagans rather than as children of God. Pinocchio's temporary change into a donkey serves to remind us of our falls, not merely into natural ways, but also into sin when, like animals, we are ruled by our appetites. And Pinocchio's actually becoming a boy at the end of the story, although only after living worthily of boyhood, may remind us of our glorious destiny of divinization and union with God, if we pass successfully through our period of testing and learn to live like divine beings.

Thus Pinocchio's probation and his failures will help us to understand a problem that faces us now. We have discussed the center of conflict between natural activity and our supernatural destiny, and the sense in which it may be said that there is a conflict. Now we need to know the reasons for the conflict. In the present conference we will set down and explain two reasons. The first is that since God has raised us to the supernatural plane, He expects us to live supernaturally. Secondly, the commandment of love, which rules the supernatural world, requires us to act from supernatural motives.

First: The Fact of Our Elevation

Just as Pinocchio, in order to realize the promise of becoming a boy, had to learn to act in a manner worthy of boyhood, so we, in order to attain to our inheritance as children of God, must live on the divine plane. Our lapses to the human level, through merely natural actions and intentions, are an infidelity to our supernatural calling and are, therefore, in conflict with it. They are like Pinocchio's infidelities when he acted as a marionette rather than as a boy. Because of our elevation, God wishes us to stay on the higher plan of action, wishes us really to live as sons of God. This requires the renunciation of a merely natural way of life. Since grace raises us to a participation in the divine nature, it is fitting that we should be imitators, not only of noble and high-minded men, but of God.

As a consequence of our supernatural elevation, therefore, when we attempt to live natural lives—bearing in mind that a natural life is a good life—we are in conflict with our supernatural destiny. We are not carrying out God's plan, we are not aiming at the good which He has determined should be the goal of all human existence. Taking natural motives at their best—that is to say, considering them as purified of all the sensuality and egotism which are so likely to spoil them in practice—they are infinitely lower than any supernatural motive. The supernatural order to which we belong, the perfection of the Christian life which we ought to seek, is not to be reached by motives of the natural order. Our destiny as sons of God, regulated by the great precept of love, requires that divine love be the dominant force of all our actions. Those who are anxious to make progress in the spiritual life should be careful to see not only that their actions are correct, but also that they are as fully as possible inspired by divine charity.

Other examples besides Pinocchio will help to make this matter clear. Suppose that one musician in an orchestra insists on playing out of key, or wants to play a melody different from all the other members of the orchestra. Will the others, or the director, or the audience, like his performance, even though considered individually it is very good? Hardly. Whatever his special excellence may be, he will now have to conform himself to what is done by the orchestra in which he plays. Or suppose that this individualistic musician insists on playing a certain piece in the key of C, when the rest of the orchestra is playing it in the key of D, to which it has been transposed. Will his playing harmonize with that of the others? Now we have been transposed, so to speak, to the supernatural order, and it is in accordance with the rules and requirements of this order that we must live. Refusal to do so places us out of harmony with our fellow-Christians, puts us into conflict with the demands of our supernatural destiny.

Again, a student who leaves one school to attend another cannot introduce the customs and traditions of the former into the latter. He will have to learn and to conform to the customs and the traditions of the school that he now attends. If he fails to do so, he will soon be told that it would be better for him to go back where he came from. It does not matter how excellent the former customs were; he must learn the new ones if he wishes to remain where he is now. So we also, introduced into the supernatural world, must live according to the rules and demands of that world. Our hankering for the world of nature, for the natural world and its ways, is, to say the least, an act of ingratitude to the merciful God Who has given us a share in His life. And if we wish to keep the privilege that He has made ours, then should we not also accept the responsibilities that go with it?

A final example: Suppose that a king would bring a young peasant lad into his court with the intention of making him a prince. He chooses this particular boy because of the excellent qualities he sees in him. Still, once the boy has come to the court, he will be expected to lay aside his peasant ways and adopt the manner of the court. When the king gives him the clothing of the prince; when he provides tutors to teach the prince-elect the manners proper to his station, if the boy would refuse to put on the clothes and refuse contemptuously to learn the manners of the court, all so new to him, then the king would surely refuse him also the honor of becoming a prince. The peasant lad might say, "I am not accustomed to these manners and these clothes, and I do not wish to change my ways." To which the king's natural reply would be, "Now that you are at the court, you must accept the manners of the court; peasant manners are praiseworthy indeed, but not proper here; if, therefore, you wish to observe the manners of peasants, you will have to leave the court and go back to your peasant home." We are like that peasant. We have been called by the King of Kings to His heavenly court to be His children, children of the most high God and therefore princes of the heavenly kingdom. And now, like boors, we refuse to put on the manners of the court and to observe the rules of our new home. We say that we are not accustomed to them, that it is hard for us to be saints, that one has to get along in the world, and other excuses of a similar kind. To which our Lord answers, "You are children of God, heirs of heaven, princes of the heavenly kingdom; if you wish to retain this honor and claim your inheritance, you must leave the ways of mere men, however good these may be, and adopt the manners fitting in My heavenly court."

Second: Love Requires Supernatural Motives

The second reason why there is a conflict is that love demands supernatural motives of us and, therefore, living by natural motives puts us into opposition with this demand of divine love. The great rule that guides us in God's world is the rule of love; and this rule when brought down to the details of our everyday actions requires that they be regulated by love. To do otherwise is to neglect our special responsibility and duty as Christians.

It is love, in the first place, which explains the need for detachment and for contempt of the world and of creatures. Some persons, as soon as they hear the phrase "contempt of creatures," mistakenly think that it implies some evil in creatures. They call the doctrine of detachment or of the contempt of the world Jansenistic, because the Jansenists did hold that there was something intrinsically evil in human nature and in mere natural affection for the things of the world. But contempt for the world does not necessarily mean that there is evil in creatures. If the Jansenist thinks that the love of creatures is evil because he regards human nature itself as evil, the true Christian practices contempt of creatures for an entirely different reason and motive. He does so because he believes that creatures are good and that therefore he should prefer God to them. It is love, not hatred, nor any fancied evil in the world, which requires detachment and contempt of the world.

Let us consider an example. Two young men are friends—we will call them James and John. They go to school together, work together, play together, and are fast friends over a period of many years. Then there comes a time when they both meet a young woman, whom we will call Mary, and both are attracted to her; in fact both fall in love with Mary and wish to marry her. What happens to their friendship for each other? Will it survive? There is at any rate a possibility that it will not. The former friends now become rivals. And why? Not because there has been any intrinsic change in their characters; the virtues which they possessed formerly, and which they admired in each other, are still present in them; there is no change for the worse, there is no evil in either of them. Yet now there is a tension, a rivalry, a jealousy between them. What causes the jealousy is not any evil in their character but the affection both have for Mary. Further, suppose that one of them, James, marries Mary. Mary must now give all her affection to James; she can no longer flirt even innocently with James's rival. Love is jealous and exclusive, so Mary must give all her love to her husband. She cannot occasionally spend an evening with John. James would object to that, even though he would admit that John is a fine man and would retain his friendly feelings towards John. In other words, Mary would have to treat John as if he were evil. The fact that he is a virtuous and a good man would not be sufficient reason, in the eyes of James, who loves Mary, for her to become intimate with John.

Now apply all of this to the relationship between the soul and God. It is a just and exact parallel. Our relationship to God is one of love. The great law of the supernatural world, we have said repeatedly, and must keep insisting, is love. When the Sacred Scriptures teach us this relationship of the soul to God, they use two examples which bring out in the most direct and graphic way possible the fact that it consists in love. We are called children of God--that is one of the examples. As children, St. Paul tells us, we have the right to say "Abba," which means "Father," since we have received a spirit of adoption as sons. (Rom. 8, 16) What is the relationship of a child to its parents except that of love, intimate, tender and strong? If then we desire to study and to know our relationship to God, and the duties it entails, surely we ought to take this parallel given to us by the Scriptures themselves and analyze it. Our duties to God are similar to those of a son towards his father. They are the duties of love.

The other example brings home to us the fact that this love of God is of a kind even more intimate and tender than that of children for their parents. Jesus calls Himself the bridegroom. Now a bridegroom is a man who has a bride, and we know that Jesus in a human sense had no bride. Why then does He call Himself a bridegroom? Who is His bride? The Church, of course; and that means every soul within the Church. Mystical writers are fond of representing the soul very concretely as the bride of Christ. But this is not limited to those souls who have reached the heights of mystical prayer and union with Christ. Every Christian soul is a bride of Christ. And the relationship of a bride to the bridegroom is one of love. Again, therefore, if we wish to study the relationship of the soul to God, we should go to this parallel, this example given to us by Jesus. Our duties towards God are shadowed forth in the duties of a bride to her bridegroom; our love for God is illustrated concretely by the love of the bride for the bridegroom. Since God is a Spirit, the love of God is a difficult thing for us to grasp and to practice; men speak of loving God, but are often vague about how they can show their love for God. Jesus, in giving us these concrete illustrations, teaches us what is meant by the love of God and how we may express that love.

We can compare God and the world to James and John. As James and John are friends, thus also God and the world are, so to speak, friends. God made the world and the world is good; God Himself, after creating the world, looked upon it and saw that it is good. Why then should they become rivals? Why should we practice contempt for the world? That is the question which those who are scandalized at this doctrine invariably ask. And the reason is the same that we have seen operating to make James and John rivals. Love makes them rivals, the love which each has for Mary; and it is love which makes God and the world rivals, the love which each of these has for our soul and the efforts which each makes to court and win the affections of our soul.

God woos us; all through the Old Testament He frankly represents Himself as a Lover, spurned and scorned by an adulterous people. And it is this love that we have, this power of loving, that creates opposition between God and the world. Nothing evil in the world, then, creates it, but simply our love. If we love the world, God is jealous; and if we love God, the world is jealous. This is no exaggeration. When men love God, the world is Jealous. You have seen the world interfere whenever men or women wish to consecrate their lives to God in religion or in the priesthood. The world points out that this is foolish and needless, and even Catholics will try to persuade their relatives not to follow a religious vocation. If a man wishes to give his life to a business career, the world does not try to dissuade him because that is according to the world. But since the world is jealous of God, it will try to dissuade souls from giving themselves to Him. The same thing happens when laymen wish to show some special devotion to God by large alms, by long periods of prayer, or by any other special exercise of piety. The jealous world interferes at once and exclaims that all this is foolish, needless, wasteful, and that we should guard carefully against carrying religion too far! Or again, you have heard men say that certain churches are too big, or involve too great an expenditure of money. That is because such people hate to see money spent on God; you would never hear the same men object to the huge amounts of money that are spent on some vast temple of finance, a skyscraper in a large city. They do not object to the latter because the world distastes it, but they object to the former because the world is jealous of God.

The converse is also true: God is jealous of the world. This we have remarked in an earlier conference, but now we can view this truth in its proper context. If you are tempted to object to this characterization of God as jealous, you should reflect that it comes from His own inspired words: *"I am a jealous God,"* (Deut. 5, 9) He tells us in the Old Testament. And the demand of love that He makes upon us is a demand of a jealous Lover: *"Thou shall love the Lord thy God with thy whole heart with thy whole soul and with thy whole strength."* It is the demand of an exclusive, entire, and jealous love—the demand of a Lover. Of course when we say God is jealous, we do not mean that we can hurt God by refusing to love Him. Since God is perfect, we cannot really injure Him. Yet He is angry and indignant by our failure to give Him our love. Throughout the Scriptures, we have said, He represents Himself as a Lover; and His people when they give their love to the world He calls adulterers, just as Mary, once she is married to James, would be an adulteress if she gives her affections to John.

We are then, in a sense, married to God; every soul is His bride. Because of this, must we withdraw our love from the world. Yet this withdrawal implies no evil in the world. It implies and means only one thing--that we should love God with our whole hearts. Thus it is love, not any taint in the world, which demands our detachment from the world and contempt for creatures.

But perhaps you will say that although Mary, after marrying James, cannot love John still she need not treat the latter with contempt; why then, admitting that we should not love the world, should we practice contempt of the world?

These phrases, "contempt" and "hatred" for the world do not, again, mean that the creatures made by God are bad or hateful. They are used, and are of value, to show that these creatures, however good, are, in comparison to God, paltry worthless, as nothing. So also in ordinary conversation we speak of trivial and unimportant things as contemptible. You may think that we could better dispense with a usage that is likely to be misunderstood unless patiently explained. But is not human language always subject to limitation, and must we not always explain and define what we mean? Besides, this usage has been consecrated by the Scriptures, by the long tradition of spiritual writers, and by the Liturgy of the Church. If we do not understand it, then surely our thinking is at fault; we do not have the mind of God, but are so accustomed to the wrong thinking of the world that we do not even understand spiritual doctrine. Truly, as St. Paul said, the sensual man cannot understand the things of God!

The things of this world are good, and we can see them and appreciate their excellence. The things of the supernatural world are infinitely better, but, because we cannot see them, it is most difficult to appreciate their sublime beauty and attractiveness. If, however, realizing the goodness of earthly things, we nevertheless hold to a conviction that, in comparison with the things of God, they are little, contemptible, and as nothing, then will we be raised to at least some dim realization of the goodness and lovableness of God. Here is the reason why the Church has consecrated this usage, the reason also why we should faithfully retain it.

It may be added that, despite the objection, human lovers do observe a similar logic. They are so possessed by the beauty of the one they love that they have no eyes for others and treat these others as if they did not exist. Before Romeo met Juliet, and was in love with Rosalind, he was not interested in hearing of Juliet despite enthusiastic reports of her loveliness; but after falling in love with Juliet, he no longer had any regard for Rosalind and forgot about her entirely.

Let us now consider the relationship of these principles to the matter of motives. The guiding principle may be stated in the following axiom: *We get our motives from the object of our love.* This, we have said already, is what a motive is: the grip which the will, or the heart, takes on an object which it chooses as good. Or again, a motive is an act by which the will chooses some good as an end and disposes other actions towards the attainment of this end. As a consequence, whatever we love will determine the motives of our actions. We are told in the Scriptures, for example, that Jacob as a young man worked fourteen years for Laban in order to marry Rachel. He first worked seven years, and then Laban, the father of Rachel, deceitfully gave him Lia, instead of Rachel, in matrimony. Upon discovering this, Jacob worked for seven more years, tending sheep, in order to obtain the hand of Rachel. Now let us ask, what was Jacob's motive during this prolonged labor? It may seem a presumptuous question, since the realm of motives and intentions is not one that we can safely penetrate. Still, once we know the object of a person's love, we can also know his motives. There are four motives which Jacob might possibly have had. He might have worked those fourteen years out of love for Laban; he might have worked simply out of love for work; he might have worked out of love for the sheep; or finally, he might have worked out of love for Rachel. And no one will doubt why he did it—his motive was determined by his love for Rachel. He got his motive from the object of his love; and so do we.

Therefore, if we love God, we will get our motives from the love of God. If we love the world, on the other hand, we will get our motives from love of the world. Or, to put it differently, if we love God our motives will be supernatural, whereas if we love the world our motives will be natural. Since a Christian is bound by the first and greatest commandment to love God, then it follows that his motives ought to be supernatural.

To see this concretely, let us go back to our example. Mary is now married to James after a period of indecision when she was attracted to both James and John. But now her love has been declared and consecrated in marriage. No more can she give her affections to John. But let us suppose that Mary announces one fine day, that she is going to go out and spend the evening with John, or that John is going to come and spend the evening with her. How would James react to that? Would he immediately forbid it? Perhaps, but first he might ask a question. You all know what that question would be. If Mary would make such an announcement to him, there would rise spontaneously to his lips the sharp inquiry, "*Why*—why are you going to see John?" In other words, "*What is your motive* for seeing him or receiving him?" That is the question that love asks: Why? Now if Mary could give a satisfactory answer, James could not reasonably object. If Mary should say, "He owes us some money, and he is coming over to pay it," then there would be a sufficient motive, and James would not object, since he would profit by the visit as well as Mary, Or suppose Mary would say, "I have invited him over because he can give us information that will help you to get a better job," or "because he can help us to find a suitable home for ourselves." Certainly in these cases James would not object. But suppose, in response to his insistent "Why?" that she would say "Well, I have invited John over simply because I like him, I am fond of him, I love him in fact, and I wish to spend the evening with him!"—then surely James would object. Love is exclusive and will not tolerate any such sharing of itself. It is not John that James objects to, but Mary's affection for John; and he inquires into her motive to discover whether or not there is any affection present. He understands, as love always understands, without any analysis, that motives come from the object of one's love.

In the example, we can distinguish two kinds of motives. If Mary has a motive of genuine utility, or of necessity, for seeing John, then her husband will not interfere. But if her motive for seeing John is one of love, then James will strenuously protest and refuse his permission.

In our relationship to God, which is one of love, everything is the same. When we go to the world, which we now realize is God's rival, God is concerned with our motives. When we use creatures, God, Who loves us and desires our love, is interested in knowing whether or not our affections rest upon these creatures. Therefore, when we utilize the creatures of the world, He asks us the question prompted by love, "Why?" ("What is your motive?") So if one, let us say, is eating, God does not object to this. God has created us and knows our needs in this respect! What He does ask is the question love always asks: "Why? *Why* are you eating that piece of bread?" If we can answer that we have a motive of utility, that we are eating it to gain strength, then God does not object. Or, if we can say, "We are eating it to sustain ourselves in order that we may better serve you, O Lord," then God will object still less. He puts the creatures of the world here before us precisely that we may use them to serve Him and glorify Him. But if we use creatures of this world out of love for them, and when the question of love is put to us, we can only reply that we are using these creatures because of our affection for them, then assuredly God will object. His love is a jealous and exclusive love also, and He requires that we love Him with all our hearts. Accordingly, in our dealings with creatures, in relation to God, we can likewise distinguish two kinds of motives: motives of utility, and motives of love. In our living daily in the world, in our innumerable contacts with creatures, our rule should be to use them for utility. In this case, God will not object to our using creatures, and we will be able to live devout and holy lives even among the things of the world. The reverse of this rule, equally valid, is that we should never use the creatures of this world out of love or affection for them. Our affections belong to God, and God, like a jealous husband, will be displeased when we use creatures of the world out of love; for this is like a wife leaving her true husband for companionship with his rival.

Thus our motives are a matter of love. We must make them supernatural because of the commandment which ordains that we love God with our whole heart, with our whole soul, with our whole strength, and with our whole mind. Natural motives are an affront to God's love. The rule governing motives therefore is this: for creatures, motives of necessity or utility only; for God, all motives of love. And now, before leaving this consideration of love in relation to motives, we will point out two important practical corollaries which follow from it.

The first is this: Since we get our motives from the object of our love, then our motives, especially our habitual motives, will reveal the object of our love. Our motives are like an indicator or a gauge on a machine or boiler, showing the pressure of the boiler or the condition of the machine. A man driving an automobile keeps his eyes on the dial that points to the gasoline supply, as also on the various instruments that indicate the condition of the battery, the oil, and so forth. So should we also, as we proceed along the way of life, keep our eyes on our motives if we wish to know the spiritual condition of our soul. We may be very complacent in the belief that we love God. But the Scripture says that *"Not everyone who says to me, 'Lord, Lord,' shall enter the kingdom of heaven; but he who does the will of my Father in heaven shall enter the kingdom of heaven."* How can we know whether our love is from the lips only or much deeper, from the heart and soul? If our motives are habitually supernatural, then we can safely conclude that we do love, or desire to love, or are trying to love God. But if, in looking into our hearts, we discover that our motives often or usually proceed from an affection for the good things of the world, then it is clear that, whatever the profession of our lips, our practical and actual love is for the pleasures and comforts afforded by the creatures of the world.

The second corollary is this: The principle or rule, that we get our motives from the object of our love, enables us also to know what it is that we do love. Even saints fall occasionally into imperfections; but what spiritual masters and writers especially warn us against is the habitual affection or attachment for creatures. Occasional imperfections, which do not proceed from any habitual attachment, do not produce lasting harm in the soul. What causes such harm is the attachment, the habitual love for, and clinging to, creatures. Therefore it is useful to know how we may detect in our use of creatures whether or not we have an attachment for them. And we can state concerning this, on the basis of what has been said already, that when we use a creature habitually, without any necessity, or without a motive of utility, this is an indication that we have an attachment for it. Suppose that Mary tells James that she has invited John over for the evening, and to his inevitable, "Why?" responds by giving a motive of utility, as explained just a moment ago. John is going to bring over some furniture for their house, we will say. But suppose that the following evening she again tells James that John is coming over for the evening. Once more James asks the question of love, "Why?" Again, we will suppose, she is able to give a motive of utility: more furniture perhaps. But if this performance is repeated a third and a fourth and a fifth and more times, will not James suspect, and have reason to suspect, that there is something deeper than mere utility in these frequent meetings between John and his wife? He will suspect, and as it goes on he will know, that there is affection. Likewise, if we use the creatures of this world frequently without any reason or utility, it reveals to God, and may well reveal to ourselves, an attachment for that creature. I say to God, I am going to eat this chocolate, I am going to use this creature. In the secrecy of my soul God asks, "Why?" I answer, "Not out of affection, but out of utility." Then I say again to God, "I am going to eat this other chocolate." Again God asks "Why?" and once more I assure Him, "Out of utility." But suppose I continue this, eating chocolate after chocolate, taking indulgence after indulgence, without any real utility, then God will certainly know that I am using and enjoying this creature, not because of a genuine utility, but rather because I have an attachment, an affection, for that creature. We may therefore set down as a rule for detecting an attachment for a creature: the repeated use of that creature without utility or necessity betrays attachment.

What we have learned in this conference may now be summarized in a number of slogans or mottoes, which are also rules of action. We get our motives from what we love. Therefore, we must, to express in practice our love of God, act from supernatural motives. Our use of creatures should be regulated by motives of necessity or utility but should never proceed from motives of love. Motives of love should be reserved for God. Finally, an attachment for creatures is revealed by a habitual use of that creature without real need or utility.

Let us think upon these things. And may God bless you.

"O God, since Thou hast prepared for those who love Thee such good things as human eye hath never seen, pour into our hearts such an experience of Thy love that we may obtain these Thy promises which surpass all desire by loving Thee in all things and above all things. Through Our Lord Jesus Christ Thy Son Who liveth and reigneth with Thee in union with the Holy Spirit, God world without end. Amen."

(Collect, Fifth Sunday after Pentecost)

THE CONFLICT BETWEEN NATURE AND THE SUPERNATURAL: WHY NATURAL MOTIVES MUST BE MORTIFIED

My dear friends in Christ--

A certain religious is said to have told St. Bernard that he was content to remain permanently in the spiritual condition in which he was at that time. "I do not consent to be worse," said the religious; "and I do not desire to be better."

"You ask what is impossible," replied the saint; "if you do not wish to proceed, you must fail."

This anecdote, with the important spiritual lesson it contains, will serve to introduce us to a new aspect of our subject, that is, it will help us to realize the effect of our failure to remove the conflict of which we have spoken, the effect, that is, of our neglect to mortify natural affections and motives in order to live wholly on the supernatural plane.

But first, a brief resume is in order at this point. After studying the harmony between nature and grace we took up the conflict which, as a result of spiritual sluggishness and tepidity, may exist between our natural activity—or the free disposition of our natural activity—and our supernatural calling. So far we have devoted two conferences to considering this conflict, first locating its center, then going on to state the reasons for it. These reasons show us, in a positive way, why we should abandon merely natural affections and motives in order to live as divine beings. It remains to study what may be called the negative or shadowed side of the picture, that is to say, to inquire why we must give up natural motives, why these motives are displeasing to God, what will happen if we fail to abandon them. This negative side is of great practical importance also for it reveals the cause of spiritual deterioration and shows us the process at work. Not to go forward is to go backward, not to progress is to retrogress: this principle, given to us in the saying of St. Bernard, who does but speak for the whole of Christian tradition, summarizes what may be called the law of spiritual deterioration. The truths we now possess give us a key to the understanding of this law and thus gain valuable insights for our warfare against sin.

In the present conference we shall set down three reasons why God hates natural motives, three reasons, therefore, why we should mortify such motives.

First: God Has Revealed This

The first reason is simply that God has told us that natural motives must be removed. If we do not mortify them, He will do so by the afflictions He sends us. He has Himself said that by His own Providential action on the soul He will purify it of affection for creatures, hence of natural motives. The Scriptures are full of statements which disclose this purpose, this divine determination of emptying our hearts of natural affections. Let us consider just one. *"Over this you rejoice; though now for a little while, if need be, you are made sorrowful by various trials, that the temper of your faith more precious by far than gold which is tried by fire — may be found unto praise and glory and honor at the revelation of Jesus Christ."* (I Peter, 1, 7)

In this passage the inspired word not only indicates the fact of which we are speaking, but also gives a fine illustration to assist our understanding of it. Gold is treated with fire in order to remove its blemishes and make it pure. God intends to purify us likewise and He does so by means of the chastening fire of afflictions, which He Himself sends or at least permits to come upon us. The Divine intent, therefore, behind all such sufferings is that we be purified, and by purification is meant the removal of affections for creatures. What causes us to suffer is our being separated from some creature or pleasure or satisfaction that we love. It is because we cling to something with our hearts that its loss causes us pain. Thus, by means of trials, God breaks the attachments that we have for the goods of this world. Through separations effected by Providential trials—separations even from creatures that are good and praiseworthy—God is preparing us day by day for His heavenly kingdom, purging our hearts from the dross of earthly attachments. Such purification is correlative with sanctification, is inseparable from sanctification, is the under side or shadowed side of sanctification. That is why detachment and mortification are so necessary for holiness. And it is also why suffering is so useful in the hands of Providence.

The need and the reason for our purification by the fire of suffering follows, of course, from our supernatural elevation. Because we have been raised to the Divine plane, God desires that we should enlist all our energies and all our affections in the pursuit of the Divine Good Himself; hence His determination to purge us of our tendency to hold by our affections to created goods. Thus God aids our efforts and compensates for our failure to remove the conflict that exists between our divine vocation and our natural activity when the latter is not properly oriented to our supernatural end.

Second: Natural Motives Affront God

The second reason why God hates natural motives is that they are an insult to Him. This is evident from an axiom already given and explained, namely, that we get our motives from the object of our love. As supernatural motives reveal a love for God, so natural motives indicate an attachment for the creatures of the world, and the world is God's rival for our affections. We are wedded to God by love, and surely it is an insult to Him when we constantly act out of love, not of Him, but of His rival, the world. Suppose that Mary unexpectedly gives James a gift. James is puzzled and says to her, "Well Mary, I surely appreciate this, but I do not understand the reason for it. Today is not Christmas, it is not our anniversary, it is not my birthday." "No," replies Mary, "but it's John's birthday, and I wish to give you this out of affection for John!" How would James receive this gift? What would he do with it? Assuredly he would not keep it or cherish it. Can we then expect God to look with pleasure upon our actions, even when these are not morally evil, if they are animated by love for creatures?

Here is another example. Suppose that James gives Mary a bouquet on her anniversary, and she, on examining the bouquet, discovers that underneath some bright paper camouflage of flowers, she has really received a large bunch of weeds; she would not be pleased or honored, but rather insulted. Let us suppose, further, that she asks James the reason for this, and tells him that she doesn't like the weeds that he has brought her. And James, we will imagine, replies, "Yes, I know that *you* don't like them, but *I* do!" That is what we do when we offer to God actions performed out of attachment for sense pleasure, and therefore pleasing to us, but not manifesting any love for Him. Our actions, outwardly good, or at least not sinful, are very often really weeds because of their worldly motivation, and yet we presumptuously offer them to God thinking that we are honoring Him.

Third: Natural Motives Lead to Sin

The third and final reason why we must mortify natural motives is because these motives lead to sin. Now observe what we are saying. We are *not* saying that natural motives are sinful. What we wish to state is that natural motives which are good or apparently good nevertheless lead to sin. Natural motives we know are such as come from a love of creatures; and it is the love of creatures that leads to sin. Therefore, even apparently innocent natural motives are already imperfections that predispose the soul towards evil and set in motion the forces that carry it ultimately even into mortal sin. The reason for this is that in our present supernatural state, in which all our love should be directed to God, affections for creatures have a tendency to distract us from God, cause us to neglect God's service, lead us away from God, and finally carry us into sin.

Did you ever reflect that the love for some creature is behind every sin? Avarice is caused by the love of money, gluttony by the love of food, intemperance by the love of drink, impurity by the love of sensual pleasure, anger by the love of our own wills. And so in every case; it is the love of some creature that causes us to sin.

Now this is by no means the same as saying that the love of creatures is sinful. We have been insisting right along that the love of creatures is morally good or blameless; and we insist on it still. What we add here is that the love of creatures, although in itself without blame, tends in the long run, unless it is restrained and mortified, to lead us into sin. To understand this, simply bear in mind, on the one hand, our elevation to the pursuit of supernatural good and, on the other, the weakness and waywardness of our fallen nature. And if it seems a contradiction to say that something that is not sinful yet leads to sin, remember that on the physical level eating, which is not only good but necessary to nature, also becomes, when indulged in indiscreetly or to excess, a cause of disease and therefore harmful to nature.

If a man fasts for one hundred days and falls over dead on the hundredth day, his death is no more to be attributed to his last day's fast than his first day's. With each day he has been growing weaker, his strength has been ebbing from him, and yet he has remained alive until this final collapse. So it is with mortal sin, the final collapse of the soul; it comes directly from one final natural motive by which a forbidden pleasure is chosen, and yet it cannot be said to be wholly due to this last sinful motive apart from the countless harmless natural motives that preceded it. These preceding natural motives were mere acts of self-indulgence; and since such acts are not sinful, certainly not gravely sinful, the soul remained in the state of grace during the time that they were being committed and thus seemed strong and healthy. Nevertheless, this constant self-indulgence was undermining its strength, and when its weakness had become very great, then it was no longer able to resist the allure of a sinful "good," i.e., of an apparent good. Those who do not deny themselves in legitimate pleasures will in the end be unable to deny themselves sinful pleasures.

To gain a fuller knowledge of this, let us consider the nature of sin. We will introduce here a definition of sin as old as Catholic theology, derived ultimately from the Scriptures, and clearly formulated by St. Augustine and St. Thomas, but far too little known. We take it instead of the usual Catechism definition of sin, because this definition better than others, gives us an insight into the nature of sin, especially into its origin and cause.

Sin, according to this definition, is "a turning away from God and a turning towards creatures." The cause of sin, it is apparent from this, is the love of creatures; the attractiveness of creatures woos and wins us from the love of God. This does not mean, we affirm once again, that creatures are evil or that the love of creatures is evil. We simply state that the love of creatures, although not in itself sinful, *leads* to sin.

Why is this so? Why does affection or attachment for creatures carry us into sin? Because in practice the love of creatures turns us away from God. It is not the love of creatures that is hateful to God, not therefore the turning towards creatures that is sinful; if we could turn towards creatures without turning from God, there would be no harm at all in our affections for creatures and they would not lead to sin. This is important to notice because there is a sense in which the saints love creatures—witness particularly St. Francis of Assisi—and this fact might otherwise be cited against the teaching that we should mortify the love of creatures. The saints love creatures without turning from God.

If Mary, who is married to James, should walk down the street, let us say to buy some groceries, James could not reasonably object. He would not object even if John, his former rival for Mary's affections, were the grocer—that is, provided Mary is interested in the groceries and not in John. But if she walks down the street or goes to the store out of love for John, then even her walks and her shopping trips will become a matter of jealously to James. These otherwise harmless actions become of significance to James only because of Mary's affections for John.

In a similar way, since creatures are good, the use and the love of creatures is also good. The love of these creatures becomes an issue, becomes objectionable to God, only when this love turns our affections away from Him to His rival, the world; just as Mary's walk for groceries becomes objectionable to James when it means a withdrawal of affection from him. Now the saints love creatures while being wholly detached from them. Their detachment is their guarantee against their being drawn away from God by the creatures. Nor does detachment interfere with their love for the creatures because this love is supernatural.

That is to say, the saints love creatures because these manifest the goodness of God. Their love for creatures is but an expression of their love for God; just as your fondness for your father's photograph is an expression of your love for your father and not of your love for the photographic paper. But imperfect and worldly men, less wise than the saints, are more attracted to the photographic paper, that is, to the creatures which bear God's image, than to their heavenly Father Himself. In the case of the saints, therefore, the love of creatures does not in the least withdraw their love from God but rather exercises this love. But in the case of those who are not detached, their affections for creatures, which cause them to use creatures selfishly and sensually, do withdraw their affections from God. This is why God objects to our loving creatures in the way that most men love them and in the way this expression is generally understood. It is also why the love of creatures, which are good, will nevertheless lead into sin unless it is mortified.

What happens then, when we sin, is that we are allured and attracted by the pleasure which creatures offer us, and in giving our affections to these creatures we withdraw it from God, Whom we ought to love with our whole heart. The malice of sin, therefore, consists in the turning from God, not in the turning towards creatures; yet the turning towards creatures is the cause or the principle of sin. It is what St. Thomas calls the material cause of sin—the thing which turns us from God, the material object and good which, tempting us with an immediate satisfaction, causes us to forget God and give our affection to something other than Him.

Furthermore, we do not have to commit sin to be guilty of an infidelity to divine love. After James is married to Mary, a flirtatious word spoken to other young women, a flirtatious glance now and then, does not constitute the sin of adultery. Yet such flirting is without doubt an infidelity to the entire love which he owes, and which he has vowed, to his spouse. It is a minor fault, you will say. Yet it may start him on a career of philandering, and, in any event, it will probably not be pleasing to Mary even in its beginnings, and James will be embarrassed if Mary discovers his habit of flirting. Similarly, every attachment, every natural affection for creatures, and every motive that comes from such attachments, is an infidelity to God. A minor matter, perhaps, a mere imperfection; but it is contrary to the entire love which we owe to God and which, as Christians, we have vowed to Him. Furthermore, and this is the point that concerns us now, these small infidelities are not without effect on our subsequent conduct and character; they in fact set in motion the cause of sin.

The Three Kinds of Disorder

Let us imagine God as being directly before us; then if we turn away just a little bit from Him, attracted by some creature pleasure, that is what is meant by imperfection; if we turn a little farther away from Him, by abusing creatures, though not seriously, in disregard of His laws, this is venial sin; finally, if we turn away from Him entirely, turn our backs upon Him, as it were, we commit mortal sin. These three kinds of moral disorder, although vastly different from one another, nevertheless have a common cause and roots, namely, the love of the creatures of this world. Because they are vastly different -- specifically different, as theologians say--imperfections never grow into venial sins, nor venial sins into mortal, any more than a mouse, by puffing itself up, would ever become a man. But because all have a common cause in the love of creatures, imperfections dispose the soul towards venial sins, and venial sins in turn dispose it towards mortal sins. Thus natural attachments set in motion the forces of spiritual deterioration; so that it may truly be said that such attachments and natural motives, although mere imperfections, lead finally into mortal sin. For mortal sin consists essentially in this, that we turn completely away from God and choose a creature as our supreme good and final end.

When we commit imperfections and venial sins we do not turn fully away from God, yet we do allow the attractions of creatures to take us away from fulfilling God's will perfectly. When we commit venial sin we are like a man who, sick and placed on a strict diet by his doctor, sometimes disregards that diet because of his fondness for some delicacy. Yet, although he thus disregards the diet, he does not give up his desire for good health; these small infractions will perhaps injure him but they will not wholly ruin him physically; at least he does not indulge himself with any idea of abandoning the hope of regaining health. So also, when we commit venial sin, we are indulging ourselves in some pleasure apart from the will of God, but we do not really intend to abandon God, we do not turn wholly away from Him. We nevertheless displease Him, and the cause of our doing so is the fact that we are too weak to resist the momentary gratification afforded by a creature pleasure.

The Law of Sin

Now we can easily see why it is that the love of creatures leads to sin, and why the habit of performing actions out of natural motives will multiply and accumulate sin-germs, so to speak, in our souls. If we act habitually out of natural motives, we will not be able in the long run to prevent ourselves from falling into sin. We are constantly increasing that movement of our hearts towards creatures which is the cause of sin; and the longer we act from natural motives, the more momentum we gather, as it were, carrying us towards the things of this world and away from God. Suppose that a man were to stand on top of a skyscraper, and looking down, would say to himself, "What a wonderful thrill it would be to jump from here and go down through the air—what an exhilarating feeling one would enjoy!" But then it would not be so much pleasure to fall on the sidewalk. "But here is what I will do," he says, "I will jump and enjoy the thrill, and then, before reaching the sidewalk, I will stop." Suppose he tries this. He jumps; and, as he goes down through the air, enjoying the exhilaration that he had desired, he is also gathering more and more momentum. As he comes close to the sidewalk, just a few stories above it, he says to himself, "Now it is time to stop!" But what will then stop him? The force that is carrying him downward will also dash him against the pavement. He made his mistake when he jumped; and it will be very hard for him to correct it now.

It is the same with a person having a worldly outlook and acting from natural motives. He says, in effect, "I wish to enjoy the thrill of satisfying myself with the creatures of this world.

But then I do not wish to commit sin, I do not wish to carry my pleasure to the length of doing grave evil." Suppose he carries out that policy. He begins to enjoy the things of this world, more and more each day, making it his habitual practice. He has his own philosophy which tells him that the things of this world are good and are put here by God to be enjoyed; and so he enjoys them, but without desiring to commit sin. But when the temptation to enjoy some forbidden pleasure comes, what is to prevent him from committing sin? He has given up the one principle, the principle of self-denial, which might have prevented him from falling. Now he has nothing to stop him; he is helpless. This is why men commit sin, as it were unsuspectingly, not realizing that they have come to such a length. Their sin surprises them, they did not intend it; but they are carried into it by the force of undisciplined desire and passion.

From these principles it will be clear that they are doing too little and acting too late who confine their practical efforts against sin to an avoidance of what the Catechism calls the near occasions of sin. This would be like cutting out the main roots of weeds while leaving the rootlets in the ground to grow again in time. Or like running full-speed towards the brink of a cliff and waiting until reaching the very edge before deciding to turn away. Or finally, to return to the analogy of married love, always the most direct and useful, it would be as though James would freely allow himself minor flirtations, as not being very dangerous, drawing the line only to exclude the most beautiful and seductive rivals of his wife. Apart from the fact, already noticed, that even the minor ones are infidelities of love, there is always the possibility, human nature being what it is, that the minor flirtations may become major.

This is not to make light of the rule that we should avoid the proximate occasions of sin; it is rather to show, lest we expect too much, that this rule like all others has its definite field of application and therefore its limits. For those who are accustomed to restraint and mortification, striving to remove those rootlets of sin, namely, the affections for earthly things and natural motives, this rule will be useful to apprise them of danger—a danger which long practice enables them to avoid. It will be like a danger sign near a powder magazine, warning passers-by that they are approaching a dangerous locality. But as to those whose hearts are filled with worldliness, the rule will not be sufficient as long as this condition remains. It may help a little to keep a habitual drunkard away from taverns; but it will not cure him; until he is able to mortify the desire for this pleasure of sense he will live in perpetual danger of taking hold of the occasion and the sin in one embrace. For him the rule "avoid the near occasion of sin" is of little help for the same reason that a danger sign placed only at the very edge of an abyss, would be of little help to one running full-tilt towards it.

We have reached a very important conclusion. Sins have roots, have a cause. That may seem a very trite thing to say, and yet, as a matter of fact, we habitually try to overcome sin as though this were to be accomplished by a mere mechanical resolution on our part. We seem to imagine that we can overcome sin when we please as long as we have good will and the desire to do so. We fail to take into account those strong moral forces which have gathered in our soul, forces which are directed, or misdirected, by lifelong habits. It is hard to stop these, hard to undo them in a moment; and as long as they are permitted to grow and gather strength, it will be constantly more difficult to counteract them. The struggle against sin becomes so difficult that we are apt to be discouraged, or at any rate to fall frequently; and to expose oneself to the danger of falling frequently is likewise to expose one's self to the danger of falling finally.

Let us imagine sins as weeds growing in the garden of the soul. Weeds have roots, and the way to get rid of the weeds is to dig out the roots. Suppose a gardener, heedless of such common sense, tries to remove weeds from his garden or lawn simply by cutting them off or by running a mower over them. The weeds vanish; but after some rain and sunshine, they will of course soon reappear; and as long as the gardener does not remove the roots, they will come up over and over again. If he is wise, and really wishes to get rid of the weeds, as well as save himself some labor, he will in the first place get a trowel and dig out the weeds by the roots and throw them away. Then the weeds will not come back—at least those same weeds will not come back.

When we sin, the cause of that sin is a love of creatures manifested concretely in natural motives, since we get our motives from what we love. And when we go to confession, we may be very sorry for the sin indeed; but if we do not clear our heart of the love of creatures, the sin will recur. When we receive the sacrament of penance, confessing our sins without going to the labor of removing their cause, we are like the man who removes the weeds by means of the mower. That is why, after we come from confession, and perhaps very soon after, we fall into the same sins again. We do not understand these repeated falls and are saddened by them; for we are sincere in our intention to overcome sin. Sometimes we are discouraged, hardly able to put aside the terrible thought that the temptations are too great for our strength. But of course this is not so at all; we have simply not taken the common-sense procedure of looking for and removing the cause of sin. We thought that we could eliminate sin from our lives mechanically, by a mere resolution. But this cannot be done.

Now it can be seen why the definition of sin as a turning from God and a turning towards creatures is of such decisive importance. It is a truth to be taken and memorized and studied and meditated upon. It opens up to us the pathology of sin—that is, the causes of sin and of its growth—and therefore it gives us a hope, a well-founded hope, of overcoming evil in our lives. But without a realistic procedure, based on such knowledge, our efforts to overcome evil, however well-intended, are likely to be futile.

Let us conclude these observations by quoting the Apostle St. James who vindicates this teaching. He says (4,4) *"Adulterers, do you not know that the friendship of this world is enmity with God? Therefore, whoever wishes to be a friend of this world becomes an enemy of God."* Do not imagine that this is not spoken to all worldlings because here St. James address adulterers. In the Sacred Scriptures the word adulterer is often used in a spiritual sense as referring to those who, instead of giving their love to God, to Whom it belongs, give it to the world. This is the sense in which it is used here: Adulterers are those who love the world. And these, St. James says, are enemies of God and their friendship with the world is enmity with God.

He speaks here broadly, without any distinction of the various kinds of disorder—imperfections, venial sin, and mortal sin—and his words leave us in no doubt of the opposition between the love of this world and the love of God.

It should be obvious by this time how foolish and futile is the advice sometimes given by worldly persons who say that we may enjoy the things of the world, exhorting us only to avoid mortal sin. If we enjoy the things of the world without restraint, it will be morally impossible to avoid mortal sin. The enjoyment of the things of the world is precisely that which leads to mortal sin. Therefore, seeking pleasure in the things of the world while attempting at the same time to avoid sin is like trying to swim without getting wet or to play in the mud without getting dirty. If you are enjoying the things of the world, you will find it difficult indeed to stop short of sin. This counsel, to enjoy the things of the world while avoiding mortal sin, may sound very pious and prudent and moderate; actually it is exhorting us to an impossibility, and those who attempt to follow it will do so at their own terrible cost. That many persons fall into mortal sin, are surprised by their fall, is due to the fact that they are living worldly lives, are attached to the things of this world, and therefore reap the harvest of such attachments. He who thus sows the wind will assuredly reap the whirlwind.

Let us think upon these things. And may God bless you.

> *"Thy gifts, O God, free us from the fascination of earthly things and ever give us new strength by their heavenly nourishment. Through Our Lord Jesus Christ Thy Son Who liveth and reigneth with Thee in union with the Holy Spirit, God, world without end. Amen."*
> (Postcommunion, Fourth Sunday after Pentecost)

THE TWO MENTALITIES

My dear Friends in Christ--

Most novels and stories reach their climax in marriage. The lovers, after many vicissitudes, are happily united; and the reader is left to hope that they will live happily ever after. Unfortunately, real life does not always fulfill the promise of the stories. The lovers do not always live up to their vows; even when they are not guilty of gross infidelity, their romance often wears off, the honeymoon stage passes, their affection for each other sometimes cools and they come to live selfishly, each devoted to himself.

Something like this frequently happens also in the relation of the soul to the Divine Spouse to whom it is wedded by grace. Indeed, the cooling of marital love that too often takes place serves as good illustration of the daily spiritual lives of large numbers of Christians, of our large promises and feeble practice, of our ardent profession of love for God and our actual devotion to ourselves. The parallel likewise provides a concrete answer to a question or objection that has perhaps been forming in your minds in reference to the doctrine of the preceding conferences.

We have been insisting on the central importance of supernatural motivation in our daily lives. Now from the time of your childhood most of you have been taught to make a Morning Offering every day, by means of which you each morning consecrate, with an appropriate formula, all the deeds that you are to perform during the day. At this point you ask, therefore, "Do we not sufficiently supernaturalize our actions by reciting the Morning Offering? After all"—you continue—"what has been said in these conferences reduces itself to this, that we should make a morning offering each day, and that this will be enough to make all the actions of the day supernatural."

Certainly the custom of making a frequent or daily offering of our actions to God is most commendable. So is it commendable and holy when a couple sincerely pronounce marriage vows. Yet the vows do not end their problem but rather begin it. Or, if it ends one set of problems, it begins another and a more difficult series. They must now live up to their vows; and the circumstances of daily life, together with their own weaknesses, make this at times difficult; they are at any rate liable to fall from the high devotion which they have vowed to one another in the enthusiasm of their love. The practical realization of this love will now require of them persevering effort, daily self-conquest.

The making of a daily or frequent offering of our good deeds to God may be likened to the making of marriage vows. And while we praise the custom, we must realize that no mere formula of words, no mere verbal protestation, can dispense us from the effort and from the sacrifice involved in doing all for God and not merely to please ourselves. Really to do all to please God means that we will do nothing merely to please ourselves. This is a large and very generous sacrifice of pleasure and comfort. If we are unprepared for such daily recurrent self-denial, yet go on protesting to God that we do all for Him, then surely we are acting hypocritically rather than virtuously.

To put matters a little differently: No mere formula of words is sufficient to redirect all the passions and desires of life if they are moving in a direction contrary to that expressed in the prayer. If a man is living a natural or worldly life, it will take more than the pronunciation of some words to consecrate all his actions to God. That consecration must come from the will, from a new disposition by which his actions, instead of being dedicated to the accomplishment of worldly ends, are in truth directed towards God. You would not dream of attempting to dam a torrent by holding a lady's silk handkerchief before it. And you cannot stop or control the torrent of human passions by means of a few words. The morning offering is useful and efficacious *if* we are truly living Christian and supernatural lives. It will not be very helpful if we are living natural lives. Another kind, a deeper kind of effort—what may be called deep-therapy—will be required to effect a change in this case.

Suppose that James calls on Mary, armed with a box of candy. After taking off his hat and coat he sits down, opens the box, and explains that he has brought it for her on her birthday.

Then he takes a piece of candy and eats it himself, without offering any to Mary. After this he eats another piece and another, and still another. In fact he eats it all himself. Perhaps Mary—to remind him of her presence—asks him, "Why did you say you brought that candy, James?" And he answers, as he swallows piece after piece, "I brought it in honor of your birthday."

Yes, the example is ridiculous; but it is a true description of what many of us are doing daily in relation to God. We make a morning offering, consecrating all our actions to God, and then as soon as we get up from our knees we begin to perform our actions, not for God at all, but for our own selfish, worldly motives. We go through the day under the delusion that these actions are for God because they are not sinful and because we have made a verbal consecration in the morning. But if we would stop to analyze our motives, we would see that we are actually performing them in most cases for our own pleasure, or at any rate that a great deal of selfishness is mixed up in them. In this case making the morning offering is simply a means by which we deceive ourselves, adorning worldly lives with an external devotion. Such a practice will not make our lives supernatural. To accomplish this object, we must detach ourselves from creatures and pleasures, out of love for which we usually perform our actions; then we will be in a condition to perform our actions truly for God. Thus, inward detachment and the purification of the will from self-indulgence are necessary elements in the practice of supernaturalizing actions by means of a morning offering. Indeed, these alone can make this practice really fruitful.

Another example. Suppose a man goes to work in the morning, and, bidding good-bye to his wife, says that he is going to perform every action of his day out of love for her. That is his morning dedication, his morning offering, so to speak. Then he starts down the street, and he is not very far away from home when one of his cronies invites him into a tavern for a few drinks. Instead of going on to work, to take care of the interests of his wife and family, he goes in and wastes some time and money at the tavern. Is he doing this for the love of his wife as he promised? Next he goes to the office, and let us suppose that he flirts a little with some of the girls that work there. Nothing serious in this, just a few pleasantries—but could he truthfully say that he is acting out of love for his wife? Then in the afternoon, we will further suppose, he steals off to a show or to a ball game instead of taking care of his duties. Once again, can he say honestly that he is doing this out of love for his wife? Has he not really performed all these actions out of mere self-love, or out of love for these enjoyments? Now he goes home in the evening, and, greeting his wife, tells her again how great his love is for her and says that all during the day he has been thinking of her and everything that he has done he has done out of love for her. Surely he is a hypocrite. It is the same kind of hypocrisy that we practice when, pledging all our love to God in the morning and offering Him all our deeds, we then set out to perform them from clearly selfish motives, that is, for the enjoyment they bring. Our lives today are organized deliberately with a view to securing the greatest possible self-satisfaction and indulgence. From morning until night we pamper ourselves, not thinking of God at all, but constantly concerned with our own gratification, not acting out of love for God but rather out of love for the creatures which are offered to us on every side for our pleasure and comfort. And after a long day, dedicated to such self-enjoyment, we have the effrontery to kneel before God at night and say, "Well God, all that I have done today I have done simply out of love for you." Thus, you see, the use of the morning offering can be a very important part of a Christian life, but it is not the whole of the Christian life, nor a substitute for the Christian life. If we are striving to be purified and detached, then this practice will help to make and keep our motives truly supernatural, but not otherwise.

The Two Mentalities

It is thus apparent that the value of our offerings and the merit of our daily actions depends very largely on our habitual outlook and practice, or on what may be called our mentality. Two such mentalities may be distinguished: the mentality of those who, guided by worldly wisdom, love the things of the world. The other is the unworldly mentality of those who truly love God and strive to use creatures in His service rather than for their own pleasure. And it must be said that if the worldly-minded wish to consecrate their works to God, they cannot do so unless they become unworldly and mortified. Otherwise their works will have little merit in the sight of God. Just so a careless husband, if he wishes to be reconciled with his wife and to love her with entire fidelity, must give up all the flirtations in which he has been indulging.

Suppose that James, who is something of a flirt, is married to Mary. When Mary sees him talking to other women, knowing his character, she will be suspicious and jealous. Sometimes her suspicions will be fully justified; at other times, no doubt, James will speak to these other women out of necessity or for some legitimate end. Nevertheless, even when he has a just reason, James will be suspected by his wife because of his known character; and these suspicions will probably be correct on most occasions, too, for James, because of his weakness, will not be able to restrain himself from mixing a little pleasure with business even when he has a good reason for talking to others besides his wife.

So it is with God and an imperfect soul who is attached to the creatures of the world. Such a soul has a customary way of acting; he uses creatures, not out of love for God, but out of love for them or for the selfish pleasure they afford him. Sometimes his use of creatures is necessary, as in eating, but even then his weakness will be such that he will act here too out of love for pleasure. Thus all his actions will be more or less imperfect. Imperfection, in other words, will be habitual, and as long as he continues in this course, he can scarcely say that he is doing all that he does out of love for God, no matter how many prayers he offers. God, on His part, will be displeased with such a soul, who is constantly flirting, as it were, with His rival, the world.

Suppose on the other hand, that James is an absolutely faithful husband. Then, when Mary sees him talking to others, she is untroubled, being secure in the possession of his love. Thus, also, when a Christian who truly loves God uses the creatures of this world, he will use them only for God, or for utility, with the final intention of pleasing God, for that is his habitual desire and tendency. Moreover, even if in a given case

143

this truly Christian soul forgets to refer his action explicitly to God, still it would be supernaturalized through his habitual disposition and intention. Since he does not act out of any love for creatures, and prunes back by mortification every tendency in this direction, his ordinary supernatural motive persists to sanctify all his actions. Thus, in imperfect souls all actions are more or less imperfect; on the contrary, in devout souls, all actions are meritorious.

This example clearly illustrates the utility of the morning offering. If we have the mind of Christ, if we are detached from creatures and truly love God, then an offering made to God each morning will, like the careful aim of a skilled marksman, direct all our actions towards God.

To sum up. The quality and the purity of our motives, hence the supernatural vitality of our actions, is determined by our mentality, that is, by our habitual spiritual outlook and practice. There are two such mentalities. First there is the natural, or pagan, mentality, which tends to make the love of creatures the motive force of our actions, thus depriving them more or less of supernatural life and merit. Then there is the supernatural, or Christian, mentality which, by purging the will of affection for creatures, makes it possible for charity, becoming active through supernatural motives, to be the living influence of all that we do.

The Question of Intentions

At this point another difficulty may suggest itself to some minds. These will perhaps remind me that there is controversy among theologians as to what kind of intention is required to make actions supernaturally meritorious. Some theologians say that an habitual intention is sufficient; and one already has what is here called an habitual intention if he is in the state of grace, to which infused or habitual charity is inseparably attached, and fulfills all the ordinary duties of Christian life. A habitual intention is thus one that is formed and never retracted although perhaps little is done to carry it out; as when a student, by the mere fact that he goes to school, devotes himself to study although through laziness or negligence he fails to get down to actual study. Thus if a habitual supernatural intention is sufficient for obtaining increases of grace and merit, it would not be necessary for us to undergo the labor of supernaturalizing and purifying our intentions; the mere fact that we go to Mass on Sundays and fulfill the other basic duties of Christian life would imply the intentions of seeking a supernatural end and would therefore direct in a general way all our actions that are not sinful to a supernatural end.

However, this teaching is only what theologians call a probable opinion. That is to say, it is not wholly without foundation; there are certain considerations that give it some probability; but it is not a definite, certain, unassailable truth. Moreover, it is not the teaching of the Church; it is not defined as Catholic doctrine. It is not even the general opinion of theologians; on the contrary, it is opposed by many of these, including St. Alphonsus Liguori, prince of moral theologians, who require a definite supernatural intention formed frequently enough to persist as a real influence over our daily actions.

Now while it is sometimes permissible to base our conduct on a probable opinion, it is not safe nor permissible to do so when there is question of something necessary for salvation. Assuredly then, the opinion which admits the habitual intention as sufficient for merit is not safe since we are here dealing with the very actions by which we hope to merit salvation. Too much is at stake; it would be too risky to place the whole weight of one's hope for salvation on a teaching that may finally prove untrue and inadequate. It would be like deliberately and defiantly getting into a leaky boat to make a long and hazardous trip. It might be necessary to use such a boat if no other is available and one is in great danger; but one would surely be foolish to choose it as a matter of principle or policy. Similarly, if it may be hoped, on the basis of the opinion we are here considering, that many of our actions may be salvaged from worthlessness; still we would be foolhardy indeed to gamble all our hopes for holiness and final happiness on its possible truth. Consequently, even those theologians who advance this opinion warn us that in practice we ought to form supernatural motives and renew them frequently. For example, Father Joseph Noldin, who strenuously defends the minimum opinion, speaks as follows at the conclusion of his treatment of the subject:

"Since this opinion, which we say is preferable, is not certain, the just man should frequently form supernatural intentions, especially the motive of love: for where we are dealing with the conditions required for merit, the probability of an opinion is of no help, but only the truth. Indeed, even if the truth of this opinion is not to be doubted, the faithful should be taught, by apt motives, to work for the *most perfect intention,* especially the intention of charity *frequently renewed.* For the more perfect an intention is, and the more frequently renewed, especially a supernatural intention, the more does it help; and sometimes, indeed, it is necessary, for strengthening the will against temptations and for constantly fulfilling the more difficult laws of Christianity."

In brief, when we enter the sphere of practice, the controversy disappears. This controversy belongs to the area of speculative or theoretical theology. In practice all theologians agree that Catholics should strive to make their actions supernatural by a frequent repetition of a supernatural intention.

Of course, even the opposite teaching which requires a supernatural intention as a necessary condition for merit is only probably true. But its probability is on the safe side. There need be no fear in adopting it. That is why all agree on it as the basis for practice. To take it as the norm of practice is like taking a cruiser for a trip that might be attempted in a skiff, although only at great hazard.

One point more in connection with the question of natural motives. For the sake of argument, let us suppose that the opinion which holds that good natural motives are sufficient, is true, safe and practical; it is a large supposition: and even then we would have to say that natural motives are still not adequate for realizing the fullness of Christian life, hence would not be cultivated by those aspiring to Christian perfection. If the habitual supernatural intention possessed by everyone in the state of grace exerts any influence at all upon actions actually performed from natural motives, this influence would be but small; the impulse of grace, which alone can make actions supernaturally meritorious, would be so faint in this case that one aspiring to a full Christian life would never rest satisfied with such motives. The reason is that whatever the general tendency of grace in the soul, the immediate practical propulsion of its actions in the instance considered comes from natural motives; and these, no matter how excellent in their own way, are of infinitely less value than supernatural motives. If you were riding in a small sailboat, you could help your progress by using oars also, although of course most of your speed would be due to wind and sails; but if you were to keep the sails furled, then no matter what their possibilities of helping you, the actual work must be done by the oars and progress will be slow. In a similar way, supernatural motives forward the powerful movement of grace. On the other hand, natural motives keep grace bound up as it were while they themselves give to the actual immediate momentum to our actions; and this would be intolerably slow for a true Christian.

The least impulse of charity, or of any supernatural virtue, moving our actions is infinitely superior and vastly more meritorious than the best natural good taken as motive. The supereminence of charity over the best that nature can do is that of an entirely different order, like that of sensation over plant life, or of human thought over sense knowledge; but these examples, although the best available, are powerless to convey to our minds the height of supernature and its activity over nature and all it can perform. Thus if we made it a set policy and practice to act out of even the best natural motives, we would be constantly losing or refusing grace that we might easily obtain. Suppose that a fond parent would each day offer his child some precious gift; can you imagine the child willfully and carelessly throwing these gifts away as soon as received, or refusing them altogether? That is what we do when we insist on acting out of natural motives when supernatural motives bring us so much more grace.

Renewing the Intention

What, then is required? How often should we renew our supernatural intention? Should it be renewed for each action? That is, should one form a fresh actual intention for every work or duty performed? By no means; this would be a practical impossibility. What we should do is to renew our supernatural intention frequently, as frequently as possible. How frequently each of us will be able to do this will depend to some extent on the nature of our occupations, that is, how absorbing these are, but it will depend above all on whether we have a supernatural mentality and how much we love God.

Really, to consider the matter in itself, that is, abstractly, there is no need to repeat an intention at all; for an intention, once made, tends to persist of its own inner vitality until it is deliberately retracted or replaced by another. Once you form a definite intention of going to New York, you need not repeat it over and over until you get there; it will persist and eventually get you to New York unless you change your mind. Strictly speaking, therefore, it would be enough to form one supernatural intention in a life time. Even a daily morning offering, from this point of view—that is, in theory—is superfluous. But the practical contingencies of human life and the vigilance of the human spirit to intrude its views and its motives into our actions makes it imperative that the Christian in us be vigilant also, making sure that our actions are in truth supernatural by renewing and purifying our supernatural intention.

Imagine that you put a glass of fresh water on the window sill. That is, you call it fresh, but it has been in existence for a long time; you call it fresh because, although it remains always the same, there is a tendency for it to be contaminated from the outside by dirt, and it must therefore be freshly purified before it is acceptable to us. On the window sill also the water tends of itself to remain the same and even to stay pure; but if you leave it uncovered, dust and insects will get into it. In a similar way, although a supernatural intention, once formed, tends to persist, nevertheless our natural desires and impulses are so alive and eager to substitute themselves for the influence of grace and charity, thus contaminating our general supernatural intention, that we must remain alert to see that a truly supernatural motive, and not a natural motive subtly intruding itself, is the force actually impelling our actions.

For this reason, St. Alphonsus urges that in practice we should renew our supernatural intention before every important action of the day. And Father de Caussade, an outstanding spiritual writer of a former day, counsels us further not only to renew our supernatural intention before each action but also to purify it in the course of our actions. The reason for this procedure is that often when we have begun a thing for God, our natural tendencies, mortified for the moment, soon reassert themselves, so that we are likely to continue and complete the action because of the enjoyment or satisfaction it affords us. Our nature is like one of those roly-poly-dolls that children play with; as often as its head is pushed down, it bobs right up again tirelessly; and as often as we put nature down, mortifying it by a supernatural intention, it will also bob up an instant later as zealous as ever to seek its own interests. That is why, although an actual supernatural intention is not strictly necessary, it is best in practice to approximate such an intention as closely as possible.

Nor is this as difficult as might seem at first sight. Remember that we need not deal with our actions singly; these are rather directed and determined by our habitual mentality. If we cultivate a supernatural mentality, supernatural motives will come natural to us. If you were going to read at night, you might do so by striking one match after another and holding them before your eyes; or by lighting a candle and placing it before you; and no doubt you would adopt the latter method. So, instead of repeating supernatural intentions one after the other, it is better to form a mentality that expresses itself spontaneously and continuously in supernatural motives. Then you will not have to stop, so to speak, before each action and brace yourself as for an effort contrary to your nature. You will be living continuously in God's presence, absorbed in Him and detached from creatures, anxious to refer your actions to God, and sufficiently free from selfishness and sensuality really to accomplish this.

When James truly loves his wife, he is faithful to her as a matter of course in all that he does; he will not think of flirting with others. If, on the contrary, his love is not deep, he will be guilty of many small infidelities; and his flirtatious habits, as we have observed, will make most of his dealings with other women, however necessary, displeasing to his wife. So, too, when we truly love God, then we will easily put aside the world's blandishments and refer our actions to Him. But for the worldly man, and only for him, it is difficult to turn to God; and because of his worldliness even his good actions will be generally spoiled and imperfect in the sight of God.

These last remarks, bringing us back to the example of marital love, return us to the heart of our problem and indicate the final resolution of the controversy over what kind of intention is required to make actions supernaturally meritorious. The controversy is all very well; and the several solutions proposed throw light on different aspects of theological truth. But the controversy and the learning involved in solving it leave one thing out of account, and that the most important thing. They leave love out of account. Do loving parents ask what they *must* do for their children? Do lovers or loving spouses debate and haggle over their mutual obligations, concerned only to know what they *must* do for each other, ascertaining their strict obligations and refusing to go a step further than is absolutely necessary to serve or help their beloved? When this happens, indeed, love is on the ebb, the romance is ending, and we will not be surprised to find the former lovers soon in the divorce court. True lovers follow an altogether different course. The parents can never do enough for their child and they nobly sacrifice themselves for its welfare. Lovers can never do enough for each other. True love seeks to serve always, it looks for opportunities to please, it lives on sacrifice, and it can never rest content as long as there is something more it can do to prove or express itself. And shall the soul, who is the spouse of the infinitely lovable God Himself, be alone exempt from this law, this joyous urgency of love? Shall he alone be excluded from this blissful service? By no means! He is invited, yes, commanded to love the Divine Spouse with his whole heart. And if he loves truly, then no more than earthly lovers, and indeed far less, will he haggle over what he *must* do or hire lawyers to find out his strict obligations. He gives all—willingly, eagerly, joyously. He would look upon the controversy as to what kind of an intention is, strictly speaking, required, much as spouses deeply in love would regard a legal suit entered by an unhappily married pair to protect themselves from each other's encroachments and demands. To such a soul as this, the goal of life is total consecration, which can be realized only if he in truth consecrates every action to God. And his greatest sorrow is that he has not and cannot ever do enough for such a Loving Master.

"Alas," he says, after his greatest exertions, *"I am an unworthy servant; I have done that which I ought to do."* (Luke 17, 9)

Let us think upon these things. And may God bless you.

> *"O God, Who dost make the faithful to be of one mind and will, grant that we Thy people may love what Thou dost command and desire what Thou dost promise; so that, amid the changing things of this world, our hearts may be fixed where true joys are to be found. Through Our Lord Jesus Christ Thy Son Who livest and reignest with Thee in union with the Holy Spirit, God world without end. Amen."*

(Collect, Fourth Sunday after Easter)

THE SERMON ON THE MOUNT: JESUS DESCRIBED THE SUPERNATURAL LIFE

My dear Friends in Christ--

The high point in the history of the entire human race came one day when Jesus, seeing the crowds, as St. Matthew says, went up the mountain and, seating Himself, uttered those beautiful and momentous words of instruction which we now call the Sermon on the Mount. This was God's revelation to man of how He, the Creator, envisioned human life and had eternally decreed that it should be lived. Through His Son He was here outlining the pattern that human life and conduct was henceforth to follow; and we know also that the Son, during His earthly career, gave a living and perfect illustration of that pattern. From this time forward, all men are obliged to study the same pattern and reproduce it in their own lives.

You know the scene, which has so often been represented by Christian artists. Jesus seats Himself a little above a vast and varied crowd of men, women, and children. The disciples come close to Him. Then He opens His mouth to teach; and in this moment, as the music of the Beatitudes is poured forth on the air, human language and human thought reach the greatest sublimity they have ever attained or ever will attain.

Yet the quiet and simple beauty of that scene, and the lofty but still simple beauty of the Savior's thought and speech, seem at times so to enthrall men that they overlook or forget the fundamental importance and the austere practical demands of the message itself. This is magnificent poetry, yes; but not only poetry: it is doctrine, divine truth, and also a very practical description of how Our Lord and His heavenly Father expect men to live and act. The Sermon on the Mount is the Manifesto of the Christian life; it outlines the practical program of Christianity; it sets forth the principles and ideals that are from now on to be the daily guide of Christians both in their individual lives and their social efforts and institutions.

It is needful and opportune at the present point in our study to look at the supernatural life as Jesus Himself described it in this Sermon. Therein we will find the official promulgation of the doctrine that we have been studying in these conferences. The Sermon will also serve as a summary of this doctrine.

As a preparation for systematic study let us make two useful distinctions. We are dealing with actions—specifically, with the difference between natural actions and supernatural actions. Jesus clearly distinguishes these two kinds of actions and He marks out the elements contained in them. In any action we may distinguish three phases or parts: first, the end, and this is some good which is chosen by the will and whose attainment becomes the goal of subsequent actions; secondly, the means, which are selected and disposed to obtain the good chosen as an end, for in order to obtain any end it is necessary to select proportionate means and to put them into use; thirdly, the result of the action. For example, the end of an artist, we may say, is to create a work of beauty; the means that he employs is his brush or scalpel; the result is a representation of some person or some scene, or perhaps of a saint.

The second distinction is concerned with the end itself. We have just seen that actions are guided in reference to some end: when you act, it is always with an end in view, and the end is a good that you desire—food, clothing, knowledge, contentment, or whatever else it may be. Altogether, philosophers classify in three groups the goods which men may choose as their ends.

There are, first of all, external goods—those things which are extrinsic to the human person who seeks them, for example money and fame. Then there are what are termed bodily goods, objects which the body needs or desires for its welfare or gratification, for example, food and drink, comfort and pleasure. Finally, there are the goods of the soul, or interior goods, things which are desired and pursued by our interior powers of mind and will, such as knowledge or contentment or joy.

With these distinctions in mind we may go on to show, first, that Jesus condemns natural actions. He condemns these actions in detail—lock, stock, and barrel, so to speak. That is to say, He condemns natural actions in their end, in the means which are used to obtain merely natural good, and in the merely natural goodness which is their issue. Because He does it so thoroughly, we may say that He condemns, not only natural actions but also the natural or pagan mentality—the whole outlook and program of conduct which expresses itself in such actions. On the other hand, in defining and enjoining upon us supernatural actions, He sets up a supernatural end, determines supernatural means, and shows His desire for a supernatural result; that is, He defines the supernatural or Christian mentality. We will now look at all these facts in order.

First: Jesus Condemns the Pagan Mentality

Jesus condemns the pagan mentality. This means that He condemns natural actions in all the three phases that we have distinguished in actions—their end, their means, and their result. Let us first consider the end of natural actions. We have seen what this end may be—it may be any of the three kinds of goods which we have enumerated—external goods, bodily goods, or interior goods. These are all natural ends to whose pursuit the men of the world give themselves.

And Jesus condemns the pursuit of all. First, He condemns the pursuit of external goods. He says, *"Blessed are the poor in spirit, for theirs is the kingdom of heaven."* Here He teaches men that they ought not to desire external goods—wealth, the treasures of the world. In the Gospel of St. Luke, Jesus is reported as saying *"Blessed are you poor, for yours is the kingdom of God."* In St. Matthew, however, it is the poor in spirit that are blessed. In other words what Jesus wants is that we remain detached from wealth, that we have no desire for it. Those who are lacking in desire for earthly treasures or who are detached from them are the poor in spirit; and they receive the blessing of Jesus. Conversely, there is a curse on those who are lacking in poverty of spirit. Jesus says, according to St. Luke, *"Woe to you rich! for you are now having your comfort."*

Fame and good repute are also external goods much sought after by men. Fame is the great goal of some men, while all humanly tend to desire it. As for reputation, Shakespeare expresses the natural viewpoint on it when he says, "He who steals my purse steals trash, but he who steals my good name takes which not him the richer makes and makes me poor indeed." But Jesus goes counter to all this human wisdom when He teaches, *"Blessed are you when men reproach you, and persecute you, and, speaking falsely, say all manner of evil against you, for my sake. Rejoice and exult, because your reward is great in heaven."*

Secondly Jesus condemns the pursuit of bodily goods. We may understand the second beatitude as applying broadly to the goods of the body. *"Blessed are the meek, for they shall possess the earth."* St. Thomas teaches us that meekness is the opposite of anger; so that we may understand by the meek those who bear quietly and patiently the deprivation of the comforts and pleasures of this world. As given by St. Luke, this second beatitude refers even more directly to bodily goods. *"Blessed are you who hunger now, for you shall be satisfied."* Jesus promises us gratification later, but He blesses our present lack, or privation, of the good things that we naturally want, the good things of the body and of sense. Here also, while giving a blessing to those who lack worldly goods, He pronounces His condemnation upon those who possess them, or at least upon those who are attached to them. He says, *"Woe to you who are filled, for you shall hunger."*

Thirdly, Jesus condemns the pursuit of the goods of the soul or of interior goods. *"Blessed are they who mourn, for they shall be comforted."* Those who mourn are those who suffer, who are filled with anxiety and burdened with troubles. And yet Jesus gives them a blessing. Why? Because those who mourn are they who have lost, in one way or another, the good things of the world, and the likelihood that such persons will be detached from earthly things is much greater than in the case of the prosperous and contented, who are prone to be complacent and satisfied in their possessions. A state in which men are less likely to become worldly-minded is, in the mind of Christ, something to be thankful for. To quote the same beatitude in St. Luke, *"Blessed are you who weep now, for you shall laugh."* For fidelity in bearing present suffering and pain, Jesus promises the reward of future joy, the spiritual and supernatural joy of the kingdom of heaven. But once again, He deliberately condemns those who are attached to the human satisfactions of the present world. *"Woe to you who laugh now, for you shall mourn and weep."* Certainly a remarkable statement, this, on the part of the Son of God; yet He makes it—He regards present prosperity, which causes worldlings to rejoice, to be a matter rather of sorrow. Nor should we wonder: prosperity tempts the heart and causes men to neglect God.

Before passing to the next consideration there are two points concerning this condemnation of human goods, or of the pursuit of human goods, that we may profitably remark. First of all, it vindicates a principle that we have stated several times in defining the supernatural life. To live such a life, it was pointed out, we ought not only to renounce evil: we ought also to renounce all the goods of the natural world. Jesus, it is evident, teaches precisely this in the first three beatitudes, the first three statements of the Sermon on the Mount. And He teaches it very clearly and comprehensively, explicitly including all the three kinds of goods to whose pursuit men generally give themselves.

In the first conference of this series the distinction between the natural and supernatural orders was called the key to the understanding of the Gospel. This fact is very apparent in the present case. Without a knowledge of this distinction, these first three beatitudes would remain unintelligible. Such a condemnation of natural goods would seem perverse and inhuman were it not known to open the way to a higher than natural good.

Moreover, in these first three beatitudes, the three basic rules of Christian living, it is manifest that Jesus cuts diametrically across the philosophy of the world. The world considers wealth a blessing, the greatest of all blessings. The world considers bodily pleasure and comfort blessings, and pursues them every minute of every day. The world considers gaiety and present laughter a blessing, and shuns the company of the afflicted, the sorrowful, and the mourning. Jesus thinks exactly the opposite. The mind of Christ flatly contradicts the mind of the world. What the world considers a blessing, Jesus calls a curse. What the world considers a curse, Jesus calls a blessing.

It is truly amazing, almost unbelievable that the Son of God would so directly put Himself in open conflict with the so-called wisdom of the whole world and put His benediction on poverty, pain, and privation. Nowhere in the Gospel better than in these first three beatitudes can we see the truly revolutionary character of Christianity and how completely it is opposed to the mind and the practice of the world. Ordinarily we do not notice this simply because we do not think about it. We are so accustomed to hearing the beatitudes that we do not pause and ask their meaning. And we never attempt to imagine what would happen if we really lived according to these truths. If we really tried to live according to the Sermon on the Mount, the sudden and sensational change would make us dizzy. Our lives would certainly be transformed. And if men on a large scale would live according to the Sermon on the Mount, they would transform society also. The world would be scarcely recognizable. Its whole economy would undergo a revolutionary change. Half, or more than half, of its cherished institutions would disappear, and new traditions, new customs, new institutions would arise: Behold, all things would become new. Social life would no longer be organized around the possession of earthly goods. Poverty would be esteemed and sought as riches now possess the hearts of men. Wars would simply vanish, for there would be no occasion of war; the root and cause of war would have been dried up by Christian detachment. We would truly be living in the kingdom of God.

And bear in mind, this is not a fantastic dream. This is the way God wants and intends our lives to be. It is not wishful thinking, but divine law. From the moment in which these words are spoken, it becomes every man's strict duty to share in the work of carrying out this divine plan for the renewal of the earth. Here is the pattern of human life as designed by the Creator Himself. Henceforth, all men will be judged according to the perfection of their conformity to this pattern.

Jesus condemns not only the goods which the pagan mentality chooses as its end, but He condemns also the means which are employed to seek these ends. It may be stated that the initial means used for obtaining any good is the intention to gain it. Suppose that your end is to get to New York, and the means available is the railroad. Although there should be a train passing your door every minute, New York would stay where it is, and you would stay where you are unless you would first form an intention in your will of making the trip. Then, once the intention is formed, you take the other steps which are necessary to reach your intended destination. Now Jesus, in condemning the means which men use to obtain their natural end, condemns this initial and primary means, the natural intention. That is to say, Jesus clearly and explicitly condemns natural intentions or motives. We have already seen that we must eliminate natural motives and we have studied the reason for this; now we will hear Jesus explicitly saying this very thing.

His teaching is found in Chapter Six of St. Matthew. First of all He lays down a general rule; then He gives three illustrations. The general rule is this: *"Take heed not to practice your good before men, in order to be seen by them; otherwise you shall have no reward with your Father in heaven."* Here He teaches that we are not to work from a natural motive, that is, not for a reward from our fellow-men. And He tells us point-blank that if we do so, we shall have no reward in heaven.

Then come the three illustrations—first, *"Therefore when thou givest an alms, do not sound a trumpet before thee, as the hypocrites do in order that they may be honored by men. Amen I say to you, they have had their reward."* The second illustration: *"When you pray, you shall not be like the hypocrites, who love to pray standing in the synagogues and at the street corners, in order that they may be seen by men. Amen I say to you, they have had their reward."* And the third: *"When you fast, do not look gloomy like the hypocrites, who disfigure their faces in order to appear to men as fasting. Amen I say to you, they have had their reward."* Mark the repetition of that refrain—*"Amen I say to you, they have had their reward."* If we work from a mere natural motive, that is, to obtain the goods of this world, God will not give us a reward in heaven. There is no mistaking the matter; the Son of God tells us so. If we work for Smith, we would not seek our wages from Jones; and if we work for the world, God will not have us seeking our reward from Him. If we desire the reward that God can give, then must we in the first place while we are here work for God. This passage vindicates all that we have said about getting rid of natural motives.

Some persons might be inclined to shrug these examples aside, saying that men no longer have trumpets blown before them to advertise their good works. No; nowadays there are other ways of gaining the same end. Men now do their good deeds in order to get their picture in the paper or their names on a bronze plaque or have their generosity immortalized in stained glass or to obtain some other similar kind of recognition for their virtue. We live in a day of advertising and publicity; these are sought as a matter of policy and on principle; so that, not only are many good deeds still spoiled by the desire for human praise, but it is almost impossible for them to escape the corrupting influence of publicity. St. John of the Cross observed that "the greater number of good works" which men "perform in public are either vicious or of no value to them or are imperfect in the sight of God since they are not detached from human intentions and interests." *(Ascent of Mt. Carmel, III, 28)* And this was long before modern means of publicity were available!

Even in the matter of contributions made to the Church or charitable causes Catholics are lured by the prospect of having their name published on lists. And many there are who would not give financial aid or in other ways assist in these good works without such publicity, in fact would withdraw their support if full credit and thanks were not given to them. So far are we from observing the Gospel Counsel: *"But when thou givest alms, do not let thy left hand know what thy right hand is doing, so that thy alms may be given in secret; and thy Father, who sees in secret, will reward thee."* (Matt. 6, 4)

Nor do we suffer loss on this account only in our larger public acts. How invariably we expect praise and thanks even for the least good we do, how prone we are to be disheartened when the desired commendation is not given. Often indeed men abandon well-doing simply because they have received no human reward. Such an attitude clearly, if we have it, reveals how imperfect and worldly are our customary motives.

Thirdly, Jesus condemns the result of natural actions. The result of a good natural life would be natural justice or righteousness, the kind of goodness that would come from conformity to the law of nature and of reason. Now the Scribes and Pharisees may be taken as a type of this natural justice, it was what they taught. But Jesus condemns their justice, saying, *"I say to you that unless your justice exceeds that of the Scribes and Pharisees, you shall not enter the kingdom of heaven."* (Matt. 5, 20)

In speaking thus Jesus does not deny the Scribes and Pharisees a kind of justice, but He says that what they have is not sufficient for salvation. Elsewhere He shows more clearly what He means, distinguishing between the authoritative teaching of the Scribes and Pharisees and their bad example. He says, *"The Scribes and Pharisees have sat on the chair of Moses. All things, therefore, that they command you, observe and do. But do not act according to their works; for they talk but do nothing."* (Matt. 23, 1-3)

Still, it is not only the example of the Scribes and Pharisees that Jesus warns His followers against. When He says that their justice cannot merit heaven He includes also their teaching, that teaching which we have just heard Him approving and urging people to observe. He condemns this teaching, not as evil of course, but as inadequate for salvation. The great crime of the Scribes and Pharisees, from which all their other offenses follow as effects, was their rejection of the supernatural. They neglected the great law of love, thereby diminishing the divine law to the law of nature and reason. And so Jesus condemns their teaching as insufficient: *"Woe to you Scribes and Pharisees, hypocrites! because you pay tithe on mint and anise and cummin, and have left undone the weightier matters of the law, right judgment and mercy and faith. These things you ought to have done, while not leaving the others undone."* (Matt. 23, 23) As to the actual conduct of the Scribes and Pharisees, it fell away even from their diminished preachments precisely because of their rejection of the supernatural, for, as we have several times observed, men cannot live perfectly even on the plane of nature without the aid of grace. The example of the Scribes and Pharisees, cloaking avarice and vainglory under a virtuous exterior, may stand as an illustration of natural justice in the concrete, that is, of natural justice as it turns out in actual fact and therefore as distinct from the ideal natural justice described by pure reason. In other words, their condemnation illustrates the foredoomed attempt to live on the plane of nature while rejecting supernatural truth and love. Their justice was an external respectability that covered inward corruption.

Nor would we be correct in thinking that since the disappearance of the Scribes and Pharisees the unhappy attempt to live virtuously without grace is no longer made. It may be seen all about us today in that careful cultivation of an external respectability and righteousness that so often covers up, as of old, vainglory and sensuality and avarice. Often, too, as a consequence of the downward movement taken by unmortified human desires, this hypocritical respectability covers much darker crimes also—dishonesty, injustice, impurity, infanticide (i.e., abortion), contraception.

Second: Jesus Defines the Christian Mentality

After removing from men, as goals of effort, the various classes of natural goods, Jesus replaces them with a supernatural end and good which all men are to seek. This end is proposed in the fourth beatitude, *"Blessed are they who hunger and thirst for justice, for they shall be satisfied."* Justice is the end which all men henceforth shall strive after. Jesus is legislating for the entire human race, and this is the goal that He fixed for human life.

Now justice in the Scriptures means holiness or sanctity. Consequently sanctity, holiness, is the supreme good which all men shall seek in their lives. Man is now directed to lay aside the feverish race for riches, for the pleasures of the body, and for merely human satisfaction in order to strive henceforth at the imitation of a divine attribute, namely the very sanctity of God. Elsewhere in the Sermon on the Mount Jesus says the same thing when He exhorts us to *"seek first the kingdom of God and his justice."* Jesus has just taught us to renounce human goods in order that we may now live divine lives.

The fact that the fourth beatitude tells us to seek for a share in a divine attribute opens the way to the correct understanding of the following beatitudes. Each of these, in fact, mentions a divine attribute which Jesus would have us imitate and introduce into our own lives. Once we know that God really wishes us to live divine lives, therefore, we can see the reason for the injunctions laid upon us in these other beatitudes. Conversely, the duty of imitating divine attributes shows that it is really supernatural holiness, and not mere natural justice, that the fourth beatitude determines as our goal. Thus Jesus says, *"Blessed are the merciful, for they shall obtain mercy."* Now mercy, in its plenitude, is one of the divine attributes; by becoming merciful, we become godlike. And this is precisely what Jesus wants us to do, that is, to reproduce the divine mercy in our lives and actions. Next we are told, *"Blessed are the pure of heart, for they shall see God."* Here we are enjoined to imitate the perfect purity of God, which is contrasted with the mere external righteousness of the Pharisees. Jesus wants us to observe complete purity, clear to the roots of our actions; He wishes us to emulate the divine purity which is without any blemish whatsoever. Again He tells us *"Blessed are the peacemakers, for they shall be called the children of God."* The Scriptures speak of God as the God of peace, and the gift which Jesus said that He came to bring us was the gift of peace. Those who live in charity with others, keeping peace with their neighbor as well as in their own hearts, have then a special relationship to God and are in a particular sense called the children of God. Finally, Jesus recognizes beforehand and clearly foretells that living a divine life will bring persecution upon those who do it; and He blesses those who bear this persecution. Jesus is perfectly well aware that He is condemning the world and going counter to the philosophy of the world. He is well aware of the ruin that His doctrine will bring on Himself. The Son of God became flesh and the brethren of His flesh rose up against Him; the light came into the world but the darkness did not receive it. And He warns His followers that they will be engaged in a similar conflict and will have to endure like difficulties.

In all this it is evident what Our Lord is driving at. He wants us to live not human lives, but divine lives. That is why He has told us to give up human and natural goods, and now places before our eyes as the object of our life-long endeavors a divine good, the divine ideal of holiness. Once more, we see that the kind of life that Jesus wants us to live is not merely super-sinful, but super-human and truly divine. This is what it means to be sons of God, elevated to a share in the divine nature.

Jesus also specifies that we shall act out of supernatural motives, even as He has condemned natural motives. In other words, as He has rejected the natural means for attaining natural ends, so now, having determined on a supernatural end for us, He points out the supernatural means that we should utilize. We find this in the same passage in which He has condemned the natural means, namely, in the sixth chapter of St. Matthew. After He has told those who give alms not to do it that they may be seen by men, He adds, *"But when thou givest alms, do not let thy left hand know what thy right hand is doing, so that thy alms may be given in secret; and thy Father, who sees in secret, will reward thee."* He adds two more illustrations, parallel to those we have observed in dealing with natural motives. Speaking of prayer He says, *"But when thou prayest, go into thy room, and closing thy door, pray to thy Father in secret; and thy Father, who sees in secret, will reward thee."* Both of these passages definitely point out to us that we should work not for any earthly end, but for God. The third illustration carries the same message. Having condemned those who fast to be seen by men, He adds, *"But thou, when thou dost fast, anoint thy head and wash thy face, so that thou mayest not be seen by men to fast, but by thy Father, who is in secret; and thy Father, who sees in secret, will reward thee."*

Finally, Jesus expects supernatural fruit; He requires a supernatural result from our efforts. He says, *"You therefore are to be perfect, even as your heavenly Father is perfect."* Here in the clearest possible terms He repeats His demand for divine holiness and described what He means by it. We are not just to be holy, but we are to be holy as God is holy. Clearly we cannot attain to the infinite degree of holiness which is God's alone. But we can imitate and share in God's holiness, that is to say, we can possess the same kind of holiness. We have already seen how we may imitate God's mercy and purity and love. There are other of the divine attributes which we may likewise imitate and make part of our lives. In this way we may become holy in the manner that God is holy. Having rejected the mere external justice which was exemplified by the Pharisees, and the mere natural justice that they taught, Jesus here requires of all a justice akin to that of the heavenly Father Himself.

Third: The Rest of the Sermon Teaches the Same

What we have given so far is a skeleton outline of the Sermon on the Mount. This Sermon contains of course many other words of our Lord, all deserving of devout meditation. Still you will find in studying it that all its other teachings may be placed within the framework of this general outline or schema; they may be added to the latter as flesh to the bones of a skeleton.

Let us notice just a few of these other teachings of Jesus.

Here, for example, is how He expresses and summarizes His doctrine concerning detachment. *"Do not lay up to yourselves treasures on earth, where rust and moth consume and where thieves break in and steal. For where thy treasure is, there thy heart also will be."* Once more, a call to the renunciation of mere human or natural goods.

Another word about the motive: *"The lamp of the body is the eye. If thy eye be sound, thy whole body will be full of light. But if thy eye be evil, thy whole body will be full of darkness, Therefore if the light that is in thee is darkness, how great is the darkness itself!"* The Fathers of the Church, in their commentaries on this passage, tell us that the eye here stands for the intention. Jesus wants us to have a single eye, that is, to keep our motives single or pure.

Concerning those who wish to serve the world and God also, you know the famous passage. *"No man can serve two masters; for either he will hate the one and love the other, or else he will stand by the one and despise the other. You cannot serve God and mammon."* Surely this corroborates the principle which states that affections for creatures and affection for God are contrary to each other.

Another passage shows how far He wishes to push our detachment; it tells us that we are not to be anxious about even the most necessary things. *"Therefore I say to you, do not be anxious for your life, what you shall eat; nor yet for your body,*

*what you shall put on. Is not the life a greater thing than the
food, and the body than the clothing? Look at the birds of the
air; they do not sow, or reap, or gather into barns; yet your
heavenly Father feeds them. Are not you of much more value
than they? But which of you by being anxious about it can add to
his stature a single cubit? And as for clothing, why are you
anxious? See how the lilies of the field grow; they neither toil
nor spin, yet I say to you that not even Solomon in all his glory
was arrayed like one of these. But if God so clothes the grass of
the field, which today is alive and tomorrow is thrown into the
oven, how much more you, O you of little faith! Therefore do not
be anxious, saying, 'What shall we eat' or, 'What shall we
drink?' or, 'What are we to put on?' (for after all these things
the Gentiles seek); for your Father knows that you need all these
things. But seek first the kingdom of God and his justice, and all
these things shall be given you besides."*

The reason that Jesus here gives for not seeking after things
to eat and drink and wear is significant. After all these things, He
says, the pagans seek. These are the goods which men naturally
desire. Today, too, we may see how the pagans seek after these
identical goods. Notice all the advertisements; what is it that they
are trying to bring before our eyes? Things to eat, things to drink,
things to wear. The world is constantly trying to tempt our
concupiscence—as if this concupiscence were not strong enough
without such prompting—and offers its temptations always in
the same way, with exactly the same bait. Jesus, on His part,
insistently demanding that we rise higher, tells us once again to
put aside our desire and our concern for these earthly goods.

Another matter. One of the great attributes of God is His
love. And in teaching us to be as gods, Jesus does not fail to tell
us to imitate God's love. In fact, when He tells us to be perfect,
this remark issues from His doctrine concerning love. He has
been talking about the love of the Father for man, and now
observes that we should be as perfect as God is perfect, so that
our love also may be perfect. But let us look at this whole
passage. *"You have heard that it was said"*—He is of course
referring to the Old Law—*"'an eye for an eye, and a tooth for a
tooth.' But* (notice this significant "but" each time Jesus contrasts
His teaching with the teaching of the Old Law) —*"but I say to*

you not to resist the evildoer; on the contrary, if someone strikes thee on the right cheek, turn to him also the other; and if anyone would go to law with thee and take thy tunic, let him take thy cloak as well; and whoever forces thee to go for one mile, go with him two. To him who asks of thee, give; and from him who would borrow of thee, do not turn away.

"You have heard that it was said, 'Thou shalt love thy neighbor, and shalt hate thy enemy.' But I say to you, love your enemies, do good to those who hate you, and pray for those who persecute and calumniate you,"—now mark the motive that Jesus gives—*"so that you may be children of your Father in heaven, who makes his sun to rise on the good and the evil, and sends rain on the just and the unjust. For if you love those who love you, what reward shall you have? Do not even the publicans do that? And if you salute your brethren only, what are you doing more than others? Do not even the Gentiles do that?"* Here again Jesus is rejecting a merely human mode of conduct, recognized even among publicans and Gentiles. He is giving us a higher, a divine, standard, and it is at this point that He utters those sublime words, *"You therefore are to be perfect, even as your heavenly Father is perfect."*

We leave to your own study and meditation and prayer the other teachings of Jesus in the Sermon on the Mount. We will bring this conference to a close by going at once to the conclusion of the Sermon. The doctrine of this conclusion is important and corroborates all that has been said. Let me first read it to you.

"Everyone therefore who hears these my words and acts upon them, shall be likened to a wise man who built his house on rock. And the rain fell, and the floods came, and the winds blew and beat against that house, but it did not fall, because it was founded on rock. And everyone who hears these my words and does not act upon them, shall be likened to a foolish man who built his house on sand. And the rain fell, and the floods came, and the winds blew and beat against that house, and it fell, and was utterly ruined."

Observe what Jesus is teaching here. Why is it that in one case the house falls and is destroyed, and in the other case it stands? Clearly the house does not fall because the rains and the floods and the storms come: a house must be built strongly enough to withstand such assaults of the elements. The reason that the one house falls is because it is built on sand; and the reason that the other house remains is because it is built on rock and is therefore able to withstand the shock of storms and floods. We may ask, similarly, why it is that some souls collapse, fall into sin, and are ruined? This is precisely the question that Jesus is here answering for us. We may ourselves have asked it many times: Why does weakness overcome us? Why do we fall, perhaps repeatedly, into these offenses? It is because we build on sand. Often we blame our falls on the violence of temptation, but this is not the explanation; just as a house must be built strong enough to shelter men against storms, so our souls must be strong enough, with the help of God's grace, to repel temptation.

The reason why we fall into sin, therefore is not because temptation is too strong, but because we have built our spiritual edifice on sand. What is this sand? It is the natural mentality. Jesus says, *"Everyone who hears these my words and acts upon them shall be likened to a wise man who built his house on rock."* In other words, anyone who lives a supernatural life, becomes as a god, rejecting the goods of nature and acting habitually from supernatural motives—this is the man who builds on rock, and his house will stand. *"But if anyone does not hear my words,"*—that is if anyone still retains his attachments for the goods of the natural order, seeks after the pleasures and the comforts and riches of this world, and acts from natural motives—he is the man who builds on sand, and his house shall fall. Jesus gives us here His analysis of the cause of sin. And the cause is the attempt, always ultimately unsuccessful, to live on the merely natural plane. Natural actions, natural motives, natural attachments for the creatures of this world dispose the soul towards sin, lead it in the direction of sin, and, therefore, although appearing innocent in themselves, are the cause of spiritual ruin. The wise man therefore, will heed this warning and build his house on the rock of the supernatural.

*"O God, since Thou dost show the light of
Thy truth to those who are in error, so that they
might return to the path of right living; grant*

unto all who go by the name of Christian, both to reject what is opposed and to uphold what is becoming to His name. Through our Lord Jesus Christ Thy Son Who livest and reignest with Thee in union with the Holy Spirit, God world without end. Amen."

(Collect, Third Sunday after Easter)

THE PAGAN MENTALITY

My dear Friends in Christ —

You have no doubt seen skilled workmen go quickly and expertly about the tasks of their trade. Perhaps, for example, you have admiringly watched masons cut and lay stone with great rapidity, and yet also with great accuracy, conforming to precise specifications and producing a work of beauty. They are able to do this because of previous training and experience, which have developed in them habits of craftsmanship; so that now they can ply their trade with great facility.

Now from our preceding discussion it should be evident that in the effort to live a supernatural life, individual actions need occupy our attention less than the mentality that regulates individual actions. If we form a spiritual and supernatural mentality, then, like the skilled workmen, we can proceed in virtue of well-formed habits, quickly and easily perfecting each action as it is performed because of deep conviction and long practice in acting from supernatural principles and motives.

In the preceding conference we have spoken of those who habitually act from natural motives and have shown how their actions lose merit; and about those who habitually act from supernatural motives, and how they habitually gain merit. Our efforts, then, should be directed towards forming right attitudes and discovering principles that will express themselves in Christian habits of living. Such a habitual mode of thought and action is what is meant by a mentality; and a mentality, conversely, may be defined as the ordinary cast of mind, formed through long habit, that gives a special bent and coloring to all one's thoughts, a special tendency and direction to all one's actions. When we have a mentality, our actions almost automatically conform to it. In daily life we cannot stop to think out each move that we make, laboriously weighing and pondering principles and motives for every action, but we swiftly measure our actions as we perform them in reference to principle already thought out and from motives already decided upon, that is, according to the characteristic mentality that dominates our lives.

The Meaning of Mentality

So also we distinguish diverse mentalities among different national groups. We say, for example, that the English have a practical bent of mind, that the French characteristically have intellectual acumen, that Germans possess intellectual thoroughness. We recognize these different casts of mind in the kind of work for which each type has a preference as well as in the manner in which each performs this work. Now each individual of these several nationalities develops his mentality from the background and environment in which he lives. He does so effortlessly. A Frenchman does not have to stop and ask himself what he must do in order to think or act like a Frenchman. An Englishman does not have to consider how to think like an Englishman, nor a German how to think like a German. Having the mentalities proper to their nationalities, they act automatically, as it were, each in conformity with his own national mentality. Or again, to make the matter even clearer a Frenchman does not have to stop and consider how he should express himself in French; this comes to him almost as a second nature. His mentality being French, he expresses himself easily and naturally in the French language, finding himself perfectly at home with its peculiarities, readily able to exploit its possibilities. But since the English mentality and the genius of the language are quite different, even though the Frenchman may speak English well, he will often have to stop and think how to translate his thoughts into the English tongue.

Thus a mentality enables us to act in a certain manner readily, habitually, easily. From a religious point of view, and in conformity with what we know now about the two levels of activity, we have distinguished two kinds of mentality: the natural or pagan mentality, and the supernatural or Christian mentality. If we think and act on a natural plane habitually, then our mentality is natural; if we think and act regularly on the supernatural plane then our mentality is Christian. Our spiritual task then, in order to bring our whole lives under the control of grace, is to lay aside the pagan mentality and to gain a Christian mentality. This is what St. Paul is exhorting us to do when he says (Rom. 12, 2), *"Be not conformed to this world, but be transformed in the newness of your mind."* There are, then, two things to be done: to put off the mentality of the world and to obtain a new mind, that is, as St. Paul elsewhere puts it, to form *"the mind of Christ."* In order to accomplish this transformation, we ought, at the start, to be able to recognize these two mentalities, that we may the more easily divest ourselves of the one and put on the other.

Both the mind and the will have a part to play in forming our religious mentality. The will's function is to desire and love the good, as also to set the other powers in motion, directing them that it may be able to obtain and enjoy the good it desires. But the will, as the philosophers say, is a blind faculty; as a blind man is led by another, so is the will guided by the mind. We may see a similar condition in the sense appetites, which are also blind. If you had never heard of ice cream or knew its goodness, you would not experience any desire for it. But when once it is tasted and enjoyed, the senses tend to crave and seek it. Similarly, on a higher level, the will, which is the rational appetite, can desire and seek and love only what the mind represents to it as good. If the mind is preoccupied with the goodness of creatures, seeing them as lovable for their own sakes, then the affections of the will reach out to embrace creatures. The life of the will is to love; it must love some good; it gives itself as spontaneously to love as does the eye to vision, the ear to hearing. If the mind is preoccupied with God, recognizing that creatures are but means of knowing and serving God, then the will gives its powers of affection to God.

Moreover, once the will allows its affections to rest on creatures, it begins to derive the motives of its actions from these affections. We get our motives from what we love. Then individual actions slowly lengthen into habits, so that soon the soul is accustomed and acclimatized to a merely natural mode of thinking and acting. Moreover, the convictions of the mind, once they are settled, tend to remain permanent; and the habit of loving creatures for the enjoyment they afford, as also the habit of acting from motives drawn from this love, become also fixed and permanent; for habits fit our actions into grooves in which they are likely to stay. Thus it is that when once a natural mentality has been allowed to form and harden, it is hard to change. Indeed, only a blast of spiritual dynamite, a real conversion in thinking and acting, can effect such a change. Meanwhile, we act spontaneously according to our mentality.

Suppose that a man, after walking for some time, becomes tired and wishes to rest. On one side of the street is a tavern; on the other side, there is a Catholic Church containing a tabernacle in which Jesus is present. The man can go for rest and refreshment to either place. Where will he go? He is free—and yet not free. His habitual mentality will direct his choice. If his mentality is pagan, then he will turn spontaneously to the tavern. It will not even occur to him that he can find refreshment before the tabernacle; to him attendance at church is the very synonym of tedium. If he goes there at all, it is to sit or kneel listlessly at a tiresome ceremony. But his face lights up with pleasure, and his step quickens, as he turns to the kind of pleasure and refreshment that the tavern offers. If, on the other hand, the man possesses a Christian mentality, detached from the things of this world, with his mind formed by the teachings of Jesus Christ, then he will spontaneously turn to the tabernacle. For him the tavern is a symbol of human degradation, of man's failure to live according to the spirit, of indulgence in the things of sense. This man knows by experience that the attachment to the things of the earth brings no true happiness, and so he turns to where, as he is fully convinced, he can find true and lasting repose. He makes his choice also without effort, without long deliberation, in virtue of a manner of thinking and acting that has become an unchanging element in his life. He has heard those words of Jesus, *"Come to me, all you who labor and are burdened, and I will give you rest."* (Matt. 11, 25) He has meditated on these words and made their truth an active principle of daily living. And so he kneels before the tabernacle and is refreshed with a true and satisfying joy. This is what a mentality can do for us.

The Basic Principle of the Pagan Mentality

The mind, in laying a foundation for a mentality, not only reveals to the will the things that are good, and therefore lovable, but it also employs its ingenuity to draw up rules of action, practical maxims or axioms, which the will then uses as aids ready at hand in obtaining what it desires. In any line of activity we need such rules of thumb. So each trade has its own tricks, as they are called. A mechanic has many rules, learned during his apprenticeship, for handling tools and working with machinery. A farmer also has certain rules, though he may not give them that name, for taking care of his soil, for deciding when and where and how and what to plant, for harvesting and storing his crops. If you were to take up the study of a language, as many of you have, you would gradually learn a number of rules of pronunciation and grammar; and in order to read or speak the language, you would have to learn by practice to apply these rules quickly and accurately. When we know a language well, like our own mother tongue, we may speak it without being able to formulate such rules very clearly. But some rules are known by almost everyone, everyone at any rate who has some education—as for example the rule that tells us that a sentence should have a subject and verb. And of course we learn more of these rules or principles as our knowledge of the language increases.

Now in a similar way, our religious mentality, whichever it may be, is reinforced by many axioms, which then aid us in obtaining the good that our affections are set upon. If your mentality is natural, you will equip yourself with a number of maxims that will explain and justify your conduct as well as aid you in indulging your desires. The supernatural mentality, as we shall see later, will buttress itself with a quite different set. These practical maxims tend to remain unchanged unless they should be violently upset and expelled by a wholly new mode of thinking; thus they contribute also to the quasi-permanent character of our mentalities.

In order, therefore, to change from a pagan mentality and to form *"the mind of Christ,"* we must be able to recognize the maxims of the pagan mentality and be zealous in hunting them down and expelling them from our minds.

What are some of the maxims of a pagan mentality? We will reserve to the next conference the task of enumerating what may be called the secondary maxims of the pagan mentality. Here we will remark its basic practical principle. Everywhere and always the basic rule of mere pagan conduct has been, "Eat, drink and make good cheer." The pagan rule of life is the rule of enjoyment. The pagan sees that the things of this world are good, and that he has a capacity for enjoying these goods. His capacities, in brief, match the attractiveness of earthly goods, and he reaches out naturally for their enjoyment. He forms this into a philosophy, and he teaches that philosophy in his school and in his literature: "Eat, drink, and make good cheer. Gather your rosebuds while ye may. Get the most out of life. Make hay while the sun shines. A man lives only once. You are only young once. Sow your wild oats while you have the chance." All these are forms in which the pagan mentality presents its basic tenet of the enjoyment of the things of this world. Then the will, armed with this principle, gives its affections to creatures and forms the habit of acting to enjoy them; and when this habit of enjoyment has become habitual, a pagan mentality has been developed.

Evidently a Catholic, a Christian, cannot accept this pagan philosophy in such a gross form. Nevertheless, the pagan mentality intrudes itself among Catholics, and we find the same basic mentality somewhat mitigated or modified. Indeed, you will often hear Catholics repeating the very axioms that we have just noted as belonging properly to the pagan mentality. Many of them are as likely as the pagan himself to insist on the enjoyment of life. If pushed to explain how far this enjoyment may go, they will say something like this: Enjoy the things of this world— only avoid mortal sin. Or again, Enjoy the things of this world— only be sure to remain in the state of grace. They salve their consciences by those two limiting clauses; they think that the Christian has done enough if he stays in the state of grace or avoids mortal sin.

We have seen that a Christian life is not merely a super-sinful life, but a supernatural life; and we have seen also that the state of grace is not the end and climax of all effort, but the beginning of a long process of spiritual growth and ought to end only in perfection. Of course it is true, as the pagan mentality says, that we should avoid mortal sin and remain in the state of grace. The paganism of these axioms appears in the first part of them, namely, in the counsel to enjoy the things of this world.

Can you point out any place in the Scriptures a word of Jesus, or of any inspired writer, which tells us to enjoy the things of this world? Is there any place in the Scriptures which tells us to eat, drink and make good cheer? Jesus uses that phrase just once; he is telling a parable, the parable of the rich fool who, forgetful of God and the things of God, gives himself to the pursuit and enjoyment of an earthly prosperity. And Jesus Himself uses that terrible word *fool* in describing the man who subscribes to that way of thinking. The Scriptures tell us that we should *"mind not the things that are upon the earth, but seek the things that are above,"* because as Christians we are supposed to be dead to the world and living only to Christ. Thus the pagan mentality is easily recognizable in these maxims, which state that as long as we avoid grave sin or remain in the state of grace we may freely indulge in the pleasures of the senses.

Assuredly it is true that the things of this world are good and that they were made by God; or better perhaps, that, being made by God, they are good. But it does not follow from this that they were made for our selfish and sensual enjoyment. You cannot use this undoubted truth—that the things of this world are good—to justify a pagan mode of thought and action. The Christian has his own way, taught by Jesus, of using creatures. It is one of our tasks in studying the spiritual life to discover how a Christian ought to use the creatures of this world. For the present we notice only that he is not to use them or to enjoy them simply as the pagan does. What such a half-hearted Christian does when he contends that the creatures of this world are good, and that therefore we ought to enjoy them, is to invoke Catholic truth to justify a pagan philosophy of life.

Three Signs of the Pagan Mentality

We may complete the definition of the pagan mentality by indicating three signs by which it may be easily recognized.

The first sign is the desire and love of riches. If we are detached from the world, then we ought also to be detached from the riches of the world. When men have their minds and hearts fixed on money, when their great ambition is to accumulate money, when they judge others by the amount of money these possess and are unhappy because of the fact that they themselves lack it, or lack as much as they wish for, certainly they have a natural or pagan mentality. If we wish to live as Christians, we must learn to use the goods of this world for God, while remaining inwardly detached from them and not taking our delight or joy in them. St. Paul, for example, says, *"For we brought nothing into the world, and certainly we can take nothing out; but having food and sufficient clothing, with these let us be content. But those who seek to become rich fall into temptation and a snare and into many useless and harmful desires, which plunge men into destruction and damnation. For covetousness is the root of all evils, and some in their eagerness to get rich have strayed from the faith and have involved themselves in many troubles."* (I Tim. 6, 7-10) The Apostle then goes on, showing the conduct proper to Christians, by saying, *"But thou 0 man of God, flee these things; but pursue justice, godliness, faith, charity, patience, mildness."* Such are the riches we should covet. Jesus Himself was born poor, lived poor, and died poor. And all of His followers, seeking to put on Jesus, must likewise be at least poor in spirit if their vocation and duty keep them amidst the goods of the world.

The spirit of riches is shown, not only in the love for money itself, but also in the love for the comforts and pleasures and luxuries over which money gives us command. Today, especially, mass methods of manufacture put at our disposal a great multitude of material and sensible goods while clever advertising seeks to prove their necessity or at any rate to tempt our concupiscence by means of them. To possess all or many of these luxuries is called the high American standard of living. Now the effort of the Christian life should rather be to simplify living and reduce our wants, not to multiply them, thereby complicating our lives with all kinds of pseudo-necessities. The Christian will emulate the Nazareth standard of living, exemplified by the Holy Family, rather than the high standard of modern living. True it is, alas, that life today in any case is more complex than formerly, and it will be hard indeed for those living in the world to realize perfectly the admirable simplicity and holy poverty of Nazareth. But undoubtedly we may keep the spirit of that holy home, and our bent should be in the direction of its simplicity.

The second sign of the pagan mentality is curiosity and worldly-mindedness. If we live for Jesus Christ, and are dead to the world, then we will be largely unconcerned with the doings of the world except insofar as we are directly involved in them or because of duty must take recognition of them. At any event we will not be idly curious, filling our minds with all kinds of distracting and useless thoughts and information. We will not go about with our eyes and ears wide open to catch everything that they can, regardless of whether the information or knowledge is useful or not, and wishing to have it simply because it is pleasant or novel or curious.

A Christian lives an interior life; that is to say, he turns his eyes inward to the Three Divine Persons Who dwell within his soul. He lives his entire life in the presence of the Blessed Trinity. He gives as much attention as he possibly can to these Divine Guests, just as you in your home would not leave some honored guest alone in your living-room while you take care of your cats and canaries, but would rather give all your energy and thought to entertaining your guest. Thus while we must perform whatever duties we have, we should retire inwardly as far as we can and honor our Divine Guests. St. John of the Cross, speaking to religious, tells them that though the world would come to an end, they should make no note of it. St. Peter Alcantara was said to be so recollected, with his eyes always cast down, that he could not even recognize the faces of his brother monks or even find the various parts of his monastery except by following others. Those living in the world perhaps cannot follow fully such counsel or conduct—it would be dangerous in an age of automobiles!—but they can follow it in spirit and keep their minds free of distracting and useless thoughts and desires. Our preoccupation with worldly news and curiosity comes from attachment to the world; it means therefore that our heart is not free from the world, that our affections are engaged with God's rival; and this is why it is a sign of the pagan mentality. Such affections too explain why we suffer so from distractions in prayer; and if we wish to rid ourselves of distractions, we ought to empty ourselves of these affections and of interest in idle matters.

In this connection, we may note, but not praise, the habit so common today of listening all day long, or much of the day, to the radio while engaged in work. How is it possible to sanctify our work when our mind is being nourished constantly with all kinds of worldly considerations or maxims or motives? How can we develop this life of the spirit when without interruption we listen to music or drama or other entertainment that to a large extent aims frankly and only at the gratification of the senses. There was a time when men and women performed their daily tasks in at least some silence. Then they had opportunity to direct their thoughts to God frequently. Perhaps many did not use the opportunity; but many, without doubt, did. But nowadays the very opportunity has been taken away. By constantly listening to the voice of the world, the energies of the soul are dissipated in endless worldly considerations and affections. A habit of prayer and inward recollection, a life of union with God, becomes impossible. Furthermore, such a constant succession of earthly pleasures, filling every instant of time and every crevice of the soul, becomes in time a thick fortification that effectively prevents any dart of heavenly love or inspiration from penetrating to the interior of the soul.

A third sign of the pagan mentality is human respect. Human respect is a habit by which we treat people according to their outward appearance or their social position or their riches. We are courteous and considerate of the well-to-do, curt and impatient with the poor or the needy: this is human respect. Clearly it indicates a heart that is attached to worldly goods and a lack of a spirit of faith. A spirit of faith sees Jesus in every soul, regardless of that soul's external condition, and desires to treat it with courtesy and love, because that soul mirrors God and has been redeemed by Jesus. Thus the Christian will strive to treat all men alike, and with like charity, without any regard to race or nationality or social status. Great concern about these external things at once betrays the pagan mentality, the mind of the world. St. James warns us against this human respect. He says, *"My brethren, do not join faith in our glorious Jesus Christ to partiality towards persons."* He tells us quite candidly that faith and human respect simply do not mix. He adds *"If a man in fine apparel, having a gold ring, enters your assembly, and a poor man in mean attire enters also, and you pay attention to him who is clothed in fine apparel and say, "'Sit thou here in this good, place'; but you say to the poor man, 'Stand thou there,' or, 'Sit by my footstool'; are you not become judges with evil thoughts? Listen, my beloved brethren! Has not God chosen the poor of this world to be rich in faith and heirs of the kingdom which God has promised to those who love him? But you have dishonored the poor man."* (James, 2, 1-6)

It should be evident that this Gospel warning against human respect contains the solution to two of the gravest problems of the world today—the national problem and the racial problem. These problems arise because men erect national and racial divisions into barriers and think it virtue to indulge in prejudice towards, and hatred for, races and nationalities other than their own. They do this because they have lost or rejected the vision given to them by the Gospel; the problems arise because they do not carry out the plan and law of God. God no more intends different nationalities and races to war with one another any more than He intends that the families of a neighborhood should fight among themselves. The division of mankind into races and nationalities, which results from human conditions of life and the laws of heredity, is also a Providential arrangement to secure communal effort, since men by nature need the society of their fellows. It is the penalty for the rejecting the teaching of Jesus that this Providential design becomes the occasion for war and catastrophe.

The Gospel teaches us to see Christ in our neighbor regardless of race or nationality or any other human difference. Indeed, were we accustomed to viewing the world with the eyes of faith, we would scarcely notice the accidental differences among our fellows, so absorbed would we be in loving and administering to the divine goodness reflected in all of them.

Thus our problems come from the malice of men, and not from God, Whom, however, so many thoughtlessly or blasphemously blame for them. The economic problem, another of the major troubles of the day, arises because of a neglect of a doctrine considered in the preceding conference, *"Seek first the kingdom of God and his justice, and all these things* — the material necessities for living on earth—*will be given to you besides."* (Matt. 6, 33) Men, disregarding this doctrine, set their affections, not on justice or holiness, but on earthly goods, and it is the rivalry and the rat fight for these that creates what we dignify with the name of the economic problem and the maldistribution of wealth. Now we can add that the grave political and social disorders arising from national and racial rivalries come also from discarding divine teaching. Our greatest difficulties, if men would live by the Gospel, would not only be solved but would vanish. But alas the human race for this long time, despite all its complaints, has shown a marked preference for hatred and strife and self-inflicted suffering to the peace of the Gospel.

Let us now think upon these things. And may God bless you.

"We beseech Thee, O Lord, incline Thine ear to our petitions and bring light to the darkness of our minds by the grace of Thy visitation, Who livest and reignest with God the Father in union with the Holy Spirit, God world without end. Amen."

(Collect, Fourth Sunday after Epiphany)

MAXIMS OF THE PAGAN MENTALITY USED TO EVADE THE GOSPELS

My dear Friends in Christ--

In the preceding conference we studied the basic principle of the pagan mentality—the rule to enjoy creatures—and observed how it is used by tepid Catholics. Besides this basic principle there are innumerable other accessory rules and maxims by which those who have the pagan mentality seek to evade the high responsibilities that are inseparable from the profession of Christianity. In other words, the pagan mentality appeals to certain principles, or quasi-principles, which result from specious reasoning, to explain and defend its negligence. Men always desire some justification for their conduct; they will not act without a rational explanation. To do so would be to condemn themselves, and no one wishes to condemn himself. We have already noticed several of these false principles. For example, the assertion that natural actions are meritorious, which is used to escape the duty of making actions supernatural. Or again, the belief that all that is necessary to make one's actions supernatural is to offer a mechanically recited morning offering. In the present conference we will consider a number of other such false principles, principles which are on everyone's lips, and which are the ordinary dodges of lukewarmness and tepidity. Altogether we will now distinguish six of them—six evasions of the Gospel teaching and of grace.

The First Evasion

The first evasion is this: This doctrine— i.e., the doctrine of supernatural living that has been the subject of these conferences—places too much emphasis on the will and on human action, the pagan mentality will say. Such emphasis on human effort is derogatory to grace; it ignores the power of the sacraments which confer grace upon souls of themselves—*ex opere operato,* as the theological phrase goes. It is grace and the sacraments that sanctify the soul; but this doctrine would seem to assert that the work of sanctification depends on the human will.

The human effort involved in supernatural living, far from being derogatory to grace and to the sacraments, follows from them. It is because we have been elevated by grace to a share in the divine life, that so much is expected of us. And of course our elevation was accomplished in the first place by baptism and continued with further subsidies of grace from the other sacraments. In a word, sacraments and grace require that we make this high effort to live a truly divine life; and the very labor of our minds and wills in making the effort is accomplished under the inspiration of grace.

We may answer this objection more fully by observing that in our sanctification there are two principles: the Holy Ghost and the human will. If we measure these two principles against one another, then it is clear that the Holy Ghost, with His graces and gifts, is far and away the more important. His is the positive work of sanctification; He elevates and divinizes, He it is that finally makes our actions supernatural and meritorious. Yet the work of the human will, although less important, is indispensable. It may be compared to the part that a wire plays in conveying electricity to give us light and heat. The wire does not create the electricity and would be quite useless unless there were a power plant in the vicinity. On the other hand the power plant would be no good to us if there were not wires to conduct the electricity to our homes. The Holy Ghost is the power that sanctifies our souls, while grace and the sacraments are the means through which He works. But He conveys His grace into our souls through our wills. In other words, He requires our correspondence with grace, and it is through the work of our faculties, especially of our wills, that we correspond with grace. Thus our wills, although contributing nothing positive to the work of divinization, are necessary that this work of divinization may go on.

Moreover, it is important to notice that the work of the Holy Ghost is not under our control; nor, indeed, is there much danger that *His* work will be neglected. We can presuppose *it,* we can take *it* for granted. What we cannot take for granted is our own efforts, for we are always sluggards, lagging far behind the inspirations of grace. Our immediate task, then, is not to arouse the Holy Ghost, but to arouse ourselves. For practical purposes we can and ought to center our attention on the labor of our own wills. This is by no means to exaggerate their importance or to underestimate the work of grace; but it is to do what is necessary in order that grace may become effective in our lives. Thus, granting the greater importance of the work of grace, we must nevertheless affirm that for us it is more practically important to attend to the part played by our own wills. God will take care of His part; let us see that we take care of ours.

Too many Catholics, including teachers and writers, are over-occupied with God' s part in our sanctification. They are concerned almost exclusively with what He does, they describe the beauties of grace and the efficacy of the sacraments, while ignoring the part played by the human will. Such a policy, although concerned with very high and lofty things, produces very little practical fruit, because it does not tell men what they ought to do in order to realize the beauties of grace in their own lives. Suppose that a hungry man were to go into a baker's shop, seeking for bread. The baker takes out a fine loaf of bread, lets him see it, lets him smell it even, thereby arousing his desire more, if this is possible; and then puts the bread back into the case. This is what is done by spiritual counsel which shows us the sublime beauty of grace and the sacraments, but fails to give us any practical procedure or method utilizing them to divinize our lives.

Or suppose a man is sick and he sends for a doctor, and the doctor, when he comes, stands by the man's bedside and makes a speech about the beauties of life and what a desirable thing is health, while offering no practical regimen to regain health and prolong life. What would you think of such a doctor? Well, those writers and teachers who spend all their time and space praising divine grace, extolling the work of God in sanctifying souls, but giving men no practical regimen for utilizing that grace and responding to the inspirations of God, are like such a doctor. True, theology must teach us what grace is and how it works, and much good is to be gained by meditating on such truths. But if spiritual teaching stops there, it is sterile. It must give us methods and procedures, a regimen for obtaining and increasing supernatural life. The patient knows that life and health are beautiful, and that is why he sent for the doctor. Catholics know that grace is a great marvel and that the sacraments are the works of God, and that is why they come into our churches and read spiritual books. But what they need to know is how to correspond with grace, how to make fruitful in their lives that grace which God gives so abundantly. And surely guides and teachers, writers and theologians, who fail to give them such practical counsel are remiss in their responsibility.

Pope Pius XII in his encyclical on the Mystical Body of Christ condemns a certain tendency among Catholics of our day to be exclusively preoccupied with the efficacy of divine grace, forgetting that they need to correspond in a positive way with that grace. Here is the passage:

"Just as false and dangerous is the error of those who try to deduce from the mysterious union of all with Christ a certain unhealthy *Quietism*. They would attribute the whole spiritual life of Christians and their progress in virtue exclusively to the action of the divine Spirit, setting aside and neglecting the corresponding work and collaboration which we must contribute to-this action. No one of course can deny that the Holy Spirit of Jesus Christ is the one source of whatever supernatural power enters into the Church and its members. For *'The Lord will give grace and glory,'* as the Psalmist says. But that men should continue consistently in their good works, that they advance generously in grace and virtue, that they strive earnestly to reach the heights of Christian perfection and at the same time do their best to stimulate others to gain the same goal— all this the Spirit from above does not wish to bring about, unless men contribute their daily share of zealous activity. 'For not on those who sleep but on the diligent,' says St. Ambrose, 'divine favors are conferred.'"

The Second Evasion

The second evasion is something like the first. The pagan mentality tells us that this doctrine of meritorious actions is derogatory to the sacraments. The sacraments, it says, are the ordinary means of obtaining grace. Why then all this emphasis on human actions? It would be better, so we are told, to forget about our own actions, and, if we desire grace, to go to the sacraments.

In answering this objection, it must first of all be stated that there is no opposition between Catholic doctrine concerning meritorious actions and the Catholic doctrine of the sacraments. In Catholic theology these things go together; it is a false mentality, seeking to escape its duties, that finds opposition where none can exist. The theology of meritorious actions is in perfect agreement with the theology of the sacraments. Of course we should go to the sacraments to obtain grace. But we may also obtain, or merit, grace by means of our actions. And the true Christian, desirous to obtain as much spiritual wealth as possible, exerts himself to make every action count as a means of obtaining grace. We should make our entire lives supernatural, every deed a part of an integrally Christian life. Some persons cannot get to the sacraments as frequently as they wish. But they can make their daily actions meritorious of grace. Even the saints and those who do have the opportunity of receiving the sacraments frequently are so in love with God, so eager to please Him, so greedy to accumulate spiritual riches, that they are not satisfied except when they are able to make everything that they do count in their tireless effort to do God's will and enjoy union with Him.

In brief, then, we may obtain grace both by meritorious actions and from the sacraments. The latter are more efficacious because they confer grace of their own inherent power, while the grace obtained by meritorious actions depends immediately on the dispositions of the one performing the action, assuming of course that he is in the state of grace. Still, both means will be used by the devout. For a Christian life does not consist in an occasional act of devotion, but in the effort to make all that we do supernatural and thereby conforming to the divine will.

It is important to notice also that by performing our actions out of a supernatural motive we enable grace to penetrate deep into our souls and into our faculties and to influence all our actions. A supernatural motive, particularly a motive of love, makes it possible for grace to enter our souls, just as an open window allows fresh air to enter into a room. Many people receive the sacraments frequently without any discernible improvement in their lives; sometimes persons will go to the sacraments for many years and yet experience spiritual deterioration. The reason for this is that although they obtain grace, and accumulate grace, it is like money lying in a bank unused, or like food that lies in the stomach undigested. It does not penetrate, does not enter into their faculties as a living influence. But by performing our actions supernaturally, as we have already seen, we make it possible for grace to become an actual living force in our daily lives.

Finally, let it be said, that the sacraments themselves become more fruitful and meritorious *for us* when we receive them out of a pure and supernatural intention. As a matter of fact, one of the requirements mentioned by Pope Pius X in the decree by which he made frequent and daily Communion again possible is a pure intention. Sometimes in teaching and exhorting to frequent communion, there is no mention of this condition. But it is certainly given, and theologians also teach us that we should not receive the sacraments out of any human or natural motive but out of a pure and supernatural motive. The purer our motive the more efficacious the sacrament will become for us. Thus, despite the fact that the sacraments give grace of themselves, we may in our own lives receive less of this grace than we should because of the fact that our souls are not disposed to receive it. We must empty ourselves of human things in order to prepare the way for the entrance of divine things. A pure intention, by voiding our hearts of earthly affections, increases their capacity for grace and love.

The Third Evasion

In the third evasion the pagan mentality defends its indulgence by saying something like this: Do you mean to assert that God will condemn me for one little natural motive? Will I go to hell because I eat one piece of chocolate? Will a man be damned because he takes one puff of a cigarette or one cigarette? Such an idea of course is ridiculous. And so the pagan mentality goes on condoning indulgence.

The pagan mind, always seeking to evade, is not in good faith. And here it simply misrepresents that situation. It is true that God will not condemn us for one act of self-indulgence. But acts of self-indulgence do not come by ones. As we have seen, a person develops habits, forms a mentality; and if one has a pagan mentality then acts of self-indulgence are numerous. If God will not condemn us for one act of self-indulgence, He may condemn us for innumerable acts of self-indulgence. Or to put the matter differently, innumerable acts of self-indulgence may well have an effect on our soul that is injurious to ourselves and displeasing to God.

A man who has contracted tuberculosis, looking at the tuberculosis germ under a microscope, might say incredulously, "Do you mean to assert that one little germ like that can kill me?" The answer is that of course one such germ will not kill him; but millions of them may, and those germs usually come by the millions.

Thus also, one act of self-indulgence, one natural motive, one cigarette or one chocolate, one bit of food taken for pleasure, or one snack taken without a supernatural motive, will not injure our souls. But many such acts of self- indulgence, over days and months and years, in which self-indulgence is the ordinary practice, will certainly injure us. And the pagan mentality makes this indulgence habitual. Nowadays also the circumstances in which we live make habitual self-indulgence possible to a degree never heretofore known. All day long we can have, and many of us do have, all kinds of indulgences. Human ingenuity and the resources of modern industry have provided countless devices for keeping us all warm and comfortable, with every sort of pleasure easily within reach. Recreation and enjoyment tend to become our constant occupation. All day in the house or the office or the store a radio is playing, cushioning each moment with sensual pleasure. Eating and drinking constantly for no other motive than the pleasure it affords; and endless other comforts and luxuries. Our very meals determined, not by the good that we can obtain through them, but merely according to our tastes, so that we come in time to be ruled by taste. All day long we are able to give ourselves some gratification each moment. Then at the end of such a day, or at the end of many of them, we ask petulantly, "Do you mean to assert that God will condemn me for one little natural motive?"

The Fourth Evasion

The fourth evasion states that natural motives, and a natural way of acting, are attractive, especially in children and the young. And so the pagan mentality avers that it would be a shame, cruel and unnecessary, to disturb such attractive conduct, such innocent pleasures on the part of children.

It may be allowed at once that there is a sense in which to act naturally is attractive. If we take the word natural as the opposite of affected, then to act naturally is certainly desirable. Nothing so offends us as affected behavior; and affected behavior is of course not required in a supernatural life. But in the moral or spiritual sense natural behavior is not desirable on the part of a Christian, whether in children or in grown-ups. Natural conduct, the self-indulgence of children, their attachment to the pleasures and the toys and the recreations of the world, seem attractive to us because we judge them by merely human standards. Of course such conduct does conform to natural standards, and since it avoids any grossness, it reveals the natural plane of action to us at its best, and so we are fond of the innocent pastimes and recreations of children and look on them benignly. Moreover, living a Christian life does not require either adults or children to give up recreation, which is indeed a necessary element in any normal life. But it does require them to give up a pagan mentality and attachment to the things of the world.

If we were accustomed to judge conduct by Christian and therefore supernatural standards, then we would not be pleased by any actions that indicate attachments to this world. The indulgences of children seem innocent because the law of concupiscence has not yet reached its final term, which is sin. Yet these indulgences, this turning to the world, will in time bear their noxious fruit; and then the conduct of the children, now perhaps grown-ups, will not be so attractive even from a human standpoint. But, at any rate, if we judge from the plane of grace, then we would desire that even children live supernatural lives and conform themselves to their status as children of God. Almighty God Himself, by giving us child saints, shows us what He desires of children and what manner of children are pleasing to Him. Saint Therese was able to say that from the time that she was three she had done everything out of love for God; and this is the kind of child that is pleasing to God. If we judge by animal standards, then the animal antics of an idiot would not displease us. But if we judge by human standards then we would be offended or saddened by such conduct on the part of a human being. And if we judge as children of God, then we will be saddened by mere self-indulgence on the part of ourselves or of others. If you read the life of the great St. Teresa of Avila, you will observe that she speaks of her early years as though she had been a great sinner. Yet we are told that she never committed a serious sin. But to her own eye, after she was converted to God, the innocent self-indulgences which she knew as a girl now offended her conscience deeply and she saw in them a mark of infidelity to God's grace.

Children should be taught to live a supernatural life from the very beginning. Their minds are docile and fresh and pure, better able to absorb the truths of religion than adults, who are spoiled by the world and the philosophy of the world. Childhood is a period given by God in which to learn divine truths and to cultivate the habits necessary to translate these truths into action. Parents should be concerned to teach these truths and their practice to children, rather than to permit or even encourage the spiritual corruption of their little ones through the slow infiltration into childish minds of the maxims of the world, maxims which will eventually rob these children of innocence and make them as worldly-minded, as callous, as imperfect, and as lukewarm as their parents. It is not cruel to children to teach them the secret of true joy and true happiness. All they will ever get from a life of self-indulgence is disappointment, unhappiness and bitterness. The Christian life, on the contrary, while demanding sacrifice, is the way of joy and peace and beatitude.

The Fifth Evasion

The fifth evasion says, "Not all natural motives lead to sin. There are also good natural motives."

Now it is true that while some natural motives are selfish, there are others which are good, as when men are impelled to act from the desire for some legitimate good or advantage, as in the business world or in social life. Nevertheless, natural motives at their best, as when men enter marriage or desire children from natural motives, are of an order infinitely lower than the supernatural; and because we are elevated to the supernatural plane and are striving for a supernatural good, we ought to cultivate the habit of acting from supernatural motives and rely only on these as the means proportioned to our end.

Furthermore, in practice, it is difficult to distinguish between good natural motives and imperfect natural motives. Many motives that seem at first to be harmless may grow up and become harmful. To get children to study, for example, we arouse their sense of competition, we appeal to their selfishness, ignoring the fact that this selfishness which we teach them will later develop into undesirable traits of character and may well bear fruit in sin. The teacher appeals to such motives to get a difficult task accomplished as quickly as possible; but the teacher will not be around when these motives, or the dispositions they foster, bear their final noisome fruit. Yet the physical absence of these teachers at the time of the harvest will not exempt them from the responsibility of sowing the seed or permitting the rootlets of the spiritual weeds of sin to remain. Thus, the only practical procedure is to get rid of all natural motives since we know that in any case supernatural motives are best and purest. Suppose that we should say to a guest, "I am going to put you in this room which was just vacated by a man suffering from tuberculosis. There are good and bad germs in the room; we do not want to disinfect it for fear of killing the good germs. You be careful only to breathe in the good germs." We doubt whether the effort would be successful. And similarily we may doubt whether the effort to act out of only good natural motives would be successful.

It is also to be observed that the natural motives which are the most powerful to gain results are most often the selfish kind. The ambition for wealth, for position, for first place, if only in a classroom, are the motives which will impel men to effort and action. But these are precisely the motives which encourage selfishness, lead to worldliness, and are therefore a disposition towards sin. Good natural motives, in the present condition of mankind, are often not a sufficiently powerful incentive to good conduct. You could hardly teach a group of undisciplined boys to behave themselves out of an abstract love for good order. You could hardly reform criminals in a penitentiary by teaching them the philosopher's ideal of conduct according to reason. Your appeal to them to practice virtue because it is reasonable would likely bear little fruit. An appeal to supernatural sanctions, to a life of eternal happiness in heaven or to eternal punishment in hell, is a more powerful incentive as well as a more meritorious way of acting.

The Sixth Evasion

The sixth evasion constantly uses the phrase "actions *in themselves*" *(in se)* to make it a policy to permit, without any further discrimination, all actions which are in themselves indifferent, that is to say, neither good nor bad. Since there is no sin in such actions, it is argued, they may be indulged in freely without any restraint whatever.

To understand the force of this objection, and to be able to answer it, we must notice the distinction that philosophers make between actions which in themselves are good or bad and actions which in themselves are merely indifferent. Indifferent actions are such as walking or talking or dancing or smoking. There are other actions which in themselves are good or bad, that is to say, their morality is determined from within, by their very structure and composition, so to speak. Examples of actions in themselves good are almsgiving and fasting. Examples of actions intrinsically evil are murder and theft. Now philosophers speak of actions *in themselves,* in order to distinguish these which are intrinsically good or bad from others which contain nothing that within themselves marks them off either as good or bad. Actions which contain no intrinsic determinant of morality are called indifferent actions.

Now while it is useful for philosophy to distinguish these two kinds of actions, we must notice that, when dealing with practice, we take into account the actual circumstances accompanying the transition into the practical order. A man may master all that books and charts say about swimming, but he would be very foolhardy to jump into deep water without learning the practical skills necessary to swim. Similarly, when utilizing moral principles, however true in themselves, we must always take into account actual circumstances and pressing necessities. When the philosophers teach that some actions in themselves are indifferent, they do not teach that any action in the concrete, that is as it is actually performed by an individual, is indifferent. Walking in itself is indifferent, but can you imagine the act of walking in itself—without someone doing the walking, and walking to a particular destination? The act of walking in itself is an abstraction; it does not actually exist as such; when it exists, it exists in a person who does the walking and is walking to a particular place for a particular purpose.

In a word, when indifferent actions are actually performed they are always clothed with a variety of concrete individual circumstances. And although when considered abstractly the actions are indifferent, when they are performed in individual cases with concrete circumstances they are always either good or bad. Their goodness or badness is not determined from within, as is the case with those actions which are good or bad in themselves, but it is determined by the circumstances in which they are performed. The man, for example, who is walking to preserve his health is performing a good action, as is the man who is walking to visit the church. But the man who is walking down the street to rob a bank is performing a bad action; and even if, on his way down the street, he sees a policeman and changes his plans, he is still guilty of a bad action: walking for him was bad because the end of his walking was bad.

There are then certain circumstances which invariably give a definite moral determination and character to indifferent actions in concrete cases. And the chief circumstance is the end or purpose of the action. The end or purpose, even of an indifferent action, makes that action in concrete reality either good or bad; and since the end of an action is fixed by the motive, it may be said that, where indifferent actions are concerned, their concrete morality, when they are actually performed, is primarily determined by the motive or intention. The man walking down the street to rob the bank commits a bad action because of his evil intention, even though he does not carry out his resolve.

Thus we may state it as a principle that in the concrete there is no such thing as an indifferent action; every action is either good or bad, either leads us closer to God or farther from Him. When the pagan mentality gives free rein to all indifferent actions, on the plea that they are indifferent, it is following a false and unreal principle. We have observed earlier that the wide field of indifferent actions is precisely the area where the Christian mentality should especially exercise itself, taking the opportunity to make these actions and also to elevate them to the supernatural level by a supernatural motive. It is false and artificial, when dealing with practical actions, actions really performed, to call them indifferent or to speak of actions in themselves. In that case we should speak of actions in the concrete, and determine whether such actions are desirable according to whether in their concrete circumstances they conform with the standards of supernatural conduct. Indifferent actions are like soft clay which may be shaped alike into something beautiful or something monstrous.

Suppose a mother sees a bottle labeled poison near the spot where her child is playing. "Is there poison in that bottle," she asks? The person addressed will not satisfy the mother by saying, "Yes. But *in the bottle* that poison will not hurt your child." The mother knows this; what she wants to know is whether the poison will hurt the child when he gets it out of the bottle, i.e., in the actual circumstances of the case, as she watches him reach for the bottle. Or again, suppose a man tells the mother that a gun hanging on the wall will not hurt her child, being on the wall. She knows this. What she wants to know is whether the gun will hurt the child if he takes it from the wall, as she sees he is trying to do. If you ask someone, therefore, whether an action is good or bad, your adviser does not solve your problem by saying that in itself the action is indifferent.

What you need to know, and what you ought to know to determine your manner of conduct, is whether in the concrete, that is when you actually perform the action, it will be good or bad *for you.* Therefore, in the concrete, every action—dancing, swimming, talking, walking—is either good or bad; and in the case of indifferent actions, this goodness or badness for us is determined decisively by the intention (there are other relevant circumstances, but these are less important in determining the morality of actions). Finally as we have already noticed, a merely good natural intention is not sufficient; with such an intention, the action may still remain on the natural plane. What we want is a supernatural intention; at least this is the only safe procedure, as it is also the most meritorious and the most loving, the most fully Christian.

Let us think upon these things. And may God bless you.

"O God, Whose only-begotten Son has appeared in the substance of our flesh, grant we beseech Thee, that we may be inwardly renewed by Him Whom we recognize to have been outwardly like ourselves. Who with Thee liveth and reigneth in union with the Holy Spirit, God world without end. Amen."

(Collect, Octave of Ephipany)

THE FRUIT OF THE PAGAN MENTALITY

Making Light of Imperfect Actions

My dear Friends in Christ —

A wife is ordinarily not jealous, at any rate reasonably jealous, when her husband gives some small fraction of his affections to such pleasures as smoking or taking a glass of beer. Therefore, it may seem hard to believe that God is jealous of small attachments to creatures and desires that we should mortify them. But let us suppose that a man becomes so fond of smoking, drinking, golf, and good fellowship that he practically lives at his club, although making an occasional short visit to his wife and scrupulously providing for her support; then her jealousy would be reasonable indeed, despite the fact that her husband is not guilty of formal infidelity.

Similarly, God would not condemn us for a small attachment or for a few natural motives. But, as observed before, we must in fact deal, not with single actions, but rather with the mentality which is the principle and source of a whole series, a really endless series, of actions. And if a man's love of the world is so great that he spends all his time in its joys and pleasures, only stopping occasionally to make a formal bow to God, as it were, by some external act of religion, then God is justly displeased. It is the habit of acting from natural intentions, the fixed natural mentality, that causes the harm.

Yet natural motives even when considered in themselves, although but imperfections, are not to be considered as being wholly without spiritual importance. St. Francis de Sales illustrates this fact by an example from the Old Testament.

Jacob so loved Rachel that he worked for Laban fourteen years to obtain her hand in marriage. One day, Rachel wanted some mandrakes that had been gathered by Lia, her sister, who was also married to Jacob, but not loved by him. Lia refused, complaining that Rachel had stolen the affection of her husband already, and was now adding insult to injury; whereupon Rachel, little valuing Jacob's great love and sacrifice for her, promised Lia the favor of Jacob's love in return for the mandrakes. St. Francis de Sales tells us that the great St. Augustine once observed some mandrakes to see why it was that Rachel coveted them. He found that they are pleasing to the sight, and have a delightful smell; hence surgeons formerly used them to intoxicate those on whom they wished to make an incision. But he also learned that they are altogether insipid to the taste, being without any flavor. For this reason, says St. Francis, they well represent worldly pleasures. These pleasures, he says, "have an attractive outside, but he who bites this apple, that is, he who sounds their nature, finds neither taste nor contentment in them; nevertheless they enchant us and put us to sleep by the vanity of their smell . . . And it is for such mandrakes, chimeras and phantoms of content, that we cast off the love of the heavenly Beloved; and how then can we say that we love Him above all things, since we prefer such empty vanities before His grace?"

Jesus has purchased our love by His own life; every time we indulge in worldly things, we are, like Rachel, casting aside this priceless love and its divine consolations for the worthless pleasure of a few paltry mandrakes. Looking at the matter in this light, surely we can see why it is that we displease God even by imperfections.

After James marries Mary, he could scarcely be accused of adultery for every flirtatious glance at another girl; and yet every such glance or word marks an infidelity to the entire love that he has pledged to his spouse; and a true lover and faithful husband would not allow himself such liberty. So every action prompted by the love of God's rival, the world, is an act of infidelity, however minute, which a true lover of God will avoid.

Thus it is that actions which proceed from natural motives, because they issue from an affection for creatures, are imperfections in a Christian. They are not morally evil, yet they mark a failure of love, a neglect, a small infidelity. They are opposed not to moral law but to the perfection of the law of total love; and we should all be striving to reach this perfection, each acting according to the degree of grace and charity that is given him.

The pagan mentality is prone to belittle such imperfections; it makes light of concern shown about natural motives. Its belief is that, even allowing that natural attachments and motives are imperfections, they are so trivial and contemptible that it is a waste of time and energy to bother about them. Its judgment is that we should save our strength for greater dangers, pointing out mortal sin as an evil alone worthy of serious opposition. It concludes, too, that we are likely to become scrupulous and small-minded as a result of preoccupation with motives. And it ends simply by deriding the whole procedure of attending to the motives of our actions.

Those who thus argue by the maxims of the pagan mentality would find difficulty in showing Scriptural or theological proof for such statements. The Scriptures tell us, *"He that contemneth small things, shall fall by little and little."* (Ecclus. 19, 1) And again the same high authority warns, *"He that is faithful in a very little thing is faithful also in much; and he who is unjust in a very little thing is unjust in much."* (Ecclus.,16, 10) Jesus Himself tells us that he who disobeys Him in the least of His commandments shall be called least in the kingdom of heaven. Thus it is important to attend to small things, allowing that they are small, lest they grow into real evils. An old adage tells us to withstand beginnings. Another warns us that an ounce of prevention is worth a pound of cure. These truisms hold also for the spiritual life. Here likewise must we withstand beginnings; here likewise through conquest of small faults should we destroy beforehand the roots of the greater ones.

The Effects of Imperfect Actions

In order to impress deeply upon our minds the practical importance of imperfect actions, let us consider their effects in the soul. Seven such effects may be enumerated.

(A) First, they are an affront to God. Suppose a child brings an apple to his teacher, and the teacher, upon beginning to eat it, discovers that the apple is filled with worms. She asks the boy if he knew this, and he replies, "Yes I did, but I thought that you could eat around the worm holes." When we present imperfect actions to God, we are doing as this boy does; we are offering God actions which we know contain some corruption, but we are doing so in the expectation that He will extract from them whatever good He can find. Or take the case of school boys or girls who, although highly talented, only partly use these talents, being careless and negligent. The teacher cannot fail such children as long as they make passing grades in their work; yet she will be distressed by the refusal of these pupils to utilize their talents. So also, although a soul may not deserve damnation by its carelessness, it does not please its Creator and heavenly Father by negligence in fulfilling the primary duty of love.

(B) The second effect of imperfect actions is that they cause undernourishment in the soul. Imagine a man who confines himself in the matter of food to eating biscuits, and, in a spirit of economy, bakes the biscuits half saw-dust and half flour; he is eating, he may protest, but he will certainly suffer undernourishment. In the same way, a soul that performs imperfect actions habitually suffers from spiritual undernourishment. If there is some love in its actions, it will merit a little grace, but not as much as God intends for it or as much as it needs for its full spiritual growth. Consequently, although it may remain, at least for some time, in the state of grace, it is half-starved and lacking in vitality, as is the case with those who suffer from bodily undernourishment or starvation.

(C) Third—and this follows immediately from the second effect—imperfect actions weaken the soul; for weakness and infirmity are the consequence of undernourishment. A diet that lacks nutritive value does not restore the used-up strength of the body, in fact it undermines this strength, hence leaves the body open and vulnerable to attack by disease germs. In a similar way, a weakened soul—a soul in which passion and appetite have become disordered through habitual imperfections—is an easy victim for temptation.

(D) Fourth, imperfect actions lessen the ardor of charity. Suppose that there are before us two containers of water; the water in the one is a hundred degrees in temperature, while that in the other is but ten degrees. Now let us put the lukewarm water little by little, a thimble-full at a time, into the hot water.

What will happen? Slowly but surely the water of one hundred degrees will lose its heat and be reduced to the temperature of the lukewarm water. It is the same with the soul and charity. Although charity may be very great in the soul, say, after the reception of the sacraments, imperfect acts cool its fervor, and if this process continues long enough, it is most likely that the soul will lose fervor altogether.

(E) Fifth, imperfect actions weaken the influence of charity, or, to put it differently, they lessen its radiation and keep it so bound up that it cannot exercise its divine influence in our lives. Let us imagine an old-fashioned carriage going along a dirt road in a driving rain. The mud splashes up and little by little dims the light of the lanterns. The same thing happens with headlights even on paved roads. The light is there; it does not go out, but the slow accumulation of dirt prevents it from shedding its full illumination. So also in an imperfect soul. Grace and charity are there—all the imperfections that can be imagined will not of themselves destroy charity—but this charity remains in the substance of the soul, so to speak, and does not manifest any influence on the ordinary daily actions; these latter are rather performed under a natural impulse, that is, from a motive derived from the love of creatures.

You will recall how Gulliver, in the tale by Jonathan Swift, fell asleep while he was in the land of Lilliput and, when he wakened, found himself bound by innumerable small cords, so that he could not move. Gulliver was a giant in comparison to the Lilliputians; they were no bigger than a man's finger and their stoutest cords were but as threads. Still, there were so many of these cords, and they were so finely drawn, that Gulliver could not move. So also when charity slumbers, imperfect actions bind the soul; and although they are but small, there are so many of them in an imperfect soul, or one having a natural mentality, and they so closely bind its powers, that even with the gigantic powers given to it by charity it is checked and hindered on every side.

(F) Sixth, imperfect actions dispose the soul to sin. We know already that sin comes from the love of creatures, that it is a turning from God and a turning towards creatures. And the first inclination of such turning occurs in imperfections, which are actions performed from love of creatures. Accordingly, a soul that commits imperfections, although it does not at once fall into sin—let us suppose that it does not fall even into venial sin, although this is a large assumption—is retrogressing, is yielding to the inclinations of the flesh, and will certainly become involved in the dark and downward law of the flesh.

Imagine two small skiffs on a swift stream. Both are going downstream, but the one oarsmen is rowing with all his might, while the other is not rowing at all. The one who rows certainly moves faster than the one who rests on his oars; yet the latter is pushed steadily downstream. In the same way, a sinner is moving faster towards ruin, pushed not only by the ordinary current of passion but speeded also by his own deliberate efforts. As for the man who commits imperfections, while he is not carried downward by the deliberate and vigorous efforts that characterize the sinner, still he is drifting in the same direction, although not so swiftly. In allowing himself to be led by natural inclinations, he is opening himself to the influence of concupiscence, and he will ultimately end in ruin also unless he resists.

Accordingly, there is an axiom in the spiritual life which runs: "Imperfections predispose to venial sins, and venial sins predispose to mortal sins." Just as disease grows until it finally destroys health, so also does the love of creatures grow until it causes men to commit serious sin. This does not mean that imperfections will grow into venial sins, nor that venial sins in turn will grow into mortal sins; no number of imperfections will ever equal one venial sin, and no accumulation of venial sins will ever reach the stature of one mortal sin. But imperfections loosen in the soul that force—the affection for creatures—which, if left unchecked, will cause, first venial sins, and then go on to produce mortal sins. Although these three classes of disorder— imperfections, venial sins, and mortal sins—are essentially different from one another, nevertheless they have the same common cause, namely, the turning towards creatures.

A doctor does not wait until his patient is dead, or at the point of death before applying a remedy. He wishes to catch disease as early in its career as possible, before it has become serious; and his chances of curing the disease are in proportion to his good fortune in discovering it at any early stage. So also the earlier we discover the factors that make for sin, the more successful we will be in avoiding sin. If we wait until we are at the verge of sin, or, worse yet, until we have fallen into it, like a man who discovers that he has cancer only when it has reached a fatal stage, we may not be ready for the effort of restraint, detachment, and mortification that will be necessary to overcome it. Thus, our spiritual efforts must be directed, in the first place, against the slightest imperfections. We must not wait for sin to appear before we get out our spiritual armory. The *logical* procedure, it might seem, would be first to remove mortal sin from our lives, and when we have succeeded in this, to work on venial sins, and then only afterwards to think of removing imperfections. When there are great faults in us, it seems almost presumptuous to pass them by and to work on tiny imperfections. Nevertheless, we know now from all that we have considered, we must not follow the logical procedure here. We must rather observe the *psychological* procedure, or the medical procedure, the way of true spiritual healing, which tells us to withstand beginnings. We should *begin* by struggling against imperfections.

This is the law of spiritual growth in reverse; in other words it is the law of spiritual retrogression. It is related to that other law, which says that there is no standing still spiritually—either we progress or we retrogress. And the moment we stop progress, we begin to retrogress.

(G) Seventh, natural motives, since they dispose the soul to sin, also imperil our salvation. We do not say that of themselves they will cause us to be lost, but they do place us in danger. If you were to ask, "Will the imperfect soul, one whose motives are habitually natural, be damned?" we cannot give an answer in terms of yes or no. But we can attempt a general answer by means of an example.

Suppose that there is a leaky boat out in the middle of a lake. Will the passengers in the boat lose their lives? We cannot say certainly; it depends on two things: on how large the leak is and therefore on how fast the water is coming in; and secondly, on how far the boat is from shore. Similarly whether an imperfect soul will be saved or lost, we may answer that this depends, first, on how fast the love of creatures is pouring into the soul through these imperfections, and, secondly how far this soul is from shore, that is from eternity. If the imperfection is small, or is somewhat counteracted by mortification, and the soul is close to eternity, then perhaps it will be safe. But if the imperfection is great, and the love of creatures is coming into the soul very rapidly, and the soul lives a long life on this earth, without mending the leaks, then its danger is very great indeed.

St. Paul, in an illuminating passage in his letter to the Romans, explains how sin occurs when he says that men are first caught in what he calls *"the law of the members"* and are thereby captivated in *"the law of sin."* The law of the members is nothing but the tendency of our natural faculties to seek their own gratification. As the eye delights in seeing and the ear in hearing, so also the mind and will, our higher spiritual faculties, take pleasure in their objects, the true and the good. And if these tendencies are not regulated and restrained, if they are not made to serve the life of grace, but are carried away by their own enjoyments, they will lead us away from God and into evil. Thus by the law of the members we are captivated in the law of sin.

Clearly, then, our spiritual struggle is in the first place against the law of the members, against the desire for pleasure and satisfaction. Too often we fight only against sin; and if we do this, we are starting too late, are giving the seeds of evil an opportunity to germinate, the forces from which sin proceeds to gather momentum. We must rather eliminate the principle of sin. This means that our spiritual efforts must oppose the desires for sense gratification. The proper sphere of spiritual struggle, the battleground of the soul that desires to please God, is not immediately against sin—when sin occurs the battle has been lost. It is rather in that twilight region, neither wholly dark nor wholly light, of natural pleasures and sensible satisfactions. Here it is that we must gird ourselves for battle and chastise our bodies lest we become entangled in the dark laws of spiritual decadence and become castaways.

The State of Tepidity—the Result of Habitual Imperfect Actions

A soul in which imperfection is habitual is a tepid or lukewarm soul. Spiritual books are full of warnings against tepidity. St. Alphonsus, for example, considers tepidity to be in a way more dangerous than that of sin. Sinful souls are more likely to know their own state, to recognize their need for repentance and reform. Lukewarm souls, on the other hand, are complacent, not realizing their danger. They believe that all is well with them since they are conscious of no grave sin and are presumably in God's grace. Yet they are in a disposition that easily leads to sin. Moreover, when they do sin, repentance will be the harder for them. For, since the hidden forces of spiritual decay have been long at work in their souls, the final effect of these forces will be harder to remove in their case than in those who commit sin unexpectedly, as it were, suddenly overcome by some great temptation; the latter, not being so enslaved by the love of creatures, will be the better able to renounce at least the sinful use of creatures and so reverse their direction. Lukewarm souls are like a man who thinks himself in good health whereas in fact the germ of some dread disease is already secretly at work in him; or they are like a man who sits comfortably in his home unaware that its foundations are rotting away and that the whole structure will soon collapse.

The Scriptures themselves have a solemn and terrible word of warning for the lukewarm: In the Apocalypse we read that our Lord, appearing to St. John in a vision, speaks thus to the Church of Laodicea: *"Thus says the Amen, the faithful and true witness, who is the beginning of the creation of God: I know thy works; thou are neither cold nor hot. I would that thou wert cold or hot. But because Thou are lukewarm, and neither cold nor hot, I am about to vomit thee out of my mouth."* (Apoc. 3,15-16)

Notice first how this text corroborates the teaching—or rather, how it teaches in the first place—that lukewarm souls are in a less desirable state in regard to salvation than sinners. God prefers not only the fervent to the tepid; He prefers even the cold, who at least are resolute and whole-hearted in their service of the earthly good that they idolize. What a fearful condemnation, this, of the lukewarm!

St. Alphonsus, commenting on this text, says that we can take food or drink that is hot or cold, but lukewarm food causes revulsion. So lukewarm souls are revolting to God and are "vomited forth by Him." This is surely a strong and startling expression; anywhere but in the Scriptures it would be offensive and its propriety likely to be challenged. In the Scriptures, which do not fear strong language, it clearly manifests the displeasure of God with lukewarm souls. St. Alphonsus adds that when we have vomited anything out, we are repelled at the thought of taking it back. So also, when God has vomited out a lukewarm soul, as He expressly says He will, there is little likelihood that He will take it back because of the improbability of such a soul being disposed to change or repent. We are reminded here of St. Bernard's saying that it is easier to convert a hundred seculars than one careless religious. The tepid are not easy to convert. *"But because thou art lukewarm, and neither cold nor hot, I am about to vomit thee out of my mouth."*

Let us think upon these things. And may God bless you.

"Guard Thy Church, we implore Thee, O Lord, with Thy perpetual mercy and, since without Thee our human weakness is ever ready to fall, by Thy help always keep it from all things harmful and lead it to all things helpful to our salvation. Through Our Lord Jesus Christ Thy Son Who liveth and reigneth with Thee in union with the Holy Spirit, God world without end. Amen."

(Collect, Fourteenth Sunday after Pentecost)

THE CHRISTIAN MENTALITY

My dear Friends in Christ —

It is time for us to define more exactly and describe more fully the notion of the Christian mentality. Already we have analyzed the notion of mentality, which, we now know, is a complexion of mind, an attitude of mind and will which becomes characteristic, and, as it were, second nature to each individual. We have learned that in forming a mentality both the mind and the will play their part: the mind by pointing out to the will that which is good, and the will by loving the good thus known; the mind also by supplying conviction and principle, the will by translating these into action and developing habits which give these principles a fixed character. Both convictions and habits tend to give the mentality a permanent character; so that once a mentality is formed and sealed, it is difficult to effect any change. What we as Christians wish to do therefore is to form a supernatural bent of mind and action, so that the habits and acts proper to the Christian life will become as spontaneous to us, as natural, as it were, as almost mechanical, and as difficult to break, as are the habits of self-indulgence and natural living fostered by the pagan mentality. We wish to learn the habits of Christian thought and action as an immigrant learns English. And if there will always remain a trace of accent in the immigrant's English, even after he is naturalized, as there will always remain in us, alas, the imperfections of the natural man, nevertheless as the immigrant may with care gain great fluency in our speech, so we also, super-naturalized citizens in God's kingdom, may gain fluency in the language of this kingdom and ease in its customs, saying with St. Paul, *"Our conversation—or our citizenship,* as the new translation has it—*is in heaven."* (Phil. 3, 20)

As the pagan mentality bases itself on naturalistic axioms of thought and action, so the Christian mentality bases itself on

Christian principles. Your purpose as a Christian, from this point of view, is to be *"renewed in the spirit of your mind,"* a renewal which is described by the same Apostle in the words having *"the mind of Christ."* We wish by meditation on the life and teachings of Jesus so to fill ourselves with His principles of thought that we will readily love the divine good that He reveals to us and spontaneously conform our actions to the norm that it sets. In speaking on this subject we will first consider the nature of the Christian mentality, taking up separately of the work done by the mind and that of the will. Secondly, we will explain how to form the Christian mentality.

The Axioms of the Christian Mentality

Perhaps there is no better way to summarize and set down with authority the basic principles or axioms of the Christian mentality than to quote those given by John of the Cross in his first book of *The Ascent of Mount Carmel.* To beginners who wish to advance in perfection he gives three rules; and we will take these three rules as a guide to forming the mind of Christ.

"First, let him have an habitual desire to imitate Christ in everything that he does, conforming himself to His life; upon which life he must meditate so that he may know how to imitate it, and to behave in all things as Christ would behave."

Since we are sons of God, we must act as sons of God; and there is no better way to do this than to imitate the only Son of God, Jesus Christ. His life and teaching should be our constant meditation, and our efforts should be to have His Spirit and influence permeate our entire lives and practice.

"Secondly, in order that he may be able to do this well, every pleasure that presents itself to the senses, if it is not *purely* for the honor and glory of God, must be renounced and completely rejected for the love of Jesus Christ, Who in this life had no other pleasure, neither desired such, than to do the will of His Father, which He called His meat and food. I take this example. If there present itself to a man the pleasure of listening to things that tend not to the service and honor of God, let him not desire that pleasure, neither let him desire to hear them; and if there present itself the pleasure of looking at things that help him not God-wards, let him not desire the pleasure or look at these things; and if in conversation or in aught else so ever it present itself, let him do the same. And similarly, in regard to all the senses, insofar as he can fairly avoid the pleasure in question; if he cannot, it suffices that although these things may be present to his senses, he desire not to have this pleasure. And in this wise he will be able to mortify and void his senses of such pleasure, and leave them, as it were, in darkness, and having this care he will soon profit greatly."

We have noticed in dealing with the pagan mentality, that its basic practical error concerns the use of creatures. It would have us to use creatures for pleasure, and it makes the search for pleasure its ordinary practice, while any specious principle that condones self-indulgence is pressed into its service. In opposition to this false use of creatures, St. John here gives us the true Christian rule of conduct for their use. We are never to use them merely for our own pleasure; we are to use them for the honor and glory of God, and purely for the honor and glory of God. Every pleasure which does not contribute towards this end is to be renounced.

"Thirdly, strive always to choose, not that which is easiest, but that which is most difficult; not that which is most delectable, but that which is most unpleasing; not that which gives most pleasure, but rather that which gives least; not that which is restful, but that which is disconsolate; not that which is greatest, but that which is lowest and most despised; not that which is a desire for anything, but that which is a desire for nothing. Strive not to go about seeking the best of temporal things, but the worst. Strive thus to desire to enter into complete detachment and emptiness and poverty, with respect to that which is in the world, for Christ's sake."

These last counsels may be even more briefly summarized in the spiritual maxim, *agere contra,* go against yourselves, that is against your natural inclinations. It is clear from these counsels that Christianity is not to be reduced to a mere avoidance of sin but is rather a renunciation of natural good: not super-sinful but in truth supernatural.

Further illustrations of the Christian mentality, and its difference from mere natural thinking, may be found in the sharp contrast which Jesus, in the Sermon on the Mount, draws between the Old Testament, which had been largely content with sanctioning the laws of nature, and the Gospel that He had come to give mankind. For example, *"You have heard that it was said to the ancients, 'Thou shalt not kill'....But I say to you"*—and in each case this *"but I say to you"* marks the contrast—*"But I say to you....If thou art offering thy gift at the altar, and there rememberest that thy brother has anything against thee, leave thy gift before the altar and go first to be reconciled to thy brother, and then come and offer thy gift."*

Another contrast: *"You have heard that it was said to the ancients, 'Thou shalt not commit adultery.' But I say to you that anyone who even looks with lust at a woman has already committed adultery with her in his heart."* (Matt 5, 27) Thus Jesus requires complete interior purity in addition to correctness of conduct.

Again: *"You have heard that it was said, 'An eye for an eye and a tooth for a tooth.' But I say to you not to resist the evildoer; on the contrary, if someone strike thee on the right cheek, turn to him the other also...."* (Matt. 5, 38-39)

A final example: *"You have heard that it was said, 'Thou shalt love thy neighbor, and shalt hate thy enemy.' But I say to you, love your enemies, do good to those who hate you, and pray for those who persecute and calumniate you, so that you may be children of your Father in heaven...."* (Matt. 5, 43-45)

To be sure, Jesus said that He came to fulfill the law and not to destroy it—a remark that certainly includes the law of nature as well as that of the Old Testament. Still, Jesus desires us to live divine lives, and divine lives, although perfecting nature, are also a mortification to nature, being a definite break from merely natural modes of conduct. And the break is all the more pronounced since the human spirit, then as now, has surrounded the ancient law with faulty human interpretations and corrupt customs.

The Part of the Will

The Christian, once his convictions are established, then begins, by means of his will, like a builder carrying out plans carefully drawn up on a blueprint, to dispose his activity in accordance with these convictions, that is, to translate them into action. He desires to live always on the supernatural plane and to direct all his actions to his supernatural end, and he does so by means of a supernatural motive, by which he aims his actions, so to speak, as an archer aims his arrows before shooting them. It is by means of love, you know, that we are aligned with our supernatural end and united with it, while it is by means of the supernatural motive that love becomes really active and influential in our lives; the supernatural motive aims each action as it occurs to the end of divine love. Through the firm convictions and sound principles formed by the mind, the will is pressed, in correspondence with grace, to undertake the work of loving God and disentangling its affections from creatures, a work arduous to nature because high above nature.

And yet, despite the difficulty involved in this super-human and divine endeavor, we have in our favor here a circumstance that in the pagan mentality, we saw, is against us. While the *attention* of the mind naturally shifts from subject to subject, just as the eye follows the successive pictures on a strip of film, so the *intention* of the will—for it is the will that forms intentions— tends of itself to persist until it is retracted. Thus once we form a supernatural intention it tends to remain, and it will therefore be easy to renew it and keep it fervent: We do not forget here what was said before about the weakness of our nature and the mischievous alertness of our natural desires and affections to intrude themselves into our actions, thus reducing the fervor of our supernatural motives. It is because of such infirmity and imperfection that we must frequently renew and purify and intensify these supernatural motives. In other words, the tendency of the supernatural intention to persist will be less strong than the natural intention; or at any rate, there are more obstacles for the supernatural intention to overcome, more opportunities for it to lose force and intensity, because here it is always working above and against nature.

As a series of points when connected becomes a line, so our motives, when we have framed the habit of directing them to God, will lengthen out into a continuous act of love, a constant living in His glorious presence, an unbroken conformity every day to His holy will. This is the purpose, indeed, of forming supernatural motives; and this is what is meant by living in the presence of God, of practicing entire conformity to the will of God. When we live like this, as a result of practice and of keeping our souls open to the influence of grace, it will be easy and not burdensome, a joy rather than a mortification, to refer all that we do to God.

Here we may profitably remember an example already given. The difference between laboriously repeating motives and making the supernatural motives a continuous act of love is like the difference between getting light by striking matches one after another and lighting a candle, which would give a continuous flame. When we begin to cultivate the habit of purifying and supernaturalizing our intentions, making and renewing our intention at the beginning of each act, we are like one who tries to read by lighting matches. It is somewhat clumsy and difficult, not quite satisfactory; but after a while, if we persevere, we will become like one who lights a candle to read: our motives will extend out horizontally into a beam of love to illuminate whatever we do all our days.

Remember, we get our motives from what we love; supernatural motives are little steps of love, each one bringing us a little closer to God, each one, if we persevere, being part of a journey God-wards, a journey that becomes ever more joyous as we proceed and in which also our progress, the further we proceed, becomes ever more rapid, until at the end, like a child who, after a long absence from home darts into the arms of its parents, we will cast ourselves eagerly in the close and unbroken embrace of our heavenly Father.

Lovers live in a kind of a trance, scarcely able to think of anything except their beloved. We, too, once the love of God has taken possession of our souls, will no longer have to be satisfied with labored and occasional glances at God. We will also live in a sort of trance—not a sensible trance perhaps, but in a deeply satisfying experience of God's interior presence, a presence urgently demanding that all our deeds be consecrated to Him, but abundantly repaying such joyous trouble by an unshakable inward peace and a secret source of refreshment amid all the duties and difficulties of our earthly pilgrimage.

When we come thus, through supernatural motives, to the practice of continual union with God and conformity to His will, we are likewise fulfilling in the most perfect way the duty of imitating Christ which the Gospel enjoins upon us and St. John of the Cross has put down as the first rule for forming the Christian mentality. For Jesus, St. Paul tells us, *"did not please himself"*—no, did not seek to gratify the inclinations even of His immaculate humanity—but rather surrendered His human will to the divine will. Accordingly, St. Paul aptly summarized the whole career and culminating sacrifice of Jesus by the words of the Psalmist, *"Lo, I come to do thy will, O God."* And Jesus Himself communicates to us the basic rule of His life and the deepest secret of His spirituality when He says, *"For I have come down from, heaven, not to do my own will, but the will of Him who sent me."* (John 6, 38) And again, *"I do always the things that are pleasing to Him."* (John 8, 29)

How to Form a Christian Mentality

God presents himself to our minds as knowledge, the science of the supernatural, for the mind grasps things to be known. That is to say, it grasps the truth of things. Thus the aspect of God seen by the mind is His truth. This is what is meant by theology: God as regarded by the mind. Now theology has two parts: it looks at divine things in themselves, abstractly or theoretically, much as scientists isolate various substances and observe them in test-tubes, in order to obtain explanations; and this is the theoretical or speculative part of theology. But theology is also practical: like such sciences as hygiene or engineering, it not only knows truth but goes on to apply it; and this is practical or spiritual theology, which is our chief concern. Practical theology may aptly be compared to hygiene or medicine because, just as these sciences take theoretical knowledge and apply it to curing disease and promoting health, so also practical theology takes all that we know from divine revelation and theological study and applies it to remedying the defects of our soul and effecting spiritual health, which is holiness.

Perhaps the practical science of architecture is a still better parallel to the work of our minds in making a practical approach to God. The Scripture makes much of it. St. Paul tells us that we are temples of God, and that the Spirit of God dwells in us. Thus the work of the spiritual life is like the work of a builder: we are engaged to build temples fit to become dwelling places of the Holy Spirit. As Christians of every age have brought together the most skilled workmen, the most precious materials, and the most beautiful works of genius in order to build and adorn churches, and make them worthy repositories for our Eucharistic King, so ought we to adorn our souls with every virtue and to cooperate with grace in all the wonderful transformations it can effect in us, that we may become truly beautiful temples into which the Holy Spirit will delight to come.

St. Paul further tells us that to build such a temple, each must work *"according to the grace of God that has been given him as a wise builder."* (I Cor. 3, 10) The following are the steps which, as wise architects, we will take to build splendid temples for the Holy Ghost.

Clearly the first thing that the architect must do is to make his decision to build, otherwise nothing will be done at all. We in turn must first decide to build, at the same time deciding also what we are going to build. It will make a great difference in subsequent practical procedure whether the architect intends to put up a hospital, a church, or a dwelling. So also we must, at the start, decide what we want to build; we must from the very beginning have a picture in our minds of the finished edifice; we must form our purpose at once and direct all subsequent work to meet this purpose. Now a temple is a holy place, and holiness is the fit preparation which we should make if we wish to have the Holy Ghost dwell within us. We should thus decide to build a temple of holiness or of perfection.

Mark: from the very first we must deliberately set out to achieve perfection. Many make a mistake here. They think that the first thing to do is to get clear of gross sin, then they can think about ridding themselves of venial sin, and only at the last set their thoughts on perfection. This is like deciding where we are going only when we finish a trip; or like deciding what sort of a building we want only after the building is finished; and a structure completed as a dwelling-place would probably not make a very good church or hospital. No, at once, from the beginning, we must have the goal of perfection in our minds; that should be the purpose, the directive idea that will determine all else that we do. Jesus has told us to be perfect as the heavenly Father is perfect, and we must courageously set ourselves to this gigantic task from the very start.

An axiom of the ancients, which explains this procedure, says that what is last in the order of execution or action is first in the order of intention, or, vice versa, what is first in the order of intention is last in the order of execution. If a sculptor is working on stone, the last thing that appears—that is, in the order of execution—is the finished product. But this finished product was the first thing in the sculptor's mind, that is, in the order of intention, since he did not begin work until he had a mental picture of what he wished to make, and had formed an intention of making it. Throughout the time of his carving, while the stone was still a crude and shapeless mass, unrecognizable to anyone else, there was in the mind of the artist a picture of the complete statue, and he was shaping the stone in reference to this mental picture.

Again, the last thing you see when you take a trip is your destination, but you had it in your mind all along; in fact, it was the first thing in your mind, having been decided upon before you undertook the journey. Likewise, the last thing on a building is the roof; but it is the first thing in the architect's mind, because it is by means of the roof that the purpose of the building, to provide shelter, is finally accomplished. In the spiritual life also, although perfection is the last thing that we shall attain in the order of action or execution, it is the first thing that we must aim at in the order of intention; it is the purpose and directive idea that should shape all subsequent work.

Having decided to build, and determined also what we are going to build, we next prepare our plans. That is one of the things that we are doing in these conferences—studying how we can build from the materials of our daily lives a work that is perfect in the sense of being holy.

We should supplement this work by daily meditation and by spiritual reading. Just as architects must spend long years in study, and then will travel all over the world to observe the great buildings put up by other architects, so ought we to learn the rules and the laws of the spiritual life, which is the science of sciences and the art of arts, and also study the great living works of this highest Christian art, namely, the lives of the saints.

This means that to live a supernatural life we must face the fact that daily meditation and frequent spiritual reading are a real necessity. Through these exercises we fill our minds with the knowledge of divine things and learn the rules and practice of the supreme art of living Christian lives.

The next step is to dig out the sand of natural motives and natural affections for creatures, in order to set the foundation of our building on a rock. Jesus, in the Sermon on the Mount, has explained to us what this sand is, and what the rock is on which we must build. The rock, we have seen, is the doctrine of supernatural living.

After we have set our supernatural foundations, we can begin with the superstructure. This is made up of all our daily actions. Our great care in the matter of building the superstructure should be to see that we use only first-class materials. If an architect, running short of stone or steel beams, would substitute planks for them here and there, his building would be very unstable and would sooner or later collapse. Accordingly, all materials of our building—our daily actions— must be of an even quality, and that the very best. In a word, every action is to be supernatural, and purely supernatural. We must therefore strive to eliminate from our actions those natural motives which make them imperfect and insufficient. These natural actions, if we put them in our building, are like straw and old rotten planks, while what we need is steel and stone.

The final step is this: in order to perfect and finish our temple, we must keep everything plumb, just as the builder does by setting every piece of material against a plumb line or level. If the builder does not do this, then his building will be both insecure and unbeautiful. Now the plumb line in the supernatural world is the ideal of perfection with which we started. We must try to make each action perfect. And we should do this, first, by doing the action well. It should be our rule not to do slovenly work for God. Sometimes men are most careful of what they do for worldly employers, but very negligent indeed in serving the Lord, as if He did not mind. But we know that He does mind; He asks perfection and requires total love. We ought therefore to use just as much care in what concerns Him as industrious men do for earthly ends—or rather, since we are laboring for a higher good, we ought to use much more care in His service. Secondly, we must try to do every action purely out of love or for some other supernatural intention that ends finally in a more perfect love of God.

Now this minute care we exercise in every action may seem like a great burden to some. But it is really not so. We must learn to do this habitually; and to do it habitually is to do it with facility and even joy. When you look at a well-built house, every door, every doorjamb, every window and every window sill, every stone—in a word, every least part of the house—is in its proper place, precisely measured and set with great care. When workmen do this for us, we do not think that they are doing anything extraordinary; we do not decorate them or give them special honors. We take it as a matter of course; it is part of their work to do this, and we expect of them the skill that is necessary for doing it. So, in working for the Lord, we must likewise learn to work rapidly and well, in virtue of habitual dispositions and practice—and not be stopping constantly to pity ourselves because we have such an exacting Lord. He is exacting, but only in the way that any true father, anxious about the training of his children, may be called exacting, and it is, in any case, for our benefit that He is strict; the success of our undertaking will not make Him happier or richer, but it will make us happier and richer. We are building a house for Him, but He really does not need our house; we are the ones who will benefit by it.

How God Presents Himself to Our Wills

God also presents Himself to our wills. Our wills are the faculties whose chief and highest act is to love. And therefore, as God presents Himself to our minds as something to be known, He presents Himself to our wills as something to be loved. When our minds are filled with the knowledge of divine things, our wills reach out spontaneously to love the divine good. We may distinguish four ways in which God presents Himself to our wills.

First, God presents Himself to our wills as their final end. God is the supreme good towards which everything in our lives should be directed. This means that for the present we should refer all our actions to Him, and in the future, when our lives here on earth are finished, we will be united with Him. And as we are working towards union with Him in the end, so ought we now, in our daily lives, be referring our deeds to Him as to their final goal. Since death changes nothing, we must begin to live this life of union in the present, in order that, when death finds us, the union having already begun may be consummated. Charity, or love, St. Paul says, is *"the bond of perfection."* (Col. 3,15) It is rightly called a bond because it unites us to God, our highest good and final end; and thereby it also perfects us by carrying us to the fulfillment of our destiny.

Second, God presents Himself to our wills in the first commandment. In giving us the commandment to love Him, God gives us the means of being united to Him already in this world. Love is union, and obedience to the commandment to love at once unites us to God. Thus St. John says, *"God is charity; and he that abideth in charity, abideth in God, and God in him."* (1 John, 4, 16) St. Gregory tells us, together with other spiritual writers, that he who loves God with his whole mind already possesses God. Indeed, Jesus Himself assures us of this: *"If anyone love me, he will keep my word, and my Father will love him, and we will come to him and make our abode with him."* (John 14, 23)

Third, God presents Himself to our wills as grace. We have seen that grace is a participation in the divine nature, and therefore, in giving us grace, God infuses into us a sharing in His own life. Together with this sharing in His nature, we come also to share in His powers, above all in His power to love; and the charity, or virtue of love, which we receive into our souls together with grace, is thus nothing less than a share in the divine love. God is love, and it is He Who gives us the power to return that love. In the same way the money which a child uses to buy a gift for his father was in the first place obtained from the father, but this fact does not lessen the value of the gift in the loving father's eyes.

Fourth, God is present in our souls as their indwelling Guest. We have seen how we are to build a temple, a temple in which God will reside, and this temple is in our own souls. St. Paul himself assures us that we are temples of the Holy Spirit, and we can have the confidence given to us by our faith that the Holy Ghost comes as a living Presence to dwell with us if we keep the divine commandments. Therefore, we ought to turn our minds and hearts away from useless and trivial things, attending rather to this Guest within our souls. How flattered and happy we are when some distinguished personage condescends to visit us in our homes, how anxious we are to leave nothing wanting in our hospitality! How much more ought we to exercise hospitality when the great God Himself comes into our souls!

It is hard to imagine that anyone would be so discourteous even to an ordinary visitor as to leave him shift for himself while the host goes off to the kitchen to play with the cat or the canary. Yet we do this when we become absorbed in secular interests to the neglect of the Divine Person Who dwells within us. Even if a housewife were forced to leave a guest to prepare dinner, she would nevertheless be back and forth from the kitchen to speak to him or render him some small service. Perhaps she would come into the parlor with paring knife and pan, doing some of her work there, anxious not to miss any of his conversation; or perhaps if he is a familiar visitor, she would invite him into the kitchen to talk to her as she works.

Now it is true that we cannot spend all our days on our knees before the Blessed Sacrament nor be withdrawn from work and wholly occupied with God. Alas, we have many tiresome and insistent duties to perform. But could we not imitate the ingenuity of this housewife? Even as we work we could dart many a glance, many a quick affection of the heart, to our interior Guest. We could do all our work in His presence; and we would not even have to run from kitchen to parlor since wherever we go He is with us.

Nor can it be said that such frequent glances at the Holy Spirit, such frequent affirmations that we will do all for Him, distract us from our duty or lessen the quality or quantity of our work. These duties absorb, more or less, the attention of our mind; but they need not, and should not, absorb the affections of our heart: our affections should rather be reserved for the end, the good, for which we work. A man may do some difficult and tedious work, not because he loves it at all, but out of devotion to his wife and family; and this devotion helps, and does not hinder, the doing of his work. He may have a picture of his wife before him, glancing at it lovingly many times each day in the course of his duties. He thereby loses a few seconds for his employer. But do you think that his employer will object, or that this loss of time will injure the quality of the man's work? On the contrary, his affection for his wife, and the thought of her, will be an inspiration to accomplish well duties that may of themselves be tedious and onerous.

When a man travels he stops occasionally to refresh himself with food and drink. Strictly speaking, this is a loss of time, since, if he did not stop, he would be farther along on his journey. But is not the strength and refreshment gained by stopping worth the slight delay? Indeed, with such pauses, or the prospect of them, he might lack the energy to continue his journey or even to undertake it in the first place. So also loving attention to God and even frequent prayerful pauses, keep us at our duties, however difficult or troublesome, and makes us perform them well also, since we dare not offer inferior workmanship to Him.

A modern writer tells about a man in Paris who always walked about with his hat in his hand in honor of the Trinity dwelling within him. We need not adopt the singularity of going hat-in-hand, but we should at any rate strive to walk about recollected and aware of that loving Presence within.

Let us think upon these things. And may God bless you.

"Grant, we implore Thee, O Almighty God, according to our belief in the Ascension into heaven of Thine only begotten Son, Our Redeemer, that our minds may also dwell in heavenly places. Through the same Lord Jesus Christ Thy Son, Who liveth and reigneth with

Thee in union with the Holy Spirit, God, world without end. Amen."

(Collect, Feast of Ascension)

IMITATORS OF GOD: BE PERFECT

My dear Friends in Christ—

Imagine that a neighbor were to come running breathlessly to your home and tell you that a man in working clothes is out in the public street preaching a new doctrine—a doctrine strange, beautiful, elevated. Imagine further that, led by curiosity, you go out yourself and find that the report is true: you hear this man, dressed in rough garb but of noble mien, utter a teaching of unearthly beauty, in language itself of matchless loveliness. The speaker is no agitator, no malcontent, no revolutionary in the ordinary sense of the term; he is seeking nothing for himself. His doctrine is wholly unrealistic as worldly men judge, but it touches the deepest needs of the heart, stirs up an indescribable hope, and indeed arouses in his hearers old aspirations, old idealisms, that have long been slumbering or forgotten, buried probably under the thick crust of the cynicism or near-cynicism that living in the world is so prone to produce. As you listen, your heart melts and is carried away. He is speaking of love and peace among men; and tears start to your eyes as you think of what this life of ours on earth might be were such teaching followed. And then, as the thoughts of this strange speaker gather to a climax, your ears are amazed, your mind is stunned, as he says, quietly enough, without a trace of fanatical heat but nevertheless with burning sincerity and ardor, *"You therefore are to be perfect even as your heavenly Father Is perfect."*

What would you think of such a man and of such a doctrine? What would you think of him back in your home when the enchantment of his eloquence is no longer heard? What would you think of him days later, when you are back in the hurly-burly of daily toil and trouble, when the charm of that unearthly eloquence seems unreal, a dream, and that sublime doctrine, too, amid these dull, prosaic daily tasks, also unreal? Surely you would think that the speaker was demented—or divine: there would seem no other possibility; these are the only alternatives. And what would your friends think when you reported the experience to them? Without doubt that the speaker you describe is demented—and yourself perhaps as well!

Now this is not imagination. It happened. You yourself were not there, but some of your fellow-men were. Jesus, of course, was the speaker. A full report of the whole occurrence has come down to us. We can at least read the report and thus relive the experience. And it is scarcely any wonder that the contemporaries of Jesus asked, *"What strange doctrine is this?"* And others said that He was beside Himself; and the Pharisees, that He had a devil. For all recognized that His was no ordinary speech, no human doctrine; and they could not grasp, or would not, that this was the Son of God.

The Meaning of the Doctrine

In several previous conferences there was occasion to quote these incredible words of Jesus, *"You therefore are to be perfect even as your heavenly Father is perfect."* How did your mind react upon hearing them? Did they startle you? Did they make you squirm uneasily, if not in your seat, at least in your conscience? They should have! Or did they fail to pierce the armor of religious apathy which too frequently wards off the shafts of even the most important religious truths? Alas, we become accustomed to hearing and quoting the words of our Savior in a merely routine way, lazily and carelessly refusing to advert to their meaning.

But their meaning, if we would allow it to penetrate our minds, would shake up all our philosophies, would revolutionize our lives, would turn us and the world we have created for ourselves all topsy-turvy. Certainly this is true of the injunction to be perfect. Jesus is here telling us to do what, every day, we say cannot be done by men, or even expected of us: He is telling us to be *perfect*. He prescribes this without limitation or mitigation of any kind, and imperatively. And if His words were spoken earnestly, they were also spoken, as it appears, almost casually, with no special vehemence or any indication that He expected His hearers to be surprised at this extraordinary demand. And since we at any rate know and accept the fact that the speaker was not demented, but divine, we must conclude that His words are to be taken seriously—as seriously as when He said, *"This is my body; this is the chalice of my blood."*

Jesus here reaffirms, brings into sharper relief, and states in the most challenging manner a truth which He had already stated in the fourth Beatitude when He said that we should hunger and thirst for justice, that is, make holiness the final goal of our lives. Henceforth, the end of all human life and effort can be no other thing than holiness. For the perfect man is the complete man, the whole man, the holy man. When Jesus tells us to be perfect, He is telling us to be saints. From this moment, made unforgettable by the amazing challenge of the God-Man, those who claim to be His followers, that is, Christians, will be distinguished from other men by this, that laying aside, or at least rigorously subordinating, all other ends whatsoever, they will give themselves up to a single-hearted quest for sanctity.

Jesus not only tells us that we are to strive for holiness but also describes the kind of holiness He wants us to have. Every day we hear men say things like this, "You cannot be a saint and live in the world." Or, "God does not expect us to be saints." Or, "People in the world cannot live as priests, or monks, or nuns." Or, "Men cannot be like angels." If you study the teaching of Our Lord, you will see that He does not, in truth, tell us to be as holy as Carmelites, or as saints, or even as angels. He tells us to be holy as God is holy. "Impossible!" you say. Yes, impossible to attain to the infinite degree of God's holiness, but not impossible to possess the same kind of holiness; or better, not impossible to share in the divine holiness. And this is what we are commanded, namely, to be holy in the manner that God is holy. The ideal placed before us is not the holiness of saints and angels; it is the holiness of God. Having been raised to a share in the divine life, we are to live as divine beings, as sons of God.

There are certain attributes of God that we cannot imitate; for example, His omnipotence. There are other divine attributes, which, as we have observed in studying the Sermon on the Mount, we can imitate—His mercy, His purity, His holiness. The holiness that we are to have is nothing of our own, but a sharing in God's; we are to be filled with this as a crystal taken from the darkness of the earth is filled and transformed by the light of the sun.

It is further manifest, from these words of Jesus, that there is only one kind of holiness in Christianity, and it is intended *for all,* that is, for laymen and religious alike; for housewives as well as for nuns, for men in the world as well as those in monasteries, for the members of active religious communities as well as for Carmelites, for diocesan priests as well as for Trappists, for truck drivers and carpenters, doctors and lawyers, as well as for priests. Consider the multitude to whom Jesus spoke and of whom He demanded perfection: farmers, shepherds, fishermen, publicans, housewives, children, hangers-on; the only group noticeable for their absence was the learned and professional religious class, the Scribes and Pharisees and Doctors.

Over the ages the words of Jesus are still addressed to "*the multitudes.*" He makes no distinction of persons. He does not even make the broad distinction between religious and laymen. This distinction came later and was made by men, namely by the great religious founders, Basil and Benedict, Augustine, Dominic, Francis, Ignatius. St. John Chrysostom remarks that Jesus knew nothing of this distinction and would have all men live as monks. Of course, religious now make three vows, thereby assuming some special obligations; but for all other things, as St. Chrysostom says, laymen and religious shall render an identical account. In other words, the basic obligations of all Christians are the same; and other than the three special obligations assumed by religious themselves, there is no instance of Jesus, when He states His doctrine saying, "But I mean this only for religious."

If to some this doctrine sounds strange, this can only be because we have so far forgotten Christian fundamentals. After all, there is only one Christianity; "*One Lord, one faith, one Baptism; one God and Father of all....*" (Eph. 4, 6) Why should we then make distinctions among ourselves, as though some Christians might exempt themselves from the Gospel law without suffering spiritual harm? Or as though the sublime ideal of the Christian life was meant for a certain spiritual elite, while all the rest of mankind are doomed to wallow forever in sensuality and spiritual mediocrity!

Why do laymen fancy that theirs is an inferior Christianity, and even boast of it? Would they boast of having an inferior make of clothing? Is their religion less important than their clothing? Those who believe in Jesus, the Scriptures say, "*are sons of God*"; and there is no better way of describing the privilege of the Christian vocation than by this phrase. Now who is more "s*on of God*"—a Christian layman or a priest? Who deserves this high title most—a diocesan priest, a Benedictine, a Jesuit, a Dominican, a Franciscan? Even the question is silly. We are *all* sons of God; we are all "*a chosen race, a royal priesthood, a holy nation, a purchased people.*" (I Pet. 2, 9) No doubt there are different degrees of grace, "*according to the measure of Christ's bestowal*" (Eph. 4, 7); but the essential element—divine sonship and participation in the divine nature— is possessed by all; even the differences in grace depend on the mystery of God's love rather than on our position in the world. Thomas More, a layman, was a greater saint than many Carthusians who were contemporary with him.

It is important to realize, then, that it is *because we are Christians* that we are "*called to be saints.*" (I Cor. 1, 2) It is baptism, not ordination or religious profession, which in the first instance, implants in the soul the seed of holiness and imposes the obligation of cultivating this new life. True indeed that a Carmelite must strive after sanctity; not, in the first place, however, because she is a Carmelite, but rather because she is a Christian; and her sister in the world, who is perhaps raising a family in a large city, has a similar duty. It is true that a priest should be, or seek to be, a saint; again, however, not in the first place because he is a priest, but rather because he is a Christian; and his relatives in the world, as also his parishioners, are also bound to seek for perfection.

These truths are of such fundamental importance that neglect or ignorance of them cannot but have the most mischievous results. Errors in this matter—and they are only too common— work such havoc in the Church that they must be put down as diabolically inspired. One of the most common errors comes from thinking that the duty of pursuing sanctity derives primarily from ordination or religious profession. It is entertained by both religious and laymen, causing the gravest spiritual injury to both groups and of course to the whole Church. For the layman at once concludes that he need not become holy, thinking that he does enough in fulfilling the minimum requirements of the natural law, he is prone to neglect the counsels and commands of the Gospel.

Religious, on the other hand, seeing that laymen live careless and worldly lives, although still retaining the hope of everlasting life and happiness, are led to relax their own spiritual efforts, defending their conduct by the sophism that the pursuit of perfection, however commendable, is not absolutely necessary. Thus both religious and laymen fall into tepidity and, what is worse, expose themselves to very grave danger of damnation.

We have said that the great religious founders were but men. Accordingly, they had not the authority (nor the intention) of founding new religions or of imposing on others the obligations to become holy. Hence it is wrong for religious to trace their duty in this matter to their rule. Religious founders established their orders to enable groups of men to live in the manner ordained by Jesus and thus attain the goal fixed by Him, but they did not dream of setting up a new goal or of inventing a new manner of life.

Of course, there is a difference between the lay and religious states. We are not concerned to deny or belittle that difference, but only to point out that it does not touch the essence or the characteristic end of the Christian life. What this difference is exactly will be seen from the following example. Suppose that for a long time I fail to pay a debt that I have contracted; then, upon my creditor's making an insistent demand for what is due him, I take an oath to pay off the debt. Since I owe the money already, why take the oath? To reinforce my obligation; also to add a second obligation, from religion, to the one which I already have in justice. Still, even were I not to take an oath, justice would demand that I pay my debt.

Similarly, all Christians are bound, *by the very fact that they are Christians,* to seek after perfection. When one takes religious vows, therefore, he does not *then* contract the obligation; of becoming holy; he does but acknowledge an obligation that exists already, reinforces it, and adds a second obligation. Now he is doubly bound to seek perfection: in the first place, because he is a Christian; and in the second place, because he has entered a particular state of life which holds him permanently to the use of special means for obtaining this end. What is not to be forgotten, however, is that the primary and essential obligation comes from baptism. Because of the particular means that the religious also adopts, he binds himself to strive for the goal of Christian life in a more perfect way, the way of the counsels. He is like a daredevil who, accepting a challenge to perform some difficult feat, says: "Not only will I do, it, but I will do it in the most dangerous and difficult manner."

What is true of religious is true also of priests. They, too, have a double obligation to seek perfection: first because they are Christians, secondly because they are priests. This holds for secular or diocesan priests as well as for priests in religious communities (although, of course, in the case of the latter, religious profession adds a third obligation).

In saying this, we come upon what is certainly the worst of all the harmful errors that are current in this important matter. For secular priests are commonly exempted by erroneous popular opinion, in which they themselves sometimes share, from the obligation of perfection. It is said that a secular priest is to live in the world and therefore cannot be governed by the same standards that rule the life of a monk. This is, of course, true within certain limits, since all are bound to strive after holiness in accordance with the duties of their particular state in life. But half-truths are dangerous when the other half is neglected; and the allowance that must be made for different duties of state does not free diocesan priests from what we have seen is the common duty of all Christians; nor from the urgent, additional need for sanctity that comes from ordination.

In the great encyclicals written by Pope Pius X and Pope Pius XI on the Catholic priesthood there is no difference made between secular and religious priests in the matter of holiness. All are urged to make the highest sanctity the primary object of their lives; and this is a duty which is represented as coming from the priesthood itself. Moreover, if the duty to seek holiness which comes from ordination is secondary and supplementary to the one which comes from baptism, it is not for that reason unimportant. If secular priests are not holy, then the whole

Church suffers. For the particular function of the secular priesthood in the mystical body is to extend the kingdom of God; its work is in the front line of the apostolate. So that if secular priests do not teach men to become holy, and also show them the way, then Catholics everywhere fall into tepidity and indifference.

Thus, from whatever side we view the matter, it is clear that all children of God have the same fundamental obligation of seeking to be perfect as God is perfect. We must, as St. Paul puts it, become *"imitators of God."* (Eph. 5, 1)

The Meaning of Perfection

Such is the broad teaching of the Scriptures and of Christian Tradition. To know it even thus is to possess an important truth and gain an important principle of action. Yet we may not leave it here. For one thing, our purpose is action; and effective action requires complete definiteness in the matter of objectives; you cannot make a trip until you know exactly where you are going; so that this general view of the purpose of the Christian life must be even more clearly described that we may outline for ourselves a definite procedure of action. Moreover, there are a number of difficulties which, if not resolved, tend to prevent our holding this great truth in perfect tranquility of mind.

The Nature of Perfection

There is, for example, that disturbing and persistent doubt as to whether perfection is possible; and clearing up this doubt, besides confirming our principle, will give us a clear notion of our destination.

What causes the doubt is the fact that we are prone to think of a mere human perfection, which is in truth impossible. Thus an adage says that "Even Homer nods," to remind us that there are flaws in the character and work of the greatest geniuses in human history. If, then, we think of perfection as a human thing, if we think of it as refinement or culture, as skill in some art or knowledge of some science, then we are right in believing that in such matters neither we nor anyone else will ever achieve perfection. The limits of our powers make such perfection an impossibility.

But you must remember that Jesus is teaching a supernatural life; the perfection He desires belongs to the supernatural world. And strange as it may sound, while mere natural perfection is impossible, supernatural perfection is not. And yet, if you reflect but a moment, you will see that this is not really strange: in the supernatural world we have grace, which gives us a share in divine powers.

We have noticed in general that perfection means holiness. St. Paul helps us to understand it further when he says that charity is *""he bond of perfection."* Charity is a bond because it unites us to God; and a bond of perfection because in uniting us to Him, it brings us to our last and our final purpose in life; thus it completes us, or, in a word, perfects us. A thing is perfect, St. Thomas explains, when it fulfills the end for which it was made; a knife is perfect when it cuts readily, a pen is perfect when it writes well. Men will be perfected therefore by that which unites them to God, their last end. This can be no other thing than charity, than love. *"He who abides in love, abides in God, and God in Him."* (I John 4, 16) Perfection is no other thing than love.

How easy and how joyous should this realization make our pursuit of perfection! How clearly it marks out for us what we must do to be perfect! How near and how attractive it renders the ideal of holiness or sanctity, otherwise so remote! For all these things—holiness and sanctity, as well as perfection—are identical with love. To advance in holiness means above all else to advance in love; all the other virtues will come in the wake of this advance. Day after day, if we go forward in the love of God, we near the goal of perfection.

On the day that we shall be able to say truly what we now say unthinkingly, that we love Cod with our whole hearts, on that day we will have arrived at the summit of perfection.

St. Thomas describes further the perfection of love that is proper to us as wayfarers on earth. We cannot love with the boundless intensity with which God loves; for God is infinite and we are finite. Nor can we as yet love as the angels and saints in heaven, whose affections are engaged wholly and uninterruptedly in loving God; the necessities of bodily existence—sleeping, for example—prevent this in our case. But what we can do, says the Angelic Doctor, is to remove from our hearts whatever is opposed to the love of God or even hinders the flight of our affections to God. In a word, we grow in love, and therefore advance in perfection, by detaching ourselves from creatures. The more we do this, the more will God fill our hearts with love and unite us to Himself.

Our understanding of perfection thus not only makes our goal perfectly clear, but also gives us a definite practical procedure. The lowest degree of perfection requires that we remove from our souls whatever is incompatible with charity, namely, mortal sin; to do this we must love nothing more than God, nothing as much as God, nothing contrary to God. The highest degree is to love God with our whole hearts. Between these two terms there are an infinite number of degrees or steps of love. Every time that we remove some attachment for the creatures of this world, we advance a step in love; every time we mortify some desire or affection, even for a good thing that hinders our affections from going wholly to God, we make progress in perfection. On the contrary, to hold on to some attachment is to come to a standstill. Now we can see why St. John of the Cross teaches that to advance in perfection we must be detached from even the least things, and if we are not, we will make no progress. A soul with voluntary attachments trying to make spiritual progress is like a man who attempts to make a long and wearisome journey through sticky mud. He will make little progress and soon he will be too tired to try at all.

The Rich Young Man

An objection to the doctrine that all men are called to perfection is sometimes taken from the Gospel story of the rich young man. Jesus, asked by this young man what is necessary to enter into eternal life, replied, *"Keep the commandments."* *"Which?"* inquired the young man. And Jesus said: *"Thou shalt not kill, thou shalt not commit adultery, thou shalt not steal, thou shalt not bear false witness, honor thy father and mother, thou shalt love thy neighbor as thyself."* To this the young man answered, *"All this I have kept from my youth; what is yet wanting to me?"* The reply of Jesus is the occasion for the difficulty: *"If thou wilt be perfect, go, sell what thou hast, and give to the poor...and come follow me."* (Matt. 19, 16-21) *"If thou wilt be perfect"*—From these words it is concluded that the pursuit of perfection is optional, not a strict obligation.

But the word "if" does not denote an option here; it is not a condition. It rather designates a consequence and should be understood as meaning "since." The young man had asked how to enter into eternal life, also what was still wanting to him. Jesus' answer therefore meant, "Since this is what you want—if you really wish to know what is wanting and how to enter life— here is the answer."

Suppose that you are ill and send for a doctor. After examining you, he says, "If you wish to get well, here is what you must do" Why does he say "if" when he knows that you do wish to get well? Obviously he does not use it to indicate a condition or an option, but rather as a consequence: *"Since* you want to get well, here is what you must do." The words of Jesus are to be understood in the same way. This is clear, not only from the context but from the other Scriptural passages where holiness and perfection are enjoined as obligatory; the other passages help to interpret this one, and this one cannot be interpreted in a manner opposed to the others. Finally, the word *"if"* does not occur in the answer of Jesus as reported by St. Mark and St. Luke. In these Gospels, Jesus is quoted as saying to the young man, after the latter boasted that he had kept the whole Mosaic law, *"One thing is lacking to thee. . . . Sell all thou hast, and come, follow me."* Thus in pointing out the conditions necessary for eternal life He is adding a new and higher requirement to the young man's obedience to the natural law.

Perfection a Precept

This Gospel incident brings us to another matter. When Jesus tells the young man to abandon his riches, He is giving what Catholic theology has come to call a counsel, that is a virtuous course of action recommended by the Gospels but not strictly enjoined by them as an obligation. Poverty, chastity, and obedience, which religious undertake by vow, are the three great counsels. A counsel is distinguished from a precept, which is a commandment setting forth an obligatory course of action and not merely a recommended and optional virtue. According to St. Thomas, the words of Jesus to the young man contain both a precept and a counsel: the precept is contained in the words *"Follow Me,"* which are an invitation to friendship and thus contain the commandment of love; the counsel is an exhortation to give up riches.

Now two questions arise. First, is the duty of tending to perfection a precept or a counsel? Secondly, what is the relation of these counsels to perfection?

To answer the first question—Is perfection a precept or a counsel?—we have only to remember that perfection means love. We ask then: Is love a precept or a counsel? And Jesus Himself answers in His reply to the lawyer who asked Him what to do to enter eternal life: *"Thou shalt love the Lord Thy God with thy whole heart, and with thy whole soul, and with thy whole mind. This is the greatest and first commandment."*

Perfection is a precept, not a counsel. Let this be carefully observed and pondered. The too common notion that it is a counsel, a notion that leads to spiritual relaxation, is without foundation in the Scriptures or in tradition. St. Thomas Aquinas, who poses for himself the very question that we have asked, answers that, since perfection is love, it is of precept. Furthermore, it is a basic precept, fixing an indispensable condition for salvation. For charity is necessary for salvation, and so in the same way is perfection, which is identical with charity.

There is, however, this difference between the precept of perfection and the other precepts. The others oblige us *at once.* For example, I am obliged at once, now, to attend Mass on Sundays, and to refrain from taking meat on Fridays. Each time I violate these precepts, deliberately and without reason, I am guilty of grave sin. On the contrary, the precept of perfection does not bind me *now,* as a thing to be immediately realized. This would be an impossibility. For perfection is a growth; it results from contiguous and prolonged effort. Thus perfection binds us a a goal, as an end towards which we should strive. I am not obliged to be perfect today; but I am obliged to strive today for perfection, and every day should see me a little farther along on the road to this goal, just as every step carries us a little closer to the end of a journey. Perfection obliges me as a destination I am obliged to reach; and just as a destination, while it is the last place we see, is the very reason for making the trip at all, so it is with perfection. And further, as we will never arrive at any destination unless we make whatever effort is necessary for progress along the way, so the duty of tending to perfection requires that we make daily progress in the love of God.

Perfection is not only a precept, it is *the* precept. Since it is love, it is the primary and essential law—*"the whole Law and the Prophets."* (Matt. 22, 40) Pope Pius XI, stated this law as follows:

Christ has constituted the Church holy and the source of sanctity, and all those who take her for guide and teacher must, by the divine will, tend to holiness of life—*"This, is the will of God your sanctification,"* says St. Paul. What kind of sanctity? The Lord Himself declared it when He said, *"Be ye perfect as your heavenly Father is perfect."* Let no one think this is addressed to a select few and that others are permitted to remain in an inferior degree of virtue. The law obliges, as is clear, absolutely everyone in the world without exception.

Precepts and Counsels

Clearly, then, we cannot maintain that Christianity is divided into two parts, the one obliged only by the commandments of the natural law and of the Church, the other by a duty of perfection voluntarily assumed. No; while it is true that the letter of the counsels obliges only those who bind themselves to observe them, perfection is a fundamental obligation for all Christians. Poverty, chastity, and obedience are the counsels; perfection is a precept. The question then remains of the relationship of the counsels to the precept.

Suppose that a man dies in New York, leaving a will by which he divides his fortune between two nephews in Chicago; the only condition being that they must come and reside in New

York to gain their inheritance. They go at once, but adopt different modes of travel, the one taking a train, the other going by air. This, of course, they may do, for the will fixes only their destination, leaving it to them to choose their mode of travel. So it is with us Christians on our pilgrimage through this world. The Father decrees that, to receive our inheritance as children of God, we must all arrive at one destination—the perfection of love. But He does not set any uniform rule or requirement as to how we are to reach this goal: indeed, He establishes several possible ways, one more perfect than the others, and while inviting some to take the more perfect way, He requires of all only that they take some way that is suitable.

Here then is the difference between the precept and the counsels: the precept fixes the end common to all; the counsels point out the best means of obtaining that end. No one, however, is obliged to choose the best means, but only an apt means.

In general, there are two ways of Christian life, two modes by which men may travel to perfection; the one is the way of the Christian religious, to whom we may compare the man who travels by air to gain his inheritance; the other is the way of the Christian laity, to whom we may liken the man who goes by train. The religious, by vowing to observe the three counsels, put aside at once those earthly goods which tend to attract and absorb the affections of the heart and thus hinder men from traveling to eternal life directly and swiftly. But the layman, although moving more slowly, since he remains among the things of the world, and is thereby prevented from concentrating all his energies at once on the service of God, is nevertheless led, by the precepts and the spirit of the counsels to the same goal, holiness of life, without which no one can see God.

The Degrees of Holiness

A common evasion of the duty to pursue holiness results from the fact that there are various degrees of holiness among the blessed in heaven. Jesus said that there are many mansions in His Father's house. Careless and lukewarm Christians cite this text as an excuse for their negligence. They are not ambitious for the highest degree of glory, they say, but will be content with a lower degree.

Now while it is, of course, true that there are degrees of holiness this fact affords no ground for spiritual indolence. The degree of our holiness and glory depends not on our own choice but on the endowment of grace received from God. In a contest, say in a school, it is the teacher's responsibility, not the pupils', to determine and award the prizes; the pupil's part is to work as hard as possible to obtain the prize, while any relaxation on his part may end in failure. Similarly, fixing our place in heaven is God's business, not ours; our task is to correspond with God's grace and, no matter how hard we work, we are all sure to lag far behind His generosity. Our task is assigned to us by the first commandment, *"Love the Lord thy God with thy whole heart, whole mind, whole soul."* We are to love without limit; and therefore we are to pursue perfection without relaxation. Only by exerting ourselves to the utmost can we reach the degree of glory determined upon for us by God.

Moreover, if all the blessed are not equally happy and holy, all are completely holy; all are perfect. If you take a number of tumblers of various sizes and fill them with water, not all will contain equal amounts of water, but all alike will be full. So in our case also, although we receive unequal quantities of grace, which will result in different degrees of glory, we will all be filled, that is, brought to the limits of our capacities, both natural and supernatural, and in this sense we must all strive for the highest perfection, we are all bound to love God with our whole hearts. To put it differently, we are all called to be saints and all must strive unremittingly to fulfill that vocation. God will determine our place in heaven and our degree of glory.

If we fail to fulfill this duty of striving for the highest sanctity, St. Augustine tells us what the result will be: "He who says he has done enough," this great Doctor states, "has already perished."

This is an observation—rather, we may call it a principle—worth pondering. It is no idle threat; no exaggeration; it is solid and sober truth. And now at the end of this series of conferences, you should be able to appreciate the profound theology that is behind that brief statement. "He who says he has done enough has already perished."

What St. Augustine means is that as soon as a soul ceases to exert itself spiritually, it sets in motion, or permits to start into motion, the forces of spiritual deterioration; and the process of deterioration, if not interrupted, will carry the soul into spiritual death. There is no standing still; one either goes forward or backward. When a man rows upstream against a strong current, it requires much labor to make even a little progress. If he stops rowing, his boat does not stand still, but begins to drift downstream, more and more rapidly, with no effort on his part. For us to obtain salvation requires a continual struggle against our passions and human desires, which tend to carry us towards the goods of earth rather than towards those of heaven; so that as soon as we cease from exertion, we do not stand still, but our affections are carried towards earthly goods and then, gathering momentum, into sin, for sin is caused by the unrestrained love of earthly things.

To put it differently: when we stop striving for perfection, we fall into imperfection; and imperfections, we know, first stop all progress and then involve us in the law of the members, disposing us towards venial sins, while venial sins in turn dispose us towards those which are mortal. There is, quite literally, no standing still. As long as we are making progress in perfection, our small in-deliberate imperfections will cause us no lasting harm; we are then like a man who, though weak, is convalescing. But if we fall into habits of deliberate imperfection we are like one whose health, although apparently sound, is in fact being secretly undermined by an unsuspected disease. Thus it is simply true that he who says he has done enough has already perished.

Therefore, although strictly speaking, to gain salvation, it is enough to avoid mortal sin and remain in the state of grace, these considerations show us that we dare not aim deliberately at a lower degree of perfection, and least of all at the lowest degree. To be sure of reaching even the lowest degree, we must strive for the highest. To do otherwise is to release the dark forces that may cause us to miss even the lowest.

A gunner does not aim his cannon directly at his target but points it up in the air, for he knows that if he pointed it horizontally, the weight of the projectile and the force of gravity attracting it to earth would cause his aim to fall short. So we also know that it would be ruinous for us if in calculating our spiritual effort, we failed to take into account the earthward pull of our passions and desires and by aiming at the lowest degree of perfection allowed them to gather force and momentum. To be sure of attaining to the lowest degree we must aim at the highest degree.

The Rule of Moderation Not Relevant to Theological Virtues

In conclusion, it may be usefully observed that these principles give us the answer to an objection that has perhaps been teasing your minds during many of these conferences. The objection is the idea that we should be moderate, that virtue lies in the happy mean, that even in matters of religion we should be careful against going to excess.

There is indeed a sense in which we should be moderate. But we should not be mediocre. To be mediocre under pretext of being moderate is to fall into tepidity and risk damnation.

I say there is a sense in which we should be moderate. The axiom, virtue is found in the happy mean, or in moderation, applies to the moral virtues: prudence, justice, fortitude, and temperance, and the others. In these we should be moderate. Thus we should not spend such long hours in prayer that we neglect our duty; nor should we fast so much as to injure our health. Yet it must be added that these dangers are not very common even for Christians: even among them, prayer is not the most frequent cause for neglect of duty, nor is fasting a common cause of illness or death. Most of us are in more urgent need of being warned against defects in these matters than against excess.

But we are concerned here with the theological virtues. And to these, the axiom, virtue lies in moderation, has no relevance at all. This rule simply does not apply to faith, hope and charity. We are not to believe in God or hope in Him or love Him moderately or to a certain extent only. We are to believe in Him and hope in Him and love Him without limit. In the matter of charity, therefore, to plead moderation is to fall into mediocrity. The only limit that charity must observe is our capacity to love; since we are creatures, and finite, we can love God only to the limit of our powers; and our wildest excesses of love will fall infinitely short of the love which God deserves. The measure of love comes from God, not from the rule of moderation; and since God is infinite, then St. Bernard tells us, "the measure for loving God is to love Him without measure."

What is true of love itself is true also of its reverse or underside, the virtue of detachment. As love should be total, so detachment should, be universal. "To love," says St. John of the Cross, "is to labor to divest oneself from affections for all that is not God."

Where love is concerned, therefore, no excess is possible; extremism is of strict obligation; moderation is a dereliction of duty; we are to love God with our *whole* hearts. And since love is identical with perfection, what is true of the former, is true of the latter. We are not to be satisfied with moral correctness in our conduct, but seek after perfection; nor are we to seek half-heartedly for a lower degree of perfection but rather exert ourselves to the limit, striving for the highest degree of perfection, the totality of love. We are to be perfect, even as our heavenly Father is perfect.

Let us think upon these things. And may God bless you.

"O God, Who dost illumine this most holy night by the glory of Our Lord's resurrection: preserve in the new children of Thy family the spirit of adoption which Thou hast given; that, renewed in body and mind, they may show forth in Thy sight a pure service. Through the same Lord Jesus Christ Thy Son Who liveth and reigneth with Thee in union with the Holy Spirit, God, world without end. Amen."

(Collect, Easter Sunday)

ABOUT THE AUTHOR

Father John Jacob Hugo in his 48 years as a priest served many communities in the Catholic Diocese of Pittsburgh. Father Hugo was born on April 20, 1911, in McKeesport, Pa. and died October 1, 1985 in an automobile accident near Greensburg, Pa. He had finished preaching a retreat two days before his death.

He began his studies at the parochial schools in McKeesport, and then went on to St. Vincent Prep School, College, and Seminary, where he was ordained a priest on June 14, 1936, by the Most Reverend Hugh C. Boyle of Pittsburgh.

His first years as a priest were spent in teaching, first at Seton Hill College, Greensburg, then at Mt. Mercy (now Carlow) College, Pittsburgh. He served as assistant pastor in St. Mary's, Kittanning; St. Alphonsus, McDonald; All Saints, Masontown; and St. Paul's, Butler. He spent five years as chaplain at the Allegheny County Workhouse in Blawnox and the County Prison in Pittsburgh. He organized street preaching in the Hill District of Pittsburgh and established the house that eventually grew into Ozanam Center, the first interracial project of the Pittsburgh Diocese.

Father Hugo was named the founding pastor of St. Germain's parish in Bethel Park, which pioneered the liturgical changes authorized by the Second Vatican Council. After a short time as administrator of St. John's parish, Coylesville, he was appointed by Bishop John Wright to pastor of St. Anne's, Castle Shannon. He was the author of a number of books and pamphlets and collaborated in preparing the post-Vatican II catechism for adults, *The Teaching of Christ*. Bishop Wright named him chairman of a new Theology Commission, an advisory body set up during this time of change and adjustment in the Church. Bishop Leonard later appointed him chairman of the diocesan Liturgical Commission as the new Catholic liturgy was being generally introduced. At the same time Bishop Leonard transferred him to a resident chaplaincy at Mt. Nazareth with the Sisters of the Holy Family of Nazareth.

The Retreats

A work close to Father Hugo's heart was the six day retreats that he organized with colleagues in the 1940's for lay people. From 1976 until his death they were conducted at Mt. Nazareth Center in Pittsburgh. Dorothy Day, co-founder with Peter Maurin of the Catholic Worker movement, promoted the retreats and returned to Pittsburgh in 1976 to make her last retreat.

Photo taken by Cecilia M. Lyons

From left: Dorothy Day, Cecilia M. Hugo, and Fr John Hugo in Pittsburgh, 1976, at the time of Dorothy Day's last retreat.

Cecilia Hugo and Father John's Books

Cecilia Marie Hugo, Fr. Hugo's sister, was an invaluable, even indispensable, help to Fr. Hugo; the present-day availability of Father John's writings is the result of her efforts. Cecilia, a teacher of the mentally handicapped in McKeesport, PA, helped out with the early Catholic Worker retreats, in Pittsburgh and at the farm in Easton.

Father Hugo was a parish priest in active ministry whose only leisure time for writing was during his days off. His priestly duties, his writing activities and his conducting of retreats left little time for reproducing what he had written. That task was generally undertaken by Cecilia, who had a little printing machine in the basement of his parents' and her house. She would print and assemble the pages into books, which for the most part were made available at Father Hugo's retreats or circulated privately among his wide circle of priestly friends.

FATHER HUGO'S FAMILY

Father Hugo inspired affection and always remained close to his family.

Some of the Hugo family in 1948, at the home of Fr. Hugo's brother Dr. Lawrence Hugo II, in North Huntingdon, PA, where Lawrence, with his wife Ruth Anne, attempted to put into practice the aspirations of the Catholic Agrarian Movement. From left to right: Father John, his nephew John, his father and mother, Lawrence and Mary Jo, his sister-in-law Ruth Anne, his niece Maryanne, and his sister Cecilia.

All four siblings of the Hugo family, in 1984, at the motherhouse of the Sisters of the Holy Family of Nazareth, Mount Nazareth. From left to right they are: Cecilia, teacher; Margaret-Ann Lyons, mother of eleven children; Fr. Hugo; and Lawrence, professor at Duquesne University.

Cecilia Hugo, Helen Rose Fielding, and Rosemary Hugo Fielding in 2004, two years before Cecilia's death. With her husband, David Fielding, Rosemary, daughter of Lawrence and Ruth Anne Hugo, is ensuring that her uncle's work continues to be available.

Father Hugo's Symbol

The symbol on the back cover appeared on the cover of most of Father Hugo's original books. It shows the cross positioned between two stylized stalks of wheat and illustrates the maxim that unless a grain of wheat falls into the ground and dies it cannot produce a harvest: the message of "the folly of the cross."

A PRAYER FOR RETREATANTS: A copy of the following prayer was found in Fr. Hugo's copy of *You Are Gods!*

At the Preface of the Mass:
"It is truly meet and just...AT ALL Times...To give thanks."

Prayer:

Teach me, Lord to live this prayer,
That I may thank Thee every day
For EVERYTHING.
I do at times give thanks for what SEEMS good:
For health, success; for love and gain;
For all that pleases Self.
And yet how thoughtless—blind—
To thank Thee not for what is truly good:
For pain, unkindness, censure, blame:
For every hurt that comes
From person, place or work.
By these keen instruments wouldst Thou,
Divine Physician,
Remove the harmful growths of Self,
To give new life; thine Own true Life,
And peace—abundantly.
But I am blind—see not Thy loving Hand;
Then, in resisting, suffer more
And spoil Thy work.
Had I accepted all with gratitude
I might long since have been a saint,
And happy
(A grateful heart cannot be otherwise).
Forgive, then, Lord,
My blindness and my squandered life,
And give me grace, this day, to see
Thy chastening Hand in all my hurts
(Nor blame Thy instruments);
The grace to take each purifying cross,

And then—
Give THANKS with all my heart!

Imprimatur: Francis Patrick Keough, Bishop of Providence
July 16, 1941
Written by "Anonymous" at Carmelite Monastery, Cleveland
Heights, Ohio

Made in United States
Orlando, FL
20 June 2022

18993616R00141